P[..]y Evans studied modern languages at C[..]bridge University before joining the editorial t[..]m at a leading London publisher. After four y[..]rs she moved to Hong Kong where she worked a[.] a journalist, before embarking on a bicycle j[..]ney around Spain. This became the subject of [..] first book, *It's not about the Tapas*, which v[..] shortlisted for the WHSmith People's Choice [..]k Awards. Her second book, *Kiwis Might Fly*, des[..]ibes her motorbike journey around New Ze[..]nd. She now lives in London.

Visi[.] the author's website at: www.pollyevans.com

Also by Polly Evans

IT'S NOT ABOUT THE TAPAS
KIWIS MIGHT FLY

and published by Bantam Books

FRIED EGGS WITH CHOPSTICKS

Polly Evans

BANTAM BOOKS

LONDON · TORONTO · SYDNEY · AUCKLAND · JOHANNESBURG

FRIED EGGS WITH CHOPSTICKS
A BANTAM BOOK : 0 553 81678 0

First publication in Great Britain

PRINTING HISTORY
Bantam edition published 2005

1 3 5 7 9 10 8 6 4 2

Set in 11/13pt Times by
Kestrel Data, Exeter, Devon.

Bantam Books are published by Transworld Publishers,
61–63 Uxbridge Road, London W5 5SA,
a division of The Random House Group Ltd,
in Australia by Random House Australia (Pty) Ltd,
20 Alfred Street, Milsons Point, Sydney, NSW 2061, Australia,
in New Zealand by Random House New Zealand Ltd,
18 Poland Road, Glenfield, Auckland 10, New Zealand
and in South Africa by Random House (Pty) Ltd,
Endulini, 5a Jubilee Road, Parktown 2193, South Africa.

Printed and bound in Great Britain by
Cox & Wyman Ltd, Reading, Berkshire.

Papers used by Transworld Publishers are natural, recyclable products made from wood grown in sustainable forests. The manufacturing processes conform to the environmental regulations of the country of origin.

For Sophie and Lee,
wishing you every happiness

Acknowledgements

China is not an easy place for a linguistically impaired foreigner to travel around, and my trip would have been all the more challenging without the help of both good friends and total strangers.

Without the assistance of Guy Rubin and Nancy Kim, there's a good chance I wouldn't have got beyond Datong. Their knowledge of China, their contacts and, on one dire occasion, their impromptu dial-a-translation service were invaluable. A huge thank you to both of them. (For more comfortable tours of China, check out Guy and Nancy's Imperial Tours website at www.imperialtours.net).

Thanks also to Yeshi Gyetsa and his team at Khampa Caravan (www.khampacaravan.com) who provided a fantastic trek into eastern Tibet.

Thanks to Annie, my guide in Yangshuo, and her mother for that amazing lunch, and to Pascoe Trott and Clive Saffery for company and alcoholic refuge.

The Sheraton Xian, the Grand Hyatt in Shanghai, and the Gyalthang Dzong Hotel in Zhongdian kindly laid on much needed interludes of five-star luxury.

I'd also like to thank all those random Chinese strangers who, with unfathamable generosity and kindness, stepped out of the mire of Chinese bureaucracy and pointed me in the right direction, escorted me onto the right bus, fixed my ticket conundrums, and beamed goodwill and friendship in my direction. It made all the difference.

And thanks as ever to Francesca Liversidge, Helen Wilson and everyone at Transworld, and to Jane Gregory, Anna Valdinger, Claire Morris and everyone at Gregory and Company for their wisdom, humour and friendship.

Contents

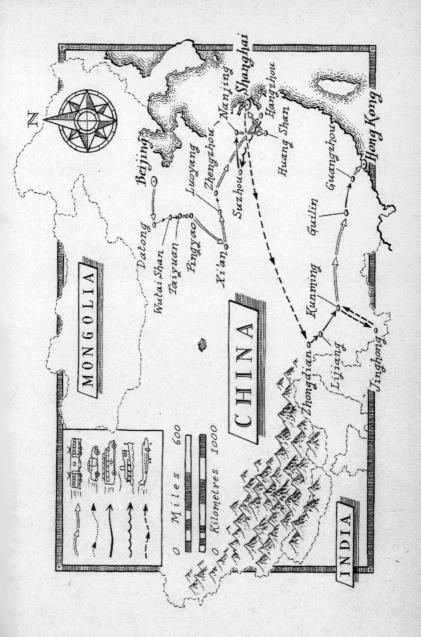

1

The Chairman is Dead

I gazed with ghoulish fascination at the withered, waxen corpse. The infamous domed forehead and rounded cheeks looked weary and wrinkled, a far cry from the jubilant, plump jowls of the propaganda posters. The embalmed cadaver of Chairman Mao lay swaddled in military uniform, his hands crossed over his chest. An orange lamp beamed through the semi-darkness onto his shrivelled, death-stiffened skin. His face glowed like a ghastly, candlelit pumpkin.

A hushed awe filled this inner chamber of the mausoleum. Nobody spoke above a whisper. The room quivered with palpable excitement. My heart was beating faster than usual; a perverse thrill tickled my skin. I felt a morbid compulsion to stop and stare at the macabre spectacle, at the mortal remains of this man who had, to such catastrophic effect, held absolute power over the most populous nation on earth. A few decades ago, a single suggestion from that formaldehyde-plumped mouth could have spelt the slaughter of a man; the disastrous economic strategies that evolved in that glowing amber head had dealt a tortured death to tens of millions. Yet beneath that taut, unyielding skin had also breathed a man who had, against incredible odds, inflamed such passion and loyalty in his people that a vast and diverse country had united and, with almost no material resources, had overthrown the foreign super-powers that threatened it.

The embalming of Mao's corpse had been an anxious affair according to his personal physician Li Zhisui, who recorded the procedure in his book *The Private Life of Chairman Mao*. The problem was that neither Li, nor anyone else in China, had attempted to preserve human flesh before. Li himself had visited Stalin's and Lenin's remains some years previously and had noted that the bodies were shrunken. He had been told that Lenin's nose and ears had rotted and had been rebuilt in wax and that Stalin's moustache had fallen off. The medical team played for time by pumping Mao's corpse full of formaldehyde.

'We injected a total of twenty-two litres,' Li wrote. 'The results were shocking. Mao's face was bloated, as round as a ball, and his neck was now the width of his head. His skin was shiny, and the formaldehyde oozed from his pores like perspiration. His ears were swollen too, sticking out from his head at right angles. The corpse was grotesque.'

The terrified medics – who could have been executed for desecrating the semi-divine cadaver – tried to massage the liquid out from the face and down into the body where the bloating could be covered with clothing. One of them pressed too hard and broke a piece of skin off Mao's cheek. In the end, they managed to restore his face to something approaching normal proportions, but then the Chairman's clothes wouldn't fit on his body and they had to slit the back of his jacket and trousers in order to button them up.

Before carrying out the permanent preservation of the body, Li sent two investigators to Hanoi to find out how Ho Chi Minh's body had been treated. When they arrived, however, the Vietnamese officials refused to divulge their secrets and wouldn't allow them to see the corpse – though someone revealed confidentially that it hadn't been a great success. Ho's nose had already decomposed and his beard had fallen off.

In the end, Li worked out a method whereby he removed Mao's internal organs and filled the cavity with cotton soaked in formaldehyde, while another group worked day and night building a pseudo-corpse out of wax just in case it all went wrong and they found themselves in need of a fake.

I wondered whether the body that lay before me was, in fact, the real cadaver or the waxen substitute. It was nearly thirty years since Mao's death; the pickling process had clearly been experimental at best. It seemed entirely possible that the real corpse could have long since rotted away and been quietly replaced with a skilfully crafted effigy.

But I wasn't allowed to linger. A dark-suited official insisted that the line of pilgrims kept moving. Silently, I filed with the coachloads of fellow tourists out of the dim mausoleum of the past and into the bright white light of contemporary Tiananmen Square.

'Follow me! Quick-a-ly!' A Chinese man dressed in a slightly soiled tracksuit top, baggy black jogging pants and scuffed pumps hollered at a white-haired Western tourist who stood in the queue that snaked around the cubic, concrete mausoleum. Amid the bedlam of loudly jabbering, camera-wielding day-trippers, the tourist nervously clutched his bag to his hip. The Chinese clasped the shoulder of the tourist's jacket and tried to pull him out of the queue. The tourist looked terrified.

He needn't have worried; I had been through the same charade just a few minutes earlier. Bags were forbidden in the mausoleum and the left-luggage office was on the other side of one of the busy roads that flanked the square. Seeing my bag, the man had grabbed me.

'Follow me! Quick-a-ly!'

We had hurtled through the square, dodging anorak-clad couples and fraught family groups. I was already struggling to keep up when Pumps had thrown himself into the multiple lanes of traffic that thronged the perimeter road. I had baulked.

'Quick-a-ly!' Pumps had shrieked across the belching fumes and honking horns.

Fearing for my life, I had followed as speedily as I could until, a few metres further on, we had reached the 'checking room'.

Pumps had grabbed my bag.

'Ten yuan,' he had said. 'Quick-a-ly.'

I had fished it out.

'And ten yuan for me,' Pumps had commanded.

This was the new China, a place where you had to move fast because time was money. It was a world that Mao, had he woken in his mausoleum a short distance away, would never have recognized. Gone were the communes; the 'iron rice bowl' – the state system that guaranteed lifelong employment – had been melted down and sold for scrap. In its place came 'socialism with Chinese characteristics' where the entrepreneurial spirit was not only permitted but actively encouraged. 'To be rich is glorious,' Mao's successor Deng Xiaoping had pronounced. After the famines and fear of recent years, the Chinese had leapt at the opportunity to create wealth.

Tiananmen Square had been central to the cult of Mao. It was here that he stood in October 1949 and proclaimed the founding of the People's Republic to the enthusiastic cheers of a hopeful, war-weary nation. The largest public square in the world, this vast expanse of grey paving stones and rigidly rectangular monuments and buildings covers an awe-inspiring forty hectares. It was originally built – in less imposing form – during the fifteenth century as the gateway to the Forbidden City from where the imperial dynasties ruled. But in the late 1950s, Mao decided to enlarge the square, to recreate this ideological landmark in his regime's own image. It was to be massive, imposing, immovable – and a uniform grey.

Mao was determined that the new square should be ready for the tenth anniversary of the People's Republic. Work started in November 1958; with the anniversary celebrations scheduled for 1 October the following year, the renovations had to be completed in just ten months. A labour force of twelve thousand 'volunteers' was conscripted. They worked round the clock in shifts of up to sixteen hours to clear the land; they built the Great Hall of the People whose auditorium would seat ten thousand and the banqueting hall where up to five thousand diners would feast.

Things had changed. In the twenty-first-century square, Mao's monuments still stood but they were surrounded by Beijingers flying kites; fashionably cut jeans and tailored jackets in purple, red and pink took the place of the blue Mao suits of yore.

In the roads around the square where, in the 1960s, the Chairman had come to inspect parades of up to one million Red Guards and to sanction their merciless ransacking of the country, shiny new BMWs and Volkswagens now streamed. Car sales in China were set to rise 80 per cent in 2003 alone. Sparkling expressways shimmered through the industrial haze – in just ten years, China had built enough new roads to circle the equator sixteen times. In Shanghai, the new Maglev train was whizzing millimetres above its magnetic tracks at a staggering 430 kilometres an hour. Two hundred and fifty million Chinese were jabbering into mobile phones.

Here in Beijing, crumbling hutongs – Beijing's ancient alleyways – were being controversially razed to make way for the clean, green city that China's capital is determined to become in time for the 2008 Olympics. The city wasn't settling for a simple facelift. It was having Botox, a nose job, and silicone implants to boot. In order to look at its best for the Games, Beijing was undergoing every cosmetic treatment on the market. Entire residential areas had been torn down and parks built in their place. Last time I had visited the city, two and a half years earlier, Beijing had three ring roads; now there were six. In 2002 alone, two million trees had been planted. Everywhere I looked, sand and cement dust filled the air. Workers wielded picks and shovels. China was under construction.

Way above my head at this very moment, on the morning of 15 October 2003, China's first man in space quite literally had stars in his eyes. As I stood and stared at Mao's pickled corpse, Lieutenant Yang Liwei was gazing out at the cosmos, perhaps tucking into one of his specially prepared space snacks as he settled into another orbit of the earth. The thirty-eight-year-old ex-fighter pilot had spoken by radio to the Party leaders; he'd chatted with his wife and eight-year-old son. Tomorrow, after twenty-one hours and fourteen orbits, China's newest hero would come back down to earth, and then soar into a rather different universe as a lustrous celebrity. He was, as he said, feeling good.

Yes, yes, so the Russians and Americans had sent astronauts into outer space forty-two years earlier. The cynics were blathering that this escapade was a scandalous waste of money for a country many of whose people lived scarcely above subsistence, and that human space adventure had gone out of fashion with A-line skirts (and they were talking about the first time). But the Chinese didn't care, for their Motherland had entered the space age. After decades of instability, strife and starvation, China had re-covered. Now she was announcing to the world with billowing jets of rocket fuel that she was a force to be reckoned with.

Alongside the economic and technological change ran a new-fangled cultural revolution. Differences in attitudes between mothers and daughters in today's China were blowing the customary inter-generational disputes into another stratosphere. In 1980, it was reckoned that a modest 15 per cent of Beijingers had indulged in premarital sex. Twenty years later, the figure had reached 80 per cent. Divorce was booming. In this country where the insidious influences of barbarians from abroad had previously been so tightly controlled, sprawling internet cafés were springing up in every town. The Chinese could access the websites of international newspapers; the more affluent apart-ment blocks had cable TV and CNN.

All this change was precisely the reason I had come here. China was haring into a new age like an out-of-control high-speed train. Yet, I had heard, while the city folk were careering forth on their expressway to modernity, some of the country dwellers were still on a very different track. They were, as ever, crawling along in carts drawn by lame donkeys, and clattering down rough-hewn roads in buses with broken seats and haphazard suspension. For the majority of China's 1.4 billion residents this futuristic leap forward with its magnetic levitation trains and supersonic rockets didn't mean a lot. If I wanted to look at the strange dichotomies of this two-tier country, the time to go there was now.

So I could glimpse things the way the people saw them, I thought I'd attempt to travel alongside the masses. I'd take sleeper trains and long-distance buses to visit China's ancient heritage sites, natural wonders and modernistic masterpieces. I'd ride a bicycle through Beijing's hutongs and I'd float on a boat down the Grand Canal.

This wasn't my first foray into China. I'd lived in Hong Kong for nearly four years and had ventured across the border a number of times. I'd arrived in the former British colony seven months after the hand-over, hot on the trail of the Asian economic crisis of October 1997 and the bird flu outbreak that led to the demise of 1.4 million chickens in the territory.

The Hong Kong Chinese had seemed to be in two minds about their reunification with the Motherland. While they were delighted to be rid of a colonial power, the Chinese Communist government provided an unnerving alternative. After the Tiananmen Square incident of June 1989, during which the Chinese government had sanctioned the deaths of hundreds, possibly thousands, of peaceful protesters, Hong Kong had descended into panic. Those who were sufficiently affluent and held the necessary professional qualifications had queued up at the gates of foreign nations

20

willing to offer them passports out. Most of these countries also required a certain minimum residency; Hong Kong's middle classes deserted the territory in their droves. Most never returned.

Their attitudes towards the mainland were complicated by the fact that the majority of Hong Kong families had themselves immigrated from China within the last sixty years. Hong Kong's war-ravaged population stood at just 600,000 in 1945; it exceeds seven million today – and procreation has played only a small part. Yet Hong Kongers tended to look down on their cousins across the border, denigrating them as unsophisticated and, worse still, poor.

Among Westerners, even those who considered themselves enthusiastic sinophiles, China seemed to inspire a love-hate relationship. It was a fascinating country with a rich history of great culture and terrible cruelty – a history whose artefacts its own people had recently decimated in an attempt to wipe out the superstition and feudalism of the past. It was an entrancing country, but one that was dirty and difficult to travel in. China was still, even in today's cosmopolitan climate, alluringly foreign – but also a hellishly frustrating place in which to operate.

Knowing these small things about China had convinced me that, if I was going to try to negotiate my way around the country on public transport, I should make some attempt at learning the language. It would be nice, at least, to master a few vital phrases: 'This bus is slower than my grandmother', 'Has this train been cleaned since the Ming dynasty?' and so on.

I'd enrolled in classes at London University's School of Oriental and African Studies and, every Wednesday evening for two terms before I embarked on my journey, I'd trekked up to Russell Square to join a small group of other misguided souls who had been cursed with the silly idea that it might be fun to learn Chinese. Together we'd sat and stared bemusedly at Wei San, our teacher, and tried to make sense of the extraordinary sounds that came from her mouth. Other evenings, I'd pored over my square-ruled notebook and painstakingly copied out Chinese characters as I'd attempted to translate sensationally dull sentences designed to incorporate every possible grammatical complexity: 'Mr Li rang me last night and told me that he would not come today', or 'Do you know that the lady who came to see him last week was his elder sister?'

What is it with language teaching that inspires this kind of intense banality? Why not liven things up a bit with sentences such as: 'Pock-Marked Chang rang me last night and said he would not annihilate my family today'? Or 'Did you know that the lady who came to see him last week was his elder sister – and that he is the father of her strange-looking child?'

Still, as the weeks had progressed, the peculiar shapes on the page had started to take on a new significance. I'd learnt to ask for one ticket from Beijing to Shanghai, and to enquire at what time the train departed. I'd learnt to pronounce astonishment at the price of plums and to declare them very expensive. I'd learnt the words for beer and wine and chocolate.

And then, not very confidently, I'd packed my bags, my phrase book and my Wet Wipes, and set off for the mystical, maddening Middle Kingdom.

2

'Might Be a Little Bit Painful . . .'

I sat on the elegant white sofa and sneezed. I was spending my first few nights in China with my friends Guy and Nancy. They had been living in Beijing for the last seven years running their luxury holiday company, Imperial Tours. Their ability to battle through China's lunatic administrative and bureaucratic complexities while – usually – retaining a modicum of sanity themselves sent them spinning into their very own stratosphere of heroism, in my book at least.

My journey around China was likely to be a challenging one and it seemed wise to ease myself into the skirmish slowly. From the cool, unflappable white of Guy and Nancy's apartment, I thought I could peer from the satisfyingly elevated twentieth-floor window and perhaps start my trip by just *looking* down at bedlam below.

Guy and Nancy knew the country well. They would be able to tell me where to go and how to get there. After years of inspecting hotels across the land in order to ascertain whether they would be up to the discerning standards of their clients, they knew which ones changed the bed linen more than once a month. They were not just familiar with the good restaurants in all the major cities, they could even tell me which dishes to order in each. They imparted vital pieces of information that as a newcomer I could never have dreamt of: I shouldn't take the bottom bunk on the sleeper trains unless I wanted to share it with a group of chain-smoking men and their noodles, because the bottom bed is used as a communal seat during the daytime. I must always negotiate my room price as the figure featured on the rate board in reception would be a vastly inflated sum displayed merely for the staff's entertainment. And I shouldn't allow a period of more than about ten minutes to pass without annihilating the battalion of murderous germs that would have taken up residence on my hands. They accompanied me to the chemist and insisted I bought several bottles of antibacterial hand-cleaning gel for those moments when soap and water wouldn't be available. Guy and Nancy seemed to have developed something of a hand-washing mania since they'd been living in Beijing, I noticed. I took it to be an ominous sign and hoped the bugs here didn't mutate at the same pace as everything else.

The problem was, one of them seemed to have set up house about my person already. I coughed and then I spluttered. The delicate white porcelain cup from which I sipped contained not a straw-coloured infusion of China's most sought-after jasmine, but a canary-yellow solution of Lemsip. With a remarkable show of feebleness, I had managed to arrive in China and instantly catch a cold. My lamentable descent into sickness at this early stage in the game didn't augur well for the weeks ahead.

Guy looked at me with a worried expression; whether this was concern for my well-being or fear that I might take up residence on his sofa for rather longer than he had anticipated, I couldn't tell. Then he had an idea.

'Some friends of ours go for a Chinese massage treatment when they get sick,' he said. 'It's called *gua sha*. Apparently they rub your back with a piece of cow horn.'

It sounded fairly kooky, to be frank, but the Lemsip didn't seem to be doing much to drive these potent oriental germs into retreat, and I was becoming desperate. A few nights from now, I was scheduled to take the sleeper train out of Beijing to Datong. I really, really didn't want to have to negotiate the nocturnal railway system of China feeling under par. And while slightly bizarre, having my back rubbed with a piece of cow horn hardly sounded arduous. I eagerly agreed to give it a try and Guy and Nancy escorted me to a nearby clinic.

I was shown to a room tastefully decorated with silks and brocade wall hangings. A young girl who spoke no English brought me a tall glass of green tea and gestured that I should undress to the waist. I did as I was told, then lay face down on the bed. A man came in. He was sinewy and youthful but, as I was about to discover, his lean forearms harboured an eye-watering strength. The masseur grinned at me. He seemed a little bit nervous.

'Er . . . is this your first time doing *gua sha*?' he asked tentatively in heavily accented English. He laughed anxiously. He had the demeanour of a person confronted with a difficult, potentially embarrassing situation. Something about him suggested that, perhaps, I oughtn't to be there.

'Yes,' I replied far too confidently.

'Aaahhh.' His grin now grew close to a fearful grimace. He clenched and stretched his muscular fingers, then clenched them again. He looked distinctly uncomfortable.

'Um,' he said, wincing. He bit his lip, then added, 'Might be a little bit painful.'

Deep within me, an uneasy suspicion started to stir. And then, before it could develop into fully fledged panic, the masseur rather cautiously picked up a brown, flat implement from the tray beside the bed and started to scrape at my back.

He didn't just scrape. He scrubbed and scoured, ground and gnawed at my back. He frayed and flayed it. With every agonizing stroke, he pressed the fine, sharp edge of the flat brown rectangle – which could have been cow horn but might just as easily have been plastic – hard into the skin of my waist then, leaning heavily so that it dug deep into my tissues, dragged it up the length of my torso to my neck. The pain was excruciating.

Trying not to scream out loud, I clenched the towel that covered the bed between my teeth.

'You can cry if you want to,' said the masseur in a matter-of-fact tone, and scraped some more.

I have a couple of moles on my back. Each time the masseur hauled the tablet over them, I felt them catch sickeningly. The pressure he was exerting was such that I worried he might pull them off. But still he continued, like a painter-decorator hacking decades-old emulsion from a wall, or a scullery maid cleaning a particularly bothersome pan. Or a butcher skinning a carcass.

I considered crying – or at least letting out a blood-curdling scream. But then the full absurdity of the situation struck me. I only had a measly cold. A couple more Lemsips should have done the job. But instead I was lying here half naked in a Beijing torture chamber – albeit one with pretty décor – enduring ludicrous levels of pain inflicted by a skinny man wielding a flat, brown slab of something. It was a ridiculous place to have come. And if this was the Chinese treatment for a cold, what would they do for pneumonia or pleurisy? Stretching on the rack? The iron maiden? Or would they just resort to the guillotine and be done with it?

I didn't cry. Instead, I started to laugh hysterically. For one blissful moment, the masseur stopped scraping in surprise. Then he, too, began to chuckle and then to roar with hilarity. He seemed to have a curious sense of humour.

Finally, after about twenty minutes, he stopped. 'OK, finished,' he said cheerfully. 'You get dressed now.'

He left the room. I rolled off the bed and staggered, slightly light-headed, over to the opposite wall where a gilt-framed mirror hung. I turned my back to the mirror and twisted my head to find out what visible damage had been done.

I couldn't believe what I saw. My whole back was covered in angry, deep-red welts and bruises. From shoulders to waist was one swollen, purplish blotch. I looked like a burns victim. Or a survivor of a punishment beating. Or road kill. I was horrified. The skin of my back had been transformed in the space of twenty brutal minutes from perfectly ordinary flesh to the kind of gruesome, gory mess you'd hope only ever to see on a television hospital drama.

The strange thing was that my back didn't hurt. It looked appalling, and felt slightly tender to the touch, but there was no stiffness or pain. I dressed, then wandered, shaken, back to Guy and Nancy's apartment, and showed them the results.

'Oh my God,' said Guy, and immediately fetched his camera to take photos.

That night I felt no better – a little more battered, slightly elated in the way that you are when you've just survived a brush with death, but my wretched flu symptoms remained. The next morning, however, they had vanished entirely. That festering, lingering cold had been stopped in its tracks and had evaporated into the ether. I was no longer snuffling; I felt renewed, invigorated and full of energy. A few days later the bruising had entirely disappeared, too. It was really very impressive. I'd never had a cold extinguished like that before. Usually a cold has to run its own grisly, determined course: first there is that ominous, mild headache, then the sneezing and streaming is followed by aches and pains, and finally there's the seemingly interminable period of very inelegant congestion. But this cold progressed as far as the initial stages of aches and pains, then I had *gua sha* and – *poof!* – the cold vanished. It was amazing.

Sha, I later found out, is the Chinese term for the congestion of blood just under the body's surface. The word *gua* means to scrape. The idea of *gua sha* is to scrape the skin in a way that encourages stagnant blood to rise, thereby promoting healthy circulation. The red marks are tiny haemorrhages as the *sha* comes to the surface. Traditional Chinese medicine uses *gua sha* to cure everything from fever to infectious diseases and digestive complaints. Apparently, if there is no toxic blood, no red marks will appear. Clearly, I had been very sick indeed.

*   *   *

Fully recovered, I felt sufficiently lively to abandon the sofa and begin my exploration of the frenzied China that ran amok beyond the safe haven of Guy and Nancy's flat. Given the Chinese fondness for riding bicycles, I had decided I'd venture into the fray of Beijing on two wheels.

Guy and I went out to purchase a bike: he said he needed one anyway so he'd buy the machine and I could borrow it for the afternoon.

During the past few years, Guy had already had two mountain bikes stolen in Beijing. This time, he said, he was going to buy a cheap heap of Chinese tin. At least that way he stood a chance of holding on to it.

Just along the street from Guy and Nancy's apartment, we found Mr Jia in a cramped shop, surrounded by old tyres and inner tubes. Outside on the pavement stood a sorry-looking line of bicycles. Mr Jia was a garrulous, ebullient man with a perfectly round face, tiny, sparkling black eyes, and barely perceptible eyebrows. He wore a bright red anorak that purported to be made by Timberland but probably wasn't.

Mr Jia had known a few modes of transport in his day. He used to work aboard an Italian passenger ship where he was the only Chinese, he told us in his jumbled, scarcely comprehensible English, and then pealed with exuberant laughter. He had sailed to New York, Miami, Finland and England. His fuzzy little suggestions of eyebrows leapt about his forehead in jaunty animation as he related his adventures.

The shinier, brand-new bikes in the line, even Mr Jia cheerfully admitted, weren't really up to much. Yes, they were gleaming right now, but when required to muscle in against mopeds and jump red lights on the streets of Beijing they'd be about as much use as My Little Pony on the course at Aintree.

His faint eyebrows slouched sadly for a moment, then sprang jovially up towards his hairline, sending his forehead into tight, wrinkled pleats.

'But this one,' he declared exultantly, his tiny eyes almost bursting with glee, 'this one very good.'

He danced to the end of the line where, all alone, spurned by its gloating, spangling companions, a tired, red contraption mooched. It looked as though it might have liked to be a mountain bike, with its straight handlebars and knobbly tyres, but it hadn't been picked for the team. It was a creaking, geriatric old thing, its stand so insecure that it frequently tumbled to the ground. It was once, a very long time ago, manufactured by Giant, as revealed by the large, white letters on its bodywork. And then, in smaller italic print, the model: Hunter. It was hard to see what Hunter could have hunted. Even the most sluggish of hedgehogs would have had plenty of time to scamper to safety when it heard those wheels grating and spokes clattering in the distance.

Mr Jia nodded and grinned, then nodded some more. Hunter, he assured us in radiantly upbeat tones, was a fabulous bike. Yes, it had seen better days and the paintwork probably dated back to the Qing dynasty, but it was a solid, dependable machine. He nodded a little harder as if to convince himself as well as us; his face, I noticed, was becoming quite pink from the exertion.

Guy and I glanced at Hunter and then at each other with doubtful expressions.

'Yes, well, I suppose it might do,' said Guy gloomily, his aspirations towards style and class crumbling away like Hunter's bodywork. 'It looks just like all the other Chinese bikes. At least nobody will steal it.'

He volunteered me to take it for a test ride. I

wobbled off down the street. The gears didn't work, but Beijing is flat so that wasn't of great consequence. The brakes seemed functional. But the best feature of all was this bike's bell. When I pressed a button on the handlebars, a speaker blared at ear-splitting volume a whole repertoire of synthesized tunes: 'This Old Man', 'Clementine', 'Frère Jacques' and 'Happy Birthday'. While the notes bleeped merrily, a red light on the handlebars flashed in time to the music.

The sound system clinched the deal. Guy handed over 260 yuan (at the time of my visit, there were about fourteen yuan to the pound) and, to the reassuring tones of 'Clementine' and much flashing of lights, I teetered off down the road to join my fellow ten million Beijing cyclists – and a few hundred thousand learner drivers.

Ten years ago, cars were used only by government officials. But that day, as Hunter and I set forth into the fray, there were around ten million privately owned cars in China. That Wednesday in Beijing alone, the authorities would have issued around two thousand licence plates for new vehicles. And for every one of them, there was a novice behind the wheel.

It could be on account of their lack of experience that the drivers of Beijing take little notice of traffic lights.

'Red, now red, hold on, I'm sure that colour means something,' they were perhaps thinking as they hurtled in an uncontrolled manner towards the junction. 'Now what was it again? Oh yes, I was meant to stop, I think, now, erm, which pedal was the brake?'

But by that time, they'd already jumped the light. Meanwhile the seasoned drivers of Beijing, the ones who passed their tests six months earlier, were hissing through their teeth, 'Bloody learner drivers,' and, with confident blasts of the horn, squeezing past them on the inside. Throw into the mêlée a few million cyclists and the odd slow-moving tricycle cart which didn't think technological advances such as traffic lights applied to them, and there was chaos on the streets.

At some junctions, traffic policemen stood about. Curiously, however, they didn't actually do anything. You'd think that in a country where the government exercises such total control it would be easy for a policeman to command the traffic. If they can introduce the death penalty for a person who fails to declare that they are infected with SARS, surely they could find a good deterrent for jumping red lights. But fear and respect didn't seem to extend to traffic policemen. At red lights the traffic flow thinned but never entirely stopped. Cars, buses, bicycles and mopeds all converged at junctions into one slow-flowing, horn-honking, bell-jangling cacophony.

In the end, though, riding a bicycle through the streets of Beijing wasn't quite as scary as it looked. The bedlam was much relieved by the fact that the main roads all had wide bicycle avenues running down each side. The pace was leisurely: millions of Beijingers pedalled unhurriedly along their way, travelling to and from work and running errands. It was almost peaceful, pottering among them, caught in the gentle flow of the city bustling about its business. Old men on tricycles drew carts to transport their wares. Children returning from school rode shinier bikes with more knobbly tyres that were almost, but not quite, mountain bikes. Women in office garb and shiny black-patent shoes remained serene and impervious to the horn-blasting, fuel-belching chaos. Somehow, their clothes remained perfectly clean amid the black of Beijing's streets.

My trousers, on the other hand, were within minutes splattered with a dark, unsightly gunge. Still, I was feeling moderately pleased with myself. First, neither Hunter nor I had yet met our demise under the wheels of a Beijing novice driver. Second, I had, with uncustomary navigational success, managed to find my way along Gulou Dongdajie and had dived left into a tiny narrow alley that led to Houhai Lake, my destination for the afternoon. This was one of Beijing's famous hutongs, the maze of narrow alleyways and walled courtyards that were first built after Genghis Khan galloped into the city at the beginning of the thirteenth century and reduced it to rubble.

Despite the rather different onslaught of Beijing's cleaning, greening machine, some hutongs stay standing. They're vibrant little back streets full of clattering bicycles, the occasional crawling car that doesn't really fit, and children in their uniform tracksuits skipping home from school. The low-rise buildings are constructed of grey brick which against the grey tarmac and grey Beijing sky gives something of a monotone look, but the tiny shops on the corners, the sun that occasionally breaks through to cast a dappled light under the trees, and the endless human chatter gives plenty of life to these busy little streets.

I wiggled through the lanes and arrived on the shores of the lake, where couples strolled and tourists snapped photos in the twilight. The lights from the bars and restaurants on the opposite bank twinkled over the water that rippled silvery blue and deep yellow in the fading light; willow trees bowed and stooped.

With the sun low, I started to head back towards Guy and Nancy's flat. Rows of red lanterns were strung from the façades of the restaurants that flanked

33

the main road. People sat on the pavement eating and chatting. Streetside shops sold snacks and drinks. The hordes of bicycles and tooting cars were making their way home for dinner now through the roads lined with newly planted trees, grass and flowers.

Then, quite suddenly, it was dark and the streets no longer looked the same. I looked at my map; I squinted at the street signs. They didn't seem to bear any relation to one another. I stopped at a kiosk and tried out my first-ever phrase of real-life Chinese – that is, spoken outside a classroom.

'*Wo zai nar?*' I asked the kiosk man – where am I? – and shrugged bewildered at the map. Remarkably, he seemed to understand. I had assumed that, despite all my efforts, my mangled tones would ensure that my simple attempt to ask directions would end up meaning something entirely different, for a simple error in timbre can alter the meaning of a Chinese word entirely. Quite feasibly, one could hope to ask for directions home but in reality say something along the lines of 'My uncle is an aardvark'.

The kiosk man didn't so much as smirk. With earnest politeness, he sent me down a road to the right; the next person told me to turn left, the next said I needed to go straight on. I had no idea where I was. The streets were packed full of jammed up cars and bicycles with no lights – including my own. Hunter clearly favoured stealth above 'be safe, be seen'.

In the end, I gave up and phoned Guy. I tried to describe where I was – there were lots of people, lots of cars, lots of bicycles with no lights . . .

'Is there anyone standing next to you?' he asked. I had a couple of million Beijingers to choose from.

'Just pass the phone to one of them,' said Guy.

I chose a tiny, gnarled, dark-skinned man in blue

overalls who was frying pancakes on a makeshift road-side stall.

'*Ni hao*,' hello, I said, then handed over the phone and, pointing at it, told him, '*Wo de pengyou*' – my friend.

He gave me a very blank look, then took the phone and held it quizzically to his ear. Then he grinned and then he started laughing. He gave me back the phone and, still chuckling, pointed the poor, lost foreigner down the street towards home.

On my last morning in Beijing, we drove out to the Great Wall. Guy and Nancy had a client who was on business in Beijing. He'd been on one of their tours the previous year with his wife and a group of friends, but had missed the Great Wall outing because he'd had to return home early. The rest of the group had subsequently told him he *had* to ask Guy and Nancy to take him to the Great Wall next time he visited China. So now that he was back in Beijing on business, he'd asked them to arrange a day trip for himself and a colleague.

The Great Wall stretches for many thousands of kilometres from the east coast of China to the Gobi Desert. It wasn't originally constructed as a single, continuous wall, though. In ancient times, the disparate kingdoms that made up this part of the world had each built their own separate walls to keep out invaders; then in 221 BC the tyrannical emperor Qin Shihuang ended the Warring States period by conquering his six neighbouring kingdoms. He declared China a single state (it is from the word qin – pronounced chin – that the name China derives) and announced his intention to join all the kingdoms' shorter walls into one very, very long one.

The First Emperor was a strong ruler; some might call him a bloodthirsty tyrant. Artists' impressions depict his long, slanting, cruel eyes with sagging, baggy pouches above a finely sculpted black beard whose tip reaches almost to his navel. Qin Shihuang imposed on his newly united subjects not only a joined-up wall but uniform systems of currency, weights and measures, and writing; he treated any attempt to revert to former ways as treason. He conscripted millions of ordinary people into the labour forces for his building projects: the Great Wall, a huge palace complex, and his tomb that houses the famous terracotta warriors.

Qin Shihuang's construction enterprises were brutal. Chinese legend has it that one life was claimed for every stone laid along the Great Wall; stories abound of dead men's bodies buried within the brick-work. One story relates the trials of a woman named Lady Meng whose husband was sent to work on this most hated of projects. One winter night she dreamt that she heard him calling out that he was cold; she packed up some padded clothes and journeyed north to deliver them. When she arrived, she found that her husband had died and wept so bitterly that her tears rent the ramparts in two. Under the broken wall, she saw her husband's bones. She travelled to the ocean and drowned herself.

During the Ming dynasty (1368–1644) there was a further effort to renovate and extend the wall. Construction lasted more than a hundred years. The work was carried out principally by the army, but two hundred crimes also carried the penalty of labour on the wall. A sentence could last for life or, worse still, perpetuity – when the convicted man died, his son had to take his place. If there was no son, another relative was drafted.

Guy and Nancy's excursion to the Great Wall incorporates none of this unpleasantness. In fact, the outing is not even a tiny bit uncomfortable. While Guy picks up the guests from their hotel and accompanies them in a leisurely way to the wall a couple of hours' drive away, Nancy packs up the lunch, visits the flower market, and drives up there in a faster, less fashionable car. By the time the guests have peeled themselves from their vehicle, gone to the loo, sorted out their cameras and tottered up the steps to the first watchtower, she's set up tables and chairs with linen covers. She's laid out white porcelain, wine glasses and a vase of roses, and strewn petals over the ground. When the guests arrive just fancying a little something to pick them up, they find smoked salmon bagels, salad, potatoes and a chilled bottle of wine complete with a waitress to serve it.

The day I accompanied her the weather was perfect; the sky was a deep, clear, flawless blue. Having bought two extra smoked salmon bagels for ourselves, we laid the tables and then, leaving Guy, the guests and the waitress to their own devices, we went for a stroll. On all sides, the Great Wall rose and fell over the hilly land. Those sandy stones, watchtowers and turrets whose construction had wreaked such hardship and misery in centuries past climbed up and dipped down, still and serene, over the green scrub and into the distance. As they wended out of sight over the far-away hills, they created a geometric silhouette on the horizon. There were scarcely any other people out here; this part of the wall has been restored, but it's not as popular with day-trippers as some other sections closer to town. We found a solitary spot and sat down to eat our bagels against the backdrop of this ancient feat of Chinese engineering.

3

Heavenly Creatures, Earthly Chaos

Waiting Hall Eight was huge and cavernous. Feeble ceiling strips cast a dim, greyish light. Every few minutes, a central fluorescent tube would flicker to life, throwing a yellowish tinge over the waiting passengers, and then it would die out once more. Down the length of the hall ran rows of bright orange plastic seats which were bolted to the floor. On the chairs and on the floor, hundreds of people sat or squatted in the gloom, waiting, chatting, and playing cards.

A scratchy tannoy interrupted the greyness every few minutes making its pronouncements in English as well as Chinese. Given that I seemed to be the only foreigner in Beijing's West Train Station at the time, this seemed to be either an elaborate courtesy or, more likely, a delusional attempt on the part of the station's authorities to convince themselves that their terminus was a hub of cosmopolitan activity, a truly international concourse. It was a peculiarly grand building, a monolithic hulk lit up orange at night – rather like Chairman Mao's waxen corpse, in fact.

As I sat on my equally orange chair and waited for my train, my mind slipped back to that infamous cadaver, and the extraordinary loyalty the Chairman had inspired. Mao was revered by the people of China. He was the man who had, at last, united their country after decades of upheavals and civil war, and led them from 1949 until his death in 1976. He evicted the foreigners who had been carving up the Middle Kingdom to create their own concessions since the middle of the nineteenth century. He vowed to cleanse the Motherland of the corruption that had poisoned it during the final, Qing dynasty and the subsequent American-backed Nationalist regime. He would douse out the opium pipes, drive away the Triads, and uphold the dignity of the common man. The populace was ecstatic. There were, however, one or two less savoury facts about Mao that, had they known them at the time, might have encouraged the masses to cheer a little less triumphantly.

To start with, the Chairman never brushed his teeth. According to his physician, Dr Li, he preferred the traditional Chinese peasant's routine of simply rinsing his mouth with tea each morning and then eating the leaves. 'As I looked into his mouth, I saw that his teeth were covered with a heavy greenish film. A few of them seemed loose. I touched the gums lightly and some pus oozed out,' Li wrote of the time he first examined Mao's mouth, when the Chairman was in his early sixties.

Additionally, the Chairman suffered from terrible constipation. During the Long March, that cavalcade of the Communist faithful to their stronghold in Shaanxi in the 1930s, he apparently suffered so badly that he made his bodyguards insert their fingers into his anus to pull out the faeces by hand.

He frequently didn't dress for days at a time, preferring to work and hold meetings in his bedroom or by his swimming pool, where he lounged in a robe. An inveterate insomniac, he lived by no established routine and frequently called upon his underlings in the middle of the night before sleeping through the day with the help of the sleeping pills to which he was addicted.

Inspired by fear, his toadying aides learned not to question his methods, nor to doubt his plans. In the late 1950s, Mao pronounced himself in favour of communal agricultural production. This was his Great Leap Forward. If the people abandoned the principles of private property and banded together into communes instead, he declared, output would soar. At the same time as reaping bumper harvests, the communes could help China to improve its steel output: they would surpass Great Britain's production in just fifteen years, Mao proclaimed. Every organization was to build a 'backyard furnace' where it would generate steel. They had no iron ore so the people threw their pots, pans and cutlery into the furnaces in order to meet their quotas. They ran out of coal so, to fuel the fires, they chucked in their beds, tables and chairs. Still falling short of their ridiculously optimistic targets, they piled in their agricultural tools – with so many hands required to manage the furnaces, they had no time to tend to their crops anyway.

The good harvest of 1958 rotted in the fields, yet still the communes had to pay their grain taxes. Fearful of punishment, the local officials grossly inflated the harvest figures, and many communes had to give almost all of their yield to the government. Many areas suffered a poor harvest the following year; in other regions the crops again weren't gathered. Famine swept China on a massive scale. More than thirty million people starved to death; some historians put the figures much higher. And the globs of metal that were churned out from these amateur furnaces in any case turned out to be useless.

In the aftermath of the Great Leap Forward, Mao was forced to take a lesser role in economic decision-making – he resigned his position as head of state, though he retained authority as the Chairman of the Communist Party – but this gave rise to a new problem: factionalism began to fester within the Party's upper echelons. The increasingly megalomaniac Mao saw power slipping from his grasp and it was this, as much as his ideological desire for perpetual class struggle, that led to his endorsement of the Cultural Revolution less than a decade later.

When his fury was triggered by a play that obliquely criticized him, the Chairman and his lackeys declared war on the intellectual classes. Encouraging students to rebel against their teachers, his government instigated a tremendous youth uprising of Red Guards who terrorized the nation with uncontrolled savagery as they attempted to destroy the 'four olds' – old ideas, old culture, old customs and old habits. This Cultural Revolution resulted in the closure of schools and universities whose students went on strike against their teachers and punished them brutally for being 'bourgeois reactionaries' and 'capitalist roaders'. Factories came to a standstill as their engineers, scientists and technicians were either sent to the countryside to be re-educated through hard labour, or jailed. The workers' production was paralysed by endless study sessions. Monasteries were desecrated. All entertainment and social activity was denounced.

The Cultural Revolution lasted ten long years, from 1966 until Mao's death.

While he preached the benefits of asceticism and a simple life to the masses, Mao himself lived opulently in his later years. As he reached his late sixties, his philandering increased. He convinced himself of the truth in the Daoist theory of sexuality: that by sleeping with as many women as possible, but not ejaculating himself, he would gain strength and virility through the absorption of vaginal secretions. At the height of the Cultural Revolution, when any form of pleasure-taking could result in accusations of bourgeois behaviour and counter-revolutionary leanings, Mao himself was, according to Dr Li, sometimes in bed with up to five women at once.

Still, the people didn't know any of this. They continued to adore him – and those who doubted stayed quiet if they wanted to survive. When *Quotations from Chairman Mao*, otherwise known as the Little Red Book, was published in the mid-1960s, the obligatory hero-worship reached truly fantastical heights. Every factory, school and commune in China was made to study the book and learn to recite the Chairman's words by heart. Posters of joyful Chinese raising their little red books to the heavens abounded. Mao had become a godhead.

'For most Chinese, a mere glimpse of Mao standing impassively atop Tiananmen was a coveted opportunity, the most uplifting, exciting, exhilarating experience they would know. The privileged few who actually got to shake his hand would go for weeks without washing, as friends and acquaintances came from miles around to touch the hand that had touched Mao and thus to partake of a transcendent, almost mystical experience,' wrote Dr Li.

Li also relates an extraordinary episode from the Cultural Revolution years. Losing faith in the students who had fuelled the movement because they were always feuding among themselves, Mao decided to bestow his favour on the workers. He therefore made a gift of mangoes (that he himself had been given by the foreign minister of Pakistan) to Beijing's factories. Each leading factory – including the Beijing Textile Factory to which Dr Li had at that time been seconded – received one mango.

'The workers at the factory held a huge ceremony, rich in the recitation of Mao's words, to welcome the arrival of the mango, then sealed the fruit in wax, hoping to preserve it for posterity. The mangoes became sacred relics, objects of veneration. The wax-covered fruit was placed on an altar in the factory auditorium, and workers lined up to file past it, solemnly bowing as they walked by,' he wrote.

Unfortunately, after a few days the mango began to rot, so the factory's revolutionary committee peeled it and boiled the festering fruit in water. Then a second ceremony was held in which each worker drank a spoonful of the mighty mango water.

I looked around the waiting hall where I now sat and considered that many of the older people in here would have lived through those desperate years. I wondered if any of them had worked at the Beijing Textile Factory and partaken of the mango water. Did these people still love Mao, or had his later mistakes turned some of them quietly against him?

A girl sitting two rows away from me turned round, stared at me, and giggled. She had clearly been born in more prosperous times – she had a chubby face and heavily gelled, permed hair that descended on either side of her round head in solid waves like sheets of corrugated metal. She seemed to find my presence here amusing. After a couple of minutes, she moved over to an empty seat next to me. Where was I from? Giggle. What was my name? Giggle. Did I like China? Giggle giggle. Her face flushed as she spoke so that it stood out like a brightly coloured beacon amid the colourless incumbents of the waiting hall.

I resurfaced from my reverie and, trying to smile, wearily answered her questions. It was just after eleven o'clock at night; I was ready for bed. Mixed with my tiredness came an acute sense of nervousness. I had at last forced myself to leave the sanctuary of Guy and Nancy's flat and venture out into the endless, bottomless Chinese unknown.

'Don't worry, the trains are fine, everyone takes them,' Guy had assured me having booked my berth on a top bunk.

I wasn't entirely sure whether I should believe him, but still, here I was, waiting to board the overnight train to Datong. It departed at eleven-thirty and would arrive at six-thirty tomorrow morning.

Taking a train in China is not like taking a train anywhere else in the world. You don't just show up on the platform with two minutes to spare and hop into a carriage. That wouldn't provide enough jobs for loyal Communist workers. So boarding a train in China ends up bearing a remarkable similarity to boarding a plane elsewhere, with the subtle difference that you do not – intentionally at least – leave the ground.

First, you enter the train station by the main door, showing your ticket to Official One. You then head for the security carousel (manned by Officials Two, Three, and Four). Having dumped your luggage on the carousel, you then have to sprint round to the other side to retrieve it before your hordes of fellow

45

passengers stamp on it. At the same time you must try not to harbour bitter feelings towards Officials Two, Three and Four who are standing around chatting and doing nothing whatsoever to help, nor indeed to spot firearms, bombs or whatever on the presumably non-existent X-ray film.

Then, reunited with your luggage, you have to locate the departures board and try to match the Chinese characters for your destination from your guidebook with one of the sequences of shapes on the board. If this fails, you can always ask for help from Officials Five or Six who can easily be identified as they stand in an authoritative manner behind little podiums doing nothing at all. The number on the board to the right of the destination indicates which waiting hall you must go to.

About half an hour before your train is due to depart, two more officials appear at a turnstile at the far end of the waiting hall. This is the sign for the entire population of the hall to leap to its feet, and push and jostle each other to get to the front first. The important thing at this juncture is to resist joining them – unless you really don't care for your current body shape and are in the market for a little free-of-charge remoulding. Finally, when everyone else has finished beating each other up and made their way onto the platform, you can saunter through the turn-stile in a leisurely manner.

The girl with the curly hair smiled. 'Where are you going?'

'Datong.'

Suddenly, the giggling stopped and the girl gasped. Her face, once rosy pink, now became pale with panic.

'Datong? *Datong?*' she yelped, and then waved at the lively mêlée of people battering each other in front of the turnstile. The turnstile officials hadn't yet arrived to take up their post; the queue wasn't moving.

'*Kuai le, kuai le*,' hurry up, she jabbered, in a manner that suggested my life hung in the balance. I was to join the unmoving queue at once. I must leap to my feet, *run*, take up my place among the crazed queue-pushers, join the joyfully jostling, shoving, heckling, haranguing throng. With great trepidation, I stood up and reluctantly plunged myself into the turmoil.

About fifteen minutes later, with only superficial bruising, I arrived on the platform. The train seemed infinitely long, its carriages disappearing into the distance. I located mine, a 'hard sleeper' furnished with rows of bunk beds three high. My ticket allocated me to a top bunk. It wasn't all that hard, really. The bed was coated in some thin padding covered by dark green plastic. Folded on top were a duvet and a small towel and, beside them, a pillow.

The people around me seemed pleasant: a middle-aged woman with her daughter, a couple of businessmen, an elderly couple. They smiled at me in a hospitable manner and helped me stow my luggage. We all found our places and climbed into our beds. Our carriage attendant appeared and exchanged our tickets for plastic discs, the lights went out, and the chatter subsided into deep, throaty snores.

4

The New Black

If Beijing is a face undergoing Botox and an assiduous eyebrow-shaping, Datong is a corn-encrusted, bunion-afflicted, hairy old toe that's never seen a pedicure. Located west of Beijing, close to the border of Inner Mongolia, it's an industrial town kept alight by its coal mines and power stations. A quarter of China's coal is mined here in Shanxi province and Datong is one of the most polluted cities in a very smoky country. (In 1998, a World Health Organization report concluded that of the ten most polluted cities in the world, seven were in China.) China still relies on coal for three-quarters of its energy; nearly a quarter of all deaths in the countryside are due to respiratory illnesses.

At six-thirty in the morning, the train station was under siege from touts. The sight of a Westerner's face threw them into a frenzy, eagerly offering taxis, hotels and day trips. Swarms of PLA soldiers stood around in the freezing cold drizzle, huddling round their packs in long, padded green overcoats with brown fur collars. I fought my way through the crowds to a licensed taxi, and asked to go to the hotel I'd booked.

We drove through the town. On the outskirts, some

of the older hovels belched acrid black smoke from their decrepit chimneys. Even the more prosperous centre was cloaked in a thick, grey haze.

The hotel was a reasonable one. The powers-that-be had allocated it four stars. It had a decent restaurant. The room was clean and the bathroom facilities worked. But I was surprised in such a seemingly salubrious place to find a collection of lotions on offer in the bathroom that suggested some kinds of business conducted here did not require a suit and tie. Next to the tiny bottles of shampoo and shower gel lay four sachets, two marked 'Man' and two marked 'Woman'.

'Eliminates pathogenic bacteria which can cause the disease of colpitis, pruritus, peculiar smell, ringworm at the thigh area and beri beri. Our product has been verified by authority organization that the rate of eliminating gonorrhoea coccus has reached 99.9 per cent,' declared the packet marked 'Woman'.

It went on. 'Using guide: Please scrub away repeatedly at the position with the product for about two to three minutes, and then wash with clean water.'

The brand name of the lotion was 'Know You Bird'. Across the front of the packet was stamped in big, black capitals: 'UNCOMPLIMENTARY'.

It seemed strange, really. The crime of organizing prostitution carries the death penalty in China, yet there seemed little doubt what was going on quite openly in this hotel. I eyed my bed with a new level of mistrust and hoped the sheets had been well boiled.

This question of when it was all right to break the law in China, and when it was downright dangerous to do so, was turning out to be less than straightforward. The Chinese are not afraid of draconian measures for malefactors. Nobody quite knows how many people are executed each year in China, but figures are reckoned to run into several thousands. Often, the final stroke is dealt by bullet in the back of the head within hours of the judge's passing sentence.

It's not just violent crimes that incur the death penalty – in China you can be executed for taking bribes, fraud, tax evasion, publishing pornography, and many indiscretions besides. (It's not just the present-day Communist regime that takes such stern measures. Across history the Chinese have been big on discipline. In the Ming dynasty, soldiers guarding the city walls were allowed only to move five paces in either direction; if any soldier abandoned his post he was decapitated on the spot. If he chatted on the job, his ears were chopped off.) But despite the possibility of severe punishment, many of China's laws are blatantly ignored. The sanctioning of prostitution in business hotels seemed to be one area towards which the authorities turned a blind eye.

I didn't feel I needed to apply any Know You Bird lotion right then – my night on the train hadn't been *that* eventful – so I skipped that part of my ablutions and instead headed out to the Yungang Grottoes, which are the only reason why anyone without an infatuation with coal would come to Datong.

On the road, donkeys pulled carts piled high with the ubiquitous black fuel. One man rode a moped, holding with one hand onto a rope tied to a donkey that charged frantically behind. The donkeys looked docile, friendly beasts with nice fluffy ears and kind eyes. I wondered what they made of pulling laden carts and galloping behind mopeds in this polluted hell-hole. The air was revolting – thick and brown. And then I arrived at the caves, the wonders of which almost sucked the coal-besmirched breath from my body.

Here, carved into a sandstone cliff face, were *fifty-one thousand* ancient Buddhist carvings. They were created in the second half of the fifth century AD, making them a staggering fifteen hundred years old. It seemed incredible that here, in this very armpit of the earth, such monumental artwork should stand. Perhaps it was the sensational contrast between the noxious, blackened town and the remarkable Buddhist statues that made them all the more astonishing. Perhaps it was because I really hadn't been expecting this: I knew there were Buddhist carvings here, but hadn't read up on them in advance and had no concept of their magnitude. Whatever the reason, I was suddenly enchanted.

I forgot about the coal, the grime and the uncomplimentary genital lotions, and wandered, awestruck, from cave to cave. The largest Buddha was nearly seventeen metres high, and said to be hewn in the likeness of one of the emperors of the Northern Wei dynasty who built their capital here at Datong. The larger, better-preserved statues had golden skin that glimmered in the light even on a drizzly day like this one. It was as though the sun itself, in a misguided moment, had descended from the heavens and decided to shine from here instead. The figures' robes shimmered rust-red and turquoise, their hair and long, curving eyebrows glowed sapphire-blue. The simple garb and serene expressions of the Buddhas contrasted with the glittering jewellery that denoted the earthly status of the bodhisattvas that surrounded them.

The walls and ceilings were filled with intricate ornamentation – lotus flowers and leaves, dragons and animals – in yellows and greens, reds and blues. Many of the carvings were tiny. Row upon row of minute statues sat in individual enclaves lining every inch of the caves' walls, their palms turned out in *abhaya mudra*, the Buddhist gesture of protection. Celestial beings glided across the ceilings; earthly creatures meditated under trees. Indian style merged with Chinese influences: a multi-armed Shiva sat upon a dragon, that all-pervading Chinese symbol of divine power.

Relief murals told the story of the origins of Buddhism. The young prince Siddharta Gautama set out on a journey on horseback and met people plagued by sickness, age and death. Realizing that these were afflictions nobody could avoid, he concluded that he could never find fulfilment on a material level. The prince therefore renounced his wealth and committed himself to a life of contemplation. One evening, as he meditated beneath a banyan tree, he achieved enlightenment. He went on to found an order of monks who preached his philosophy – that all life is suffering and that only by renouncing desire can we find happiness – and taught others to practise meditation and a contemplative life.

There are various stories about the way Buddhism first came to China. Some say an ancient explorer brought news of the religion home from his travels; others claim that in the first century AD the Han emperor Mingdi had a dream in which a golden deity flew before his palace. His advisers told him that he had dreamt of Buddha, and he therefore sent envoys to India to bring back the scriptures. Still others suggest that there was already by this time a small Buddhist community of traders or missionaries living in Jiangsu on China's eastern coast.

Whatever the origins, during the early centuries of the first millennium Chinese monks travelled to India and brought back scriptures that they translated from Sanskrit. It took several hundred years, however, for Buddhism really to take hold. The Buddha's insistence on renouncing earthly ties, including family bonds, starkly opposed recognized Confucian values. Furthermore, translation from the Sanskrit was at first haphazard and bred confusion. But by the middle of the first millennium, Buddhism was widely accepted in China.

It seemed incredible to think that, fifteen hundred years ago, on this cold, rainy hillside, monks had toiled for forty years to create these remarkable sculptures in homage to their new religion. I wondered what could have led the Northern Wei to build their capital in Datong. Presumably it was frequently cold and drizzly then as it is now. I imagined the monks shivering in their robes as they chipped away at the sandstone, reminding themselves that all life was suffering and dreaming of nirvana. It was humbling to think of them so dedicated to their religion and their art that they would undertake such an endeavour as this.

I looked out from the caves, across the road to the railway track, where goods trains blasted their horns as they drew an endless stream of coal carts through the greyness like a perpetual chain of doomed, defeated prisoners, manacled one to the next. The pollution from the coal mine, and from the trains and trucks that transport its produce, is so severe that they actually had to redirect the road in an attempt to preserve the statues here at the Yungang Grottoes – but the pervasive, black cloak of dust still hangs here.

I returned from the caves to Datong on a crowded, clattering public bus. A group of girls in their twenties chatted on their mobile phones. The bus stopped outside the entrance to the coal mine and men with wives and small children climbed on. Presumably they were off to enjoy a Sunday afternoon in the happening hub of Datong. The rain persisted, obscuring what little view there was like a dank, grey lace curtain. We drove past a building with peeling paintwork and a battered sign. 'Sunshine Holiday Hotel,' it sang. I shuddered.

The bus dropped me off on the outskirts of town and I walked for a while down the streets that buzzed with Sunday-afternoon activity. Synthesized music blared from the shops. On the streets, vendors touted fruit from carts – bananas, kumquats, cherries, grapes and apples. Others roasted chestnuts in piping hot woks, or sold baked yams from metal stoves, or toffee-coated fruit on sticks.

A group of young men hung out from the doors of a bus.

'Haa-lloooo,' they called, and laughed raucously. It didn't sound like a greeting. It was more like a catcall, or a jeering provocation. Or the desperate braying of a mangy dog who can't attract a mate.

A painfully thin man aged about thirty hawked loudly and spat a great glob of phlegm onto the pavement just centimetres from my foot. He was dressed in an ill-fitting green army uniform, but this man would surely be incapable of fighting. At the first glimpse of action, his fragile frame would have shattered into a thousand tiny shards. He must have been one of millions of poor Chinese who buy army clothes on the market simply because they're cheap and durable. I sidestepped away from the phlegm. It didn't seem healthy to walk close to fluids emanating from that man's body. A middle-aged woman picked freely at her nose. Then, in a glorious culmination of this open celebration of mucus, an old man walked past me, squeezing the tips of his nostrils as he went, and, with a mighty blast, shot two great jets of snot out onto the road.

Back at the hotel, I ventured to the dining room for some food. Ordering food in China can be difficult when one's command of the language is limited. I thought I'd just have some rice and vegetables. That surely had to be easy enough to explain.

The waitress brought me a menu with pictures. I pointed to the vegetables. Easy, foolproof, faultless, I thought. And then I realized: I couldn't remember the word for rice. Of course there was no picture for rice – it was unnecessary to advertise a staple available in every restaurant across the land.

'Just vegetables?' The waitress raised her eyebrows, then looked round at her colleagues who giggled. They huddled together near the kitchen door in their matching green silk cheongsams as though to assure themselves of a hasty escape should running for their lives become necessary.

'And some rice?' I asked weakly, but in English. And so the vegetables came all alone and stoically I munched through them, trying to look as though this was what I had wanted all along and making a mental note never again to venture into a restaurant without my phrase book.

I retired to my room where I sat on my bed and read. At nine-thirty, the telephone rang.

'Hello?' I answered it. The line went dead. Seconds later, I heard the phone ring in the next-door room and then, ever more softly, in rooms down the corridor.

Fifteen minutes later, the same thing happened, and then again at just past ten. It was with some distaste that it dawned on me: the person on the other end was probably offering those same services for which I might need the Know You Bird lotion and she was hanging up when she heard a female voice.

I stared with some revulsion at the receiver in my hand that now whined with a constant, disconnected tone. My eye wandered to the laminated sheet that constituted the hotel's telephone directory.

'S & M department,' read one entry, followed by a four-figure number. Sales and marketing, I presume.

5

'Welcome to China'

'Where do I go to take the bus to Wutai Shan?' I asked the two matching receptionists in my best Chinese, at seven-thirty the following morning. Wutai Shan is one of China's four sacred Buddhist mountains and I was going to spend a day and a night there, wandering round the temples and drinking in the calm, clean air.

'*Mei you*,' there isn't one, they replied in unison, and gave a perfectly co-ordinated blink.

The manager appeared. He was a portly man in a well-cut dark suit.

'*Mei you*,' he said, and then, in English, 'The bus left at six-thirty. I think you must go tomorrow.'

So there *was* somebody who spoke English here. Where was he yesterday when I wanted a bowl of rice?

'Or,' he said, 'you can rent a car. It will cost five hundred yuan.'

Things weren't looking good. The idea of staying for another twenty-three hours in Datong with its dust, its drizzle and its donkeys made me want to hurl myself down a mine shaft. On the other hand, this was only the second day of my attempt to tour China by public

59

transport, and to bottle out quite so early in the proceedings by taking a taxi seemed a little limp.

'Or,' conceded the manager very reluctantly, 'you could take the bus to Shahe, and then rent a car from there.'

I took a taxi to the long-distance bus station. After ten minutes or so, we pulled up in a drab, deserted forecourt.

'Where do I go for the bus to Shahe?' I asked the taxi driver.

'*Mei you*,' he said. 'But if you like, I can take you there for four hundred and fifty yuan.'

'*Mei you, mei you*,' said the bus station staff. A man went off to make a phone call.

'There's a bus at one o'clock this afternoon, or tomorrow morning at six,' he informed me when he returned.

Back outside my taxi was gone. There were two or three others parked haphazardly across the tarmac, however. Their drivers were all leaning against the bonnet of one of them, smoking and scuffing at the dirt with their shoes. When they saw me, they leapt to life.

'Five hundred,' said one.

'Four hundred and fifty,' said another.

In the end, I negotiated the fare down to three hundred and fifty yuan and set off in a small green car. The driver seemed almost deliriously happy with the way his morning had turned out.

'I'm going to Wutai Shan! I'm going to Wutai Shan! I've got a fare to Wutai Shan!' he screeched in apparent ecstasy into his radio handset as we bumped over the cracked, pitted tarmac.

'Which is better, China or England?' asked the driver, optimistic and upbeat, as we clattered over

60

potholes and past tumbledown shacks on the outskirts of Datong.

'Both are good, but they are very different,' I told him as the car's suspension twanged unnervingly.

'Who are nicer, Chinese people or English people?'

'Erm . . . well, the Chinese people are very friendly and very kind.'

We had now exhausted most of the possibilities of my conversational Chinese – I had in my repertoire only a couple of sentences regarding the movements of Mr Li that remained unused – but the ever-hopeful driver continued undeterred.

'Chinese English gobbledy gobbledy gook,' he said, or something like that.

'*Wo ting bu dong*,' I don't understand, I replied.

'*Ah, ni ting bu dong.*' Oh, so you don't understand. He shook his head sadly, then continued, 'England gookety gookety gobble?'

'*Wo ting bu dong*,' I said again.

He shrugged, undeterred. 'You in China gobbledy gobbledy gobbledy gook?'

'*Wo ting bu dong.*'

It was curious, but he just didn't seem to be getting the message. He didn't appear to understand that my inane repetition of the one phrase I had truly mastered meant that I was not going to enter into robust discussion about cultural difference, but was a goofy, good-for-nothing lump of lard who could offer him no amusement beyond the opportunity to stare through his rear-view mirror at my astoundingly large nose. It was a good fifteen minutes before he realized this and sought alternative entertainment in blasting high-volume Chinese pop from the radio and lighting up a pungent cigarette.

We clattered out of Datong and into the countryside

past endless plantations of sick, spindly saplings followed by fields of corn that were rendered ashen by the ever-present shroud of coal dust. Then, after about forty-five minutes, the pollution lifted and blue sky broke through the haze. We started to climb between rocky, terraced hills covered in grey-green scrub.

As we spiralled higher, the surface of the road deteriorated. Huge potholes progressed into great tracts of tarmac that seemed quite simply to have been ripped up. The car lunged and plunged as the driver veered from one side of the road to the other, trying to take the path with the fewest craters. Several times my head hit the roof.

'Chinese roads are worse than English roads, aren't they?' asked the driver.

'Yes,' I said.

We lapsed into a long, sad silence.

We stopped off at the Hanging Monastery at Hunyuan where, for some unfathomable reason as it seemed to me, sixth-century monks decided that it would be fun to build a monastery suspended precariously from the sheer drop of a cliff instead of on the perfectly adequate flat ground below. (I found out later that it was because the river that used to flow through the valley was prone to flooding.) Just a few metres wide, the skinny four-storey buildings teetered perilously on tiny outcrops of rock, their carved wooden balconies and curving tiled roofs attached by walkways balanced on pillars. Inside, Buddha, Confucius and Lao Tzu (the founder of Daoism) sat side by side, which seemed unusual until I worked out the monks' motivation: if you must live in a building that hangs off the front of a very sheer cliff, you'd want to curry favour from all the gods you could.

After about four hours' driving, we arrived at

Shahe. Now I understood how Datong could have a Sunshine Holiday Hotel. Compared to Shahe, Datong was an earthly paradise. The people of Shahe might quite feasibly go there for a couple of weeks' vacation, were they able to afford such a luxury. Shahe's streets were choked with queues of wheezing lorries piled high with coal. Everything was black. A group of coal-encrusted children stood by the side of the road, waiting to cross. I couldn't even conceive what it would be like to grow up in a town like this. I had always thought growing up in Derby was lacking in glamour. Next to Shahe, Derby was heaven.

We turned left at a junction and drove for a minute or two. The driver scratched his head and jabbered something I couldn't understand. I didn't reply. He muttered a little. I had no idea what he was talking about but the vibe coming from the front seat wasn't positive. Then he pulled over, stopped the car, and went to ask directions. It was only now that I realized that this man had never before been to Wutai Shan.

We turned round – we should have taken the right-hand turn – and soon the road surface improved. We drove along the flat for a while, then the road started to climb again. The contours of the hills were rounded; the scrub and rocks of earlier were replaced now by a covering of thin, bristly grass. As the air became cleaner, the driver began to smoke increasingly rapidly, until he was lighting each cigarette when he had scarcely finished the last. It was almost as if he was pining for the coal dust of Datong; perhaps the unfamiliar sensation of oxygen in his lungs was giving him a head rush. We climbed and climbed, the car groaning on the steep inclines, until the hills were coated with a light sprinkling of snow.

Now the taxi driver was dumbstruck. His eyes gaped

wide; his head pivoted from left to right to take in the snowy mountain scenery, the like of which he must never have seen before. His astonishment was itself a delight – more so really than the scenery itself. He looked about forty years old, and would almost certainly never have travelled far from Datong. I could envisage him, back in town that evening, regaling his family with what he had seen. Tomorrow morning, scuffing dirt in the bus station's forecourt, he was going to have stories that would stun them all.

We reached a mountain pass, then began our descent into Taihuai, the village at the foot of Mount Wutai, or Wutai Shan (*shan* means mountain in Chinese). Below us stretched out the honey-coloured, glazed roofs of the temples that make the place famous. Wind chimes dangled from their curled-up corners and permeated the air with melodious tones. Upon the cylindrical tiles, fiery ceramic dragons kept watch. Beneath, vivid red and yellow lotus flowers adorned the rafter-tips, while the eaves were painted with intertwined four-pronged swastikas of peace in electric blue and sea green. The sky here, far from the city, was deep blue.

The taxi driver gazed in silent astonishment. Gone were his questions, his nodding head to the blaring radio. His cigarette hung limply from his lips. He seemed never in his life to have conceived of such a place. I checked into a hotel and waved goodbye to him. He drove off back over the ravaged roads towards Datong which, I was sad to imagine, he might never find pleasant again.

The road over the mountains is apparently much better now than it was forty years ago – and it was the difficulty of the terrain that saved the Wutai Shan temples from destruction during the Cultural

Revolution. Even today, religion is viewed with mistrust by the Chinese authorities. Nobody with any religious affiliation may become a member of the Communist Party. Catholics, while allowed to celebrate Mass, are not permitted to recognize the Pope. But religion was truly abhorred by the early Communists.

When Mao came to power in 1949, he branded spiritual beliefs feudal and superstitious. It wasn't until twenty years later, though, during the Cultural Revolution, that the desecration really began in earnest. The Red Guards rampaged across the country and burned temples, mosques and churches. Monks, nuns and priests were deported to labour camps or simply tortured and executed. As a result, most of the temple complexes in China today are not the ancient edifices that once stood but recent reconstructions in the old style. Wutai Shan is exceptional: it escaped because the Red Guards never made it over the treacherous mountain paths.

Today, however, Wutai Shan is seeing an invasion of a different kind. Domestic tourism in China has mushroomed in just the last few years. With the economy roaring into a new era of prosperity, many people have disposable income for the first time. In their millions, they are jumping on tour buses and taking off to see the wonders of the Middle Kingdom.

As I attempted to tour the first few temples, I had to battle through throngs of camera-wielding visitors. Even amid the din, however, there were moments of perfect tranquillity when I would wander through an ornate doorway and find myself entirely alone in a cobbled courtyard. Multicoloured prayer flags imprinted with Buddhist wheels of life and symbols of peace fluttered from strings tied between the upturned corners of the buildings. The rounded chords of gently clanging wind chimes echoed from the walls. Occasionally a monk would shuffle by in his flip-flops and turn the heavy prayer wheels. Other monks, in robes of grey, dark red or ochre, silently swept the spotless terraces with bamboo brooms. As I wandered from one courtyard to another a harmonious chanting punctuated by the ringing of handbells emanated from a doorway.

Night was beginning to fall. I climbed down the steps of one last temple and made my way back into the village, past the souvenir stalls selling odd assortments of porcelain and, even more curiously in a place such as this, Chairman Mao memorabilia.

I ate in the hotel restaurant that night. There was no English menu and once more I failed to make myself understood. But this time I had remembered my phrase book. I opened it up on the page entitled 'Typical Dishes' and the waitress pointed to items on the list that the kitchen could muster: chilli chicken, Chinese cabbage and rice. This certainly constituted great progress in my ordering ability since the day before, when I'd eaten vegetables with no rice, though I could see that if I had to stick with this method for long I was going to be eating an awful lot of Chinese cabbage.

The other customers at the restaurant that night were crowded at the opposite end of the room onto three large, round tables. They were a tour group celebrating their holiday with endless toasting.

'*Ganbei!*' They shrieked the Chinese drinkers' call to arms again and again, leapt to their feet and poured tiny glasses of clear spirit down their throats. Their faces were becoming red and their eyes woozy. Chinese people don't generally tolerate drink well – many of them lack a certain enzyme in the liver which metabolizes alcohol – and they become intoxicated quickly and colourfully, but they make up for it with noisy bravado.

I went back to my room. The phone rang. I answered it and the line went dead. A loud burping noise emanated from the bathroom as the drain in the floor overflowed, churning out grey water and somebody else's short, black hairs.

I was determined not to miss the bus again, so I was up at six-thirty the following morning. I was heading south to Taiyuan. From there I'd take a train to the historic town of Pingyao.

Almost immediately I set foot on the road, a small white minibus drew up. The doors flew open and a man stuck his head out.

'Taiyuan, Taiyuan, Taiyuan-*Taiyuan*-TAIYUAN,' he yodelled.

I jumped aboard. Everyone seemed ecstatic to see me. Several men leapt to their feet, helped stow my luggage and insisted that I took the front seat behind the driver.

The reason they were so gladdened by my presence had nothing to do with any pleasure they might take in my company, nor with the entertainment they might derive from my witty repartee in Mandarin. It was just that the bus wouldn't depart for Taiyuan until the driver deemed it sufficiently full. And so we trailed up and down the village. The moment the man in charge of shouting spotted anybody standing by the roadside carrying so much as a handbag, he flung open the doors and, with a projection of which an opera singer would be proud, burst into his cantillation: 'Taiyuan, Taiyuan, Taiyuan-*Taiyuan*-TAIYUAN.' Once or twice, a couple of passengers warmed up sufficiently to join in with something approaching a chorus.

Half an hour later, the driver decided we had serenaded enough and we cruised, much relieved, out of the village. As we drove through the valley, past tight little mounds of tree-covered hills, we stopped every couple of minutes either to drop people off at a ramshackle handful of houses, or to pick up others who had somehow found themselves standing on the side of a road in the middle of nowhere. Before long, the bus was packed and there were people sitting in the aisle.

By now I had worked out that there were three men running the show: the driver, the money-collector (who doubled up as the yodeller), and the money-collector's mate. The latter two squatted at the front of the bus on collapsible stools or just stood chain-smoking. The driver's window was open so that a piercing, cold gale charged straight at my face, but the ventilation was a mercy.

Somehow I dozed off in spite of the glacial wind, and woke up some time later in a bus station. Money-Collector's Mate was bellowing at me in Chinese. I couldn't understand a word he said, but his gesticulations made it clear that I was to get out of my preferential front seat by the window, gather my luggage, and board another bus that had pulled up next to us.

The second bus was bigger than the first, but it stank like the breath of a tramp who has smoked sixty cigarettes a day for sixty years and never once brushed his teeth. The curtains on the window had once been grey, but had now turned a sallow, sticky brown. They were so encrusted with dirt that they were slightly stiff. The cream and purple squares of the seats' upholstery had begun to merge into an almost uniform beige. The fabric felt faintly greasy. I wondered if I might catch something.

The man behind me wheezed and let rip a racking cough. I rummaged in my bag for a bottle of anti-bacterial hand gel. I squirted a generous dollop of the alcoholic gloop onto my palms and rubbed it in with neurotic zest.

People sniffed and squatted in the aisle. Squeezing themselves onto every available surface, they turned and stared at me unwaveringly when I climbed on. Two shaven-headed monks nudged each other and pointed. I crammed myself into a seat between the window and a third Buddhist monk dressed in a remarkable number of thick, coarse robes – a heavy brown outer garment over layers of grey. His face was angular; his cheekbones stuck out over sunken hollows. His hands were gnarled and knuckly with fabulously clean, bright-white fingernails. He had a string of prayer beads wrapped several times round his wrist. He spent almost the entire journey leaning forward, his head and hands resting against the back of the seat in front. Whether this posture designated high-minded contemplation or silent agony I couldn't tell.

Personally, I was in pain. With the exception of myself and the three monks, every person squeezed on board seemed to be chain-smoking. My comfort wasn't improved by the fact that the bus seemed to be suffering from some kind of mechanical imperfection: every time it started from stationary, it juddered so violently that my head smacked several times in spasmic quick-fire against the back of the seat.

Each time we stopped, a teenage boy staggered out of the door, squatted on the side of the road and vomited. He was perspiring profusely. His face was faintly green and his pasty flesh glistened with that sweat peculiar to sickness.

What with the smoke inhalation and the repeated battering of my skull, I soon began to feel quite sick myself. Matters weren't helped by the fact that I was by now very dehydrated. The problem with this bus journey was that it offered no opportunities to pee. The men dealt with the problem easily enough. Every now and then, one of them would ask the driver to stop, and a few of them would line up on the side of the road to relieve themselves. What would happen, I wondered, if I were to alight with them, squat down by the side of the road, and empty my bladder? Just thinking about the hullabaloo that would almost certainly ensue made me cringe. The other occupants of the bus were fascinated enough just by my sitting squashed up against the monk. If I were to get out and drop my knickers on the side of the road – this part of the world didn't seem to *do* strategically placed bushes – I felt quite sure they would stand around squawking and pointing in wonderment at the milky whiteness of my curiously capacious buttocks. (Chinese women, I have noticed from discreet observation in Hong Kong's swimming pool changing rooms, don't actually have bottoms. Their backs go down and down, then their legs seem to start almost straight away.) There weren't any other women on the bus for more than a short hop so I couldn't follow their lead. The only solution I could think of was to drink nothing and so avoid the problem. It worked on one level, but failed on another. A sharp, stabbing pain ran diagonally through my head. I felt nauseous. I had been travelling for three hours – and we were still only halfway there.

We continued through small plots dotted with

70

lettuces and cabbages, apples and leeks. Among them slouched rundown one-storey houses whose bricks blended with the sandy colour of the soil. On their flat roofs, bright yellow corn dried in the sun.

There was a TV screen at the front of the bus. It was showing a movie called *Sam Hong the Happy Ghost with Supernatural Powers*. I knew this for certain because the film had English subtitles. Sam Hong was a teacher at a girls' secondary school. Most of the girls' lessons seemed to be PE for which they had to wear very tiny, tight gym knickers, or pink swimming costumes with white belts round the waist. They weren't very good at any of the sports they played but luckily for them they had Sam Hong on their side. Whenever his girls were losing, Sam Hong the Happy Ghost with Supernatural Powers would use his incredible psychic strength to twizzle them into amazing acrobatic dives, or to guide a basketball into a hoop during a match. The two Buddhist monks in the seat opposite seemed to love it. The one next to me never so much as raised his head. I began to wonder if he had died and found nirvana.

After six long hours, we finally arrived on the outskirts of Taiyuan. As we rattled along those last few kilometres into town, through piles of rubble on the road, and sat in traffic jams of trucks, I noticed to the right a gleaming asphalt highway. It was completely deserted. Either it was so brand-new it had not yet opened, or perhaps it was a toll road and none of these cranky old heaps wanted to pay. Whatever the reason, it looked like paradise to me, trapped inside that filthy, juddering bus. As far as I was concerned right then, the new China couldn't come fast enough.

When we arrived at our destination, I staggered

71

off the bus, fell into a taxi, and asked the driver to take me to the train station. He said it would cost seven yuan. We loaded in my luggage and he drove perhaps a hundred metres, then pulled into a car park across the street. On the other side of the tarmac expanse was a large, stone building with a clock tower.

'Is this the train station?' I asked drily.

'It is.' The taxi driver nodded, his face straight and unsmiling.

I clambered out and gathered my luggage and then, because I couldn't put the sentence together in Chinese right then, I told him in English, 'I'm not paying you seven yuan to drive me across the street. You should have told me where it was.'

He roared with laughter, fired up the car and chugged off still chortling. He seemed to have understood perfectly, and appeared not to care a jot. Sometimes, it seems, language learning is overrated.

I went into the station and bought a ticket for the four o'clock train to Pingyao, then deposited my rucksack at the left-luggage counter and headed into Taiyuan in search of sustenance.

I was feeling really lousy by now, sick and dehydrated. I had a splitting headache. I needed to eat and drink.

I walked down the main street which seemed pleasant enough, wide and lined with trees. There was a park on the left-hand side bursting with lush green grass. I went into a dumpling restaurant. There was no English menu, nothing to point at. There weren't even any other customers eating so I couldn't point at their food and ask for a plate of the same. The waitresses stood in a huddle and giggled at me. The establishment's sole customer, sitting alone at a bare table, stared at me as if I had just dropped by on a dumpling mission from Mars.

'Oh, forget it,' I said to them in English, and left.

I went back into the street, hungry and tired. My head was hammering. My eyes felt suspiciously watery. Things weren't looking good. One journey on a Chinese bus and I was a physical wreck – and I was supposed to keep it up for two months.

Then, slightly blurry, I saw them. On the other side of the road, rising golden above the tarmac and trees like a gateway to Eden itself: the yellow arches of McDonald's. I *never* go to McDonald's. But for once, the sight of a beaming Ronald McDonald filled my heart with cheer. I almost skipped up the steps and ordered a cheeseburger, fries and a large, large Coke. I went to the loo twice. It seemed a shame to pass up an opportunity. It was glistening, sparkling, a veritable ablutionary heaven. The cleaner was fastidiously polishing the mirror when I first went in; later she was mopping the floor. I wondered whether the job of loo-cleaner was a full-time position here in McDonald's, Taiyuan.

I travelled in a hard-seat carriage on the train. This is the way most of the Chinese travel, sometimes for twenty, thirty or even fifty hours if they have a long distance to cover. It was only an hour and a half to Pingyao. Right then, that seemed quite sufficient. My presence in the carriage was already creating something of a stir.

'Blabbedy-blabbedy *waiguoren*,' I could hear them exclaiming up and down the length of the carriage. *Waiguoren* was one of the words I had mastered. It means foreigner. My phone rang. It was Guy asking

73

how I was getting on. As I talked to him, my fellow travellers fell into a slack-jawed silence and stared at this extraordinary white woman who spoke in strange tongues.

Smoking was officially against the regulations but everyone lit up anyway. A boy sitting opposite me, who looked about ten years old, had his own packet of cigarettes and was making good progress through them. My nausea returned.

The carriage guard appeared. He was a sturdy man with a loud, booming voice. He seemed proud of the authority his uniform afforded him. As he set foot through the door at the far end of the carriage, he began to holler and waved his arms angrily. Some passengers frenziedly pretended to put out their cigarettes, others opened the windows. The guard moved on and they sneakily drew their hands back out from under the seats – as if nobody had been able to see the coils of smoke that had strangely been wisping up around them. I took two Nurofen, thanked God or Confucius or whoever for the ventilation, and started to feel better.

As the train drew into Pingyao station, I stood up and joined a line of others in the aisle waiting to get off. It was dark by now and I hadn't booked a room for the night. I was hoping to fight my way through the touts and take a taxi to the one guesthouse recommended by the Lonely Planet. If that turned out to be fully booked, it would make a perfectly horrible end to a perfectly horrible day.

My concerns were interrupted by a woman sitting in the seat next to where I stood. She stole a glance at me, then looked shyly away.

'Where is she from do you think?' the man opposite asked.

'America!' she replied emphatically. Then an expression of uncertainty crossed her face.

'*Ni shi neiguoren?*' what is your nationality, she asked.

'*Yingguoren*,' English, I said.

The people in the surrounding seats all gazed.

'*Ah, yingguoren . . . shi yingguoren*,' they confirmed among themselves, nodding and smiling as if the information somehow rather pleased them. They seemed to consider it a feasible, yet truly fascinating answer.

And then the girl in front of me in the line turned round. She was about twenty, clean and wholesome-looking. Her straight black hair was pulled back into a faultless ponytail and shone like polished lacquer. Her skin was unblemished. Her white anorak, miraculously, had not a smudge upon it. She smiled at me and, with earnest sincerity, she enunciated her words in clear, effortful English.

'Welcome to China,' she said.

6

At Home With the Wangs

I clunked through the clattering old doors of the guesthouse, into the front room that doubled up as a reception area and restaurant. Sturdy, dark-wood benches flanked square, black-lacquer tables. In the centre of each stood a wooden candlestick in which a single red candle was burning. Rows of red lanterns with yellow tassels hung from the ceiling beams. Calligraphy scrolls adorned the walls.

'*You mei you fangjian?*' Do you have any rooms? I stumbled through my best attempt at Chinese.

The woman behind the counter smiled.

'Ah, you speak Chinese!' she laughed, as if she was surprised that I had even bothered to try. Here, for the first time since I'd left Beijing, the people spoke a little English.

She showed me to my room. Red lanterns hung from the ceiling there as well. My bed was an old opium couch and the floorboards were rickety and full of character. Everything was spotlessly clean. There was even a mineral water dispenser in the corner of the room.

I spent some time standing under a piping-hot

shower, hoping to annihilate the bacteria that were, surely, at that very moment, burrowing deep into my lungs, intent on inflicting upon me a slow, agonizing, sputum-sputtering demise. China is big on disease: a mind-blowing 550 million people, that's almost half the population, carry the tubercule bacillus that causes tuberculosis; one in five people are infected with hepatitis.

I shampooed my hair three times in an attempt to eradicate the bloodthirsty lice that I imagined would have leapt, whooping with delight, from the grimy bus upholstery and onto a fresher, more succulent host. I scrubbed my fingernails and scoured my skin. And then, when I was absolutely certain that no bug could possibly have survived, I went downstairs.

Five minutes later, I was sitting at a black lacquer table and drinking chrysanthemum tea from a delicate blue-and-white porcelain bowl. The infusion was served in a large, glass pot. At first the liquid was almost clear, with just the faintest tinge of yellow, and delicate to taste. Then, as time passed and I poured myself a second, then a third bowl, the dried-up flowers that had floated as tiny balls on the surface of the water gradually opened their pink-and-white petals and the tea turned a deeper colour, with a richer, full-bodied flavour.

Somewhat incongruously, 1970s anthems reverberated from the stereo – 'By the Rivers of Babylon' and 'Yesterday Once More'. I was given a menu translated into English that featured portions suitable for a person dining alone. Sitting at one or two of the other tables in this lantern-bedecked room were the first Westerners I'd seen since I waved goodbye to Guy outside his apartment. I was both surprised and slightly disappointed by the immense relief I felt at seeing them. My trip wasn't supposed to form the basis of a study of foreigners abroad. On the contrary, I was hoping to take a look at the Chinese. Yet, after just a few days of being the only foreigner in town, of being stared at and pointed at, sometimes even laughed at and heckled, I felt almost a sense of homecoming at finding myself among these total strangers. It's not really so remarkable, I suppose. For once, I was easily able to order food – a large bowl of steaming dumplings dipped in soy sauce and vinegar. I was able to hold conversations, to compare notes with fellow travellers about their journeys. For once, I wasn't alone. The wood-panelled walls of the guesthouse blended curiously with the crooning tones of Boney M and the Carpenters to provide a welcome retreat, a safe haven from the very foreign world outside.

I slept well in my opium bed and the next morning spent a leisurely half hour or so with a banana pancake and a big mug of coffee in the guesthouse restaurant – where they were still playing the same compilation CD – before venturing out into the streets of Pingyao. Were it not for the electricity lines strung from pole to pole across the streets, Pingyao could have come straight out of the history books. Indeed, it's because of this that visitors come here at all.

Pingyao is one of the few towns in China whose Ming-dynasty walls remain intact. Several hundred years ago, it was a thriving hubbub of a place, lying as it does on the old trade route between Beijing and Xi'an. It was home to the first ever bank in China, Rishengchang. Established in the 1820s, this establishment enjoyed a monopoly in China and was even engaged in business in America and Europe. Then the Qing dynasty collapsed, revolution arose and Pingyao's commerce was trampled in its wake. The town fell into poverty. With no funds for renovations, nothing much ever changed here: the houses weren't pulled down to make way for high-rise blocks and the people carried on living in much the same way they had for centuries. Then, in 1997, UNESCO declared Pingyao a World Heritage Site so the money that now floods in from tourists is spent on renovating the old buildings rather than constructing new ones. This glossing up for the tourist trade has not come without its problems, though. The other side of the renovation coin was the eviction of large numbers of residents who were incensed at the insufficient compensation awarded to them by the government.

I wandered down the main streets whose paved flagstones had been worn smooth by the footsteps of time. A row of open-fronted shops was adorned with rust-red wooden lattices above which mural panels depicted flowers and figures. Bulbous red lanterns, now dusty with age, hung beneath the buildings' eaves. Behind one counter laden with heaps of nuts and seeds – peanuts, cashews, sunflower seeds, pistachios – a woman dressed in pink weighed out snacks into little paper bags for her customer who stood with her bicycle. Next door a tiny, wizened man who can have weighed no more than fifty kilos peddled incense sticks and temple offerings. Others sold tourist paraphernalia – yet more carved Buddhas, well-thumbed Little Red Books, old brass candlesticks and watercolours on ricepaper.

Groups of domestic tourists buzzed round the streets in large electric buggies like extended versions of those vehicles that ferry the old and infirm around airports. They rarely stepped out from the comfort of these people-movers, and when they did it was en masse, to pose for photos with the 'traditional'

80

rickshaw pullers. Dressed in silk tunics and skullcaps, these entrepreneurs passed their days sitting in the streets in their two-wheeled contraptions. When a tour group approached, one of them would pay to be 'carried'. Amid much joshing and joviality from the group, the appointed member would take up his place in the rickshaw, suitably attired in a fedora and wire-rimmed spectacles that had been lent to him for the occasion by the rickshaw puller. The latter would then pick up the wooden shafts and, with a great display of sweat and toil, would pretend to transport his customer. The hat-clad man would wave regally while the rest of his group cheered and laughed noisily as their camera shutters click-click-clicked. It was a good-humoured scene – though I have no idea what the rickshaw pullers of former days, who suffered horribly at the hands of the foreigners and wealthy Chinese they now caricatured, would have made of their descendants' hilarity.

Away from the main streets, rutted earthen alleyways stretched long and straight towards the surrounding city walls. Even here, in the parts of town that had not been dressed up for the easy passage of ancient bankers or fresh-faced tourists, the houses followed traditional architectural patterns: dark grey roofs with semicircular tiles whose pitch softened in a gentle curve towards the eaves; intricate latticed stonework on top of high brick walls. Tufty-eared donkeys stood stoic and steadfast, harnessed to wooden coal carts. Their coats blended perfectly with the biscuit-brown road and the dusky sepia of the bricks. Heaps of shiny black anthracite were piled up on the roadside; sooty clouds belched black from ancient ornamented chimneys and rose into a diffuse grey smudge against the clear blue sky.

Everywhere there were bicycles. Many sported baskets or wooden crates on either side of the back wheel that overflowed with vegetables whose vibrant green contrasted starkly with the browns and greys of the street. I climbed up onto the city walls and walked high above the houses. Signposts had been erected to instruct tourists not to throw their litter over the edge. The English translation read, 'No tossing.'

I hired a car to take me out to the Wang Family Mansion the following morning. The owner of the guesthouse had booked the driver, who was clearly a prosperous type. He was driving a shiny black Volkswagen – though his taste was cast into doubt in my mind at least by his choice of a bright pink crocheted gear-stick cover that clung tightly to the knob then flowered out into a skirt beneath.

On the road out of Pingyao, we passed a smartly dressed traffic policewoman standing peremptorily on a small platform in the middle of a junction. In her dark navy uniform and flat hat, she stood ramrod straight, her arms extended to their full commanding stretch as she directed the traffic this way and that. With a flourish of her forearms, the policewoman ordered our lane to stop and beckoned the cars coming from the right to cross in front of us. Nobody took the slightest notice. Following the example of those around him, my driver blasted his horn and cruised through regardless. Nobody, not even the policewoman, so much as blinked in surprise. They all seemed perfectly happy, continuing in their own anarchic ways.

We drove out on a long, flat road. Skinny trees struggled to grow in a spindly line between the road and the fields behind, where gaunt workers tended their scraggy crops. Huge trucks trundled along with coal heaped high; lesser enterprises – one man, his donkey and his wooden coal cart – tramped more slowly still. Others made their way on bicycles. Some men drove mopeds while their wives or girlfriends perched side-saddle behind them. It was remarkable the way they managed to stay so spruce and smart on these filthy roads. Equally surprising was the women's choice of footwear. One wore red suede stiletto boots, while another was fitted out in very high-heeled gleaming black patent shoes.

Blithely, we careered past them all, not bothering with niceties such as looking in the rear-view mirror, or checking to see if the road ahead was clear before pulling out to pass. As we overtook a coal lorry on one blind bend we met a car coming at some speed in the other direction. Involuntarily I gasped, 'Oh my God!' then, embarrassed, had to try to disguise my outburst as a grunt and a cough.

The Wang Family Mansion is not a mansion. As I discovered when we arrived there, it is a town – a vast labyrinth of stone alleyways and grey-brick courtyards, empty buildings and deserted bridges. It took more than five hundred years to construct and covers over three hectares. On top of the countless courtyard houses, now uninhabited, there are schools, gardens, gazebos and refectories. There are study areas for those taking the imperial government exams, and meeting halls. There are salons specifically for the reading of poetry.

All Chinese people with the surname Wang, all over the world, apparently descend from the Wangs of Taiyuan, who built this place. Wang means 'king'. The story goes that one of the Wang family ancestors (who wasn't called Wang but something else) was a grandson of the emperor, but he gave up his post and moved with his family to Taiyuan – a lousy choice, it must be said, if the modern-day dumpling restaurants are anything to judge by, but maybe he thought it was nice. Anyway, local residents began to call the family the Wangs as a nod to their royal blood. The Wang family went forth and multiplied, and now there are more than 100 million of them scattered about the globe, driving donkeys in Taiyuan, running chop suey shops in Vancouver, working as bankers in Manhattan, and so on.

This complex of houses and gardens, then, is meant to have special significance for Wangs the world over. It would be rather lovely, I thought, to have a bricks-and-mortar testimony to who you are and where you come from. No woad-daubed knight named Evans ever clanked through Wales in his armour and built a complex of castles for *his* descendants. As far as I'm aware, there's no labyrinth of cobbled stone streets, elegant courtyards and intricately carved doorways in, say, Swansea, where we can all go and meditate on our burgeoning family tree. (There is, apparently, an Evanstown in Mid-Glamorgan – a very tiny place consisting of about four streets and a public library – but I'm not sure that's quite the same.)

Still, I managed to overcome my feelings of bitterness towards my ancestors and their oversights sufficiently to greatly enjoy the Wang family housing scheme. To start with, it was kind of quirky to think that everyone who had lived in this enormous estate would have been called Wang. I should imagine it might have become confusing, in reality, because the Chinese aren't big on using given names when they talk to each other.

'Where are you going?' Mother Wang would have called out to Little Wang as he hitched up his robe and shuffled hastily out through the latticed doorway in his black silken slippers, his pigtail bobbing behind him.

'Just off to play with Bigger Wang,' Little Wang would have hollered back, bombing through the circular portal as fast as his flowing, floor-length garments would allow.

'Is that A-Whole-Head-And-Shoulders-Bigger-Wang, or Just-A-Bit-Bigger-Wang?' His mother would have been at a loss to know. 'If it's Just-A-Bit-Bigger-Wang, could you stop at Old Wang's and pick up some tofu for tea? Oh yes, and Dr Wang recommended a sea cucumber to treat Grandma Wang's constipation so if you could call in at Buck-Tooth Wang's medicine shop—'

But by now Little Wang would have been halfway down the cobbled lane and Mother Wang would have had no chance of catching up with him because her feet were only four inches long.

The really lovely thing about the Wang estate, though, was that it was quiet. Most of the tour groups had gone instead to the Qiao family compound, to the south. The Qiao family compound is nowhere near as big as the Wang residence, but it has the added kudos of having provided the set for the film *Raise the Red Lantern*. As a result, Wangtown is left in relative peace. I wandered through the courtyards lined with arched portals and intricate wooden doors. Ornately carved dragons snarled from the rooftops; at the gates, stone lions roared. Swirling fronds and flowers adorned the pillars; no joist or rafter was left without an ornamental touch. I slipped through doorways, explored tiny alleys, and clambered up staircases – and, before too long, I was delightfully lost in the maze. I found a courtyard, silent except for the sweet piping of songbirds in the trees. Sitting on a stone step in the sun, I contemplated life as an eighteenth-century Wang.

Over these very cobbles, men with shaved foreheads and tightly plaited queues would have stepped – for the Wang Family Mansion was built during the Qing dynasty (1644–1911) when the Manchu, the dynasty's rulers who originally came from Manchuria, forced their male Chinese subjects to wear their hair in a queue, or pigtail, as a symbol of subservience.

In the large room at the head of the courtyard, the family dignitaries would have formally received guests and put the Qing-dynasty world to rights. In those wide, horribly hard wooden chairs, family elders would have faced one other. They would have been dressed in full-length, heavy silk robes embossed with swirling golden dragons whose bulging eyeballs and protruding tongues breathed fiery authority. Over the top of their robes they would have worn three-quarter-length surcoats with wide sleeves that stopped at the elbow in order to show off the ornate flared cuffs and hems of the flamboyant robes beneath. They would have placed tasselled skullcaps lined with fur or silk on their heads, and black, rigid-soled boots on their feet. This footwear descended from the ancient Manchu nomadic tradition – it was easier for a horse-man to stand up in his stirrups and fire his arrows accurately if the soles of his boots were stiff.

Perhaps as they sat, these men would have discussed vital issues of trade between the tribes of the northern desert and the Han Chinese living on the central plains. Or they might have expressed astonishment at those new-fangled financial establishments called banks that were springing up in town, just a day's journey away.

*　　*　　*

Back at the guesthouse, I filled up on chicken, rice and vegetables before heading to the station to take the night train to Xi'an. There were six of us from the guesthouse taking the train that evening. The guesthouse booked our tickets as part of their service and even sent a man along with us to make sure we all found our seats safely.

Malcolm and Karen, a middle-aged couple from Cheshire, were taking a one-week, whistle-stop tour of China before going on to Hangzhou, where they were working in the university for a further week. There was an English boy in his early twenties who was travelling a little after spending a year teaching in Shanghai. His Chinese was even worse than mine – there was no point learning, he said, all his friends spoke English – which I thought a weak excuse until I remembered the very poor level of my own Cantonese after almost four years in Hong Kong.

Lastly, there was a German couple. The girl was very sick, her face grey and drawn. She clearly had not been sufficiently diligent with her application of anti-bacterial hand gel. Still, her boyfriend seemed to think her strong enough to lug her own substantial rucksack, despite the fact that the poor soul could scarcely stand. If anyone made me move from my bed in such a condition, let alone travel overnight on a Chinese train and carry a heavy pack, I would consider such lack of concern to be grounds for heinous retribution. I imagined the ashen-faced girl would have feverish dreams peppered by fantasies of horrible revenge as she tossed and turned on her hard bunk that night. In her wistful subconscious, perhaps, she would wait until the germ had hopped from her onto her unkind boyfriend. Then, together, they would take a journey on the most cramped and unventilated bus in China and she'd sit and whistle a jaunty German tune as he retched from the window. Or maybe she'd accidentally lock him for hours in a stinking Chinese public loo.

The subject of public lavatories was, as it happened, pungently fresh in my mind as I sat in the waiting room that night. I had had the naïve idea that it might be a good idea to pay a visit before boarding the train – the facilities on board, I thought, might be worse than the unmoving, hole-in-the-ground variety.

I was wrong.

The station loo was closed, so our escort took me to a hotel over the street. It was a respectable-looking establishment from the outside. I had high hopes for its facilities.

I walked round the back of the hotel and across a small yard as directed. The stench hit me well before I reached the door – or the entrance, more accurately, as there was no door. Inside, rough partitions crossed a shallow porcelain channel that ran lengthways down one side, dividing its length into cubicles without doors. The way the ditch was built meant that one person's waste ran directly into the cubicle of the next. But it wasn't the urine that was the problem. The really incisive, almost stabbing stench rose from the little dollops and piles of other people's slowly festering excrement that lay in a stinking landscape of hills and gullies. Some of it appeared to have been there for some time.

The smell was astonishing. It was searing, choking, gouging in its intensity. It hit me with such a physical force that my poor, excessively sensitive Western lungs constricted with frightened paranoia. What on earth was I breathing in in here? The air was so offensive it seemed remarkable that I could see straight through it. It was so thick with foulness that it ought to have been an excremental brown soup through which I had to wade rather than a transparent gas. It was so appalling I feared it might corrode my lungs like a deadly acid, perhaps consume them altogether. What would happen if I accidentally touched something? Would death be instant and dramatic like some kind of on-the-spot explosion of Ebola, or would I merely be disfigured when just the guilty finger that had done the touching dropped off?

The well-dressed Chinese women around me, meanwhile, appeared to have no such qualms. They happily straddled the repulsive ditch with a relaxed panache that featured nothing as unsightly as a wrinkled nose. I fought the urge to bring up my supper. Clearly I had led too sheltered an ablutionary life, I considered. Harpic had a lot to answer for.

I made quick work of the task in hand and, holding my breath, I made a bolt for the exit. As I marched briskly from the room, a woman crouching in the cubicle by the door chose to empty her bowels. Her back was towards me and my parting view was of a pair of perfectly white buttocks pointing high into the air with fresh faeces pouring out from between them.

Back in the waiting room, I applied my hand gel three times in as many minutes. It had been so revolting in there that cleaning my hands once or twice didn't seem enough. I was almost trembling with neurosis, quite breathless with horror at the germs I must surely have picked up. It wasn't just the loos that were squalid in this part of China, either. After less than a week on the road, all my clothes were black with grime. All around me, the phlegm was flying as the locals noisily hawked and spat. Worse still, I was starting to become rather congested myself: after just a few days of travelling, I needed with alarming frequency to blow my nose and clear my throat of the mucus that my body was churning out to fight the pollution.

'No spitting. Remember the public health,' said the signs in post-SARS China. Nobody took any notice.

Really, I thought, it's amazing that they need a birth-control policy in this country so fraught with peril. What with the choking pollution, the anarchy on the roads, the tuberculosis, the hepatitis and the pestilent state of the lavatories, it's a miracle anyone lives much beyond the age of five. You'd think they'd have to bribe people to have *more* children rather than impose crippling fines on those producing more than one.

The train arrived and we six foreigners climbed aboard. I was in another hard-sleeper carriage – but this time, the guesthouse had booked me a bottom bunk. The Chinese reckon that the bottom bunk is the best place to be, because it makes a comfortable bench seat during the daytime where they can chatter at high volume, play cards and slurp noodles with their friends. Foreigners almost universally choose either the middle or the top bunk precisely because this allows a modicum of escape from these activities.

This train had started its journey in Taiyuan, so by the time I boarded a contingent of Chinese men had already commandeered my bed. Three of them sat side by side and with great, guttural guzzling noises were shovelling instant noodles from plastic pots and sucking them into their mouths, like a row of hiccupping industrial shredders running in reverse. Some of the noodles had not made it down their gullets and were lying cold and congealed on my sheet. On the table by the bed sat a little huddle of jam jars containing varying quantities of tea. The green leaves were floating in yellowish water which in some jars was the pale colour of fresh straw, in others a dark, mustardy hue. The Chinese rarely seemed to step foot outside their homes without their jar of tea, which they replenished with hot water time and again. I showed the men my ticket for that bunk. They waved their disposable wooden chopsticks dismissively, spots of brown liquid smattering the floor.

No, no, they said to each other. The foreigner couldn't read the ticket, that wasn't the ticket for this bed, it was for somewhere else. They gesticulated towards the end of the corridor.

I took a deep breath.

'Er . . . I think perhaps this one is mine,' I stammered in my best Chinese.

There was an uncomfortable silence. The noodle-eaters went quiet and shuffled their slipper-clad feet. They glanced at each other shiftily. This foreigner really is very large, their eyes seemed to say. Although there are three of us, we can't be sure we'll win if this fight gets physical. The most cowardly of the three suddenly stood up and scuttled off; in a flash, the other two followed him and vanished from sight. Immediately I could hear the rumour chattering up and down the corridor: 'Jabber-jabber-jabber-jabber-*waiguoren*!'

And then a different voice: 'Jabber-jabber-*WAIGUOREN*!'

'*Waiguoren . . . waiguoren . . . waiguoren.*' Given that this was the only word I could understand, I wasn't entirely sure what they were saying about me. Were they merely relaying the amazing news that a foreigner was on the train? Or were they warning that the fearsome *waiguoren* had a tree trunk for a nose and eyes like bulbous turnips, and had caused the noodle-eaters terrible loss of face?

Within minutes an earnest-looking – but brave – young man came and sat beside me on my bed.

'Hello,' he said in English. 'Where are you from?'

I told him I was from England. He nodded with wide-eyed sincerity. He was a plump character with a pale circular face and round, black spectacles that made his head resemble a panda's.

'I think . . .' he said, and thought a little, 'you will go now to see the famous and glorious city of Xi'an.'

I agreed that this was my intention. A uniformed train official wielding a bin liner battled down the aisle, sweeping up empty plastic noodle bowls, polystyrene boxes, piles of sunflower seed shells, orange peel, apple cores and half-eaten chunks of lurid-coloured cake. One thing I had to say: the train was kept very clean. Despite the passengers' best attempts to carpet the floor with the remains of their snacks, the carriage attendants rose to the challenge with awesome pugnacity. Every few minutes, it seemed, they jousted through the carriage, duelling with their mops and wrestling with their bin bags. Even the loo – a metal palette in the floor at the end of the carriage – was kept clean and odourless. I would have done far better to relieve myself on the train than in the hotel by the station, after all.

The panda man turned to the table, picked up a plate of eggshells, and tipped them into the rubbish bag. I used the break in conversation to make good my escape to the restaurant car where I had arranged to meet Karen and Malcolm – who were travelling in a classy soft-sleeper – for a beer.

The colour scheme in the restaurant car was blue.

Chairs with blue covers flanked tables with blue plastic cloths. At the windows, blue curtains in a thin, shiny fabric were tied back to reveal plastic 'lace' under-curtains. A stout woman dressed in white marched up and down, taking orders and slamming down dishes and making it abundantly clear she would stand no nonsense. Each time a group of diners left, she wiped down their table with a mighty, muscular flourish of her great, beefy arm.

A few yuan bought us a couple of bottles of beer and we drank them quite happily while we surveyed the scene; then at nine-thirty, the restaurant car closed. The forceful lady sent us brusquely to bed.

Back in my carriage, a little girl in a pink tracksuit with matching pink cheeks had taken up residence on the bunk opposite mine. Her hair was tied up in two high bunches with ribbons, like a tiny Yorkshire terrier. She was entranced by her spinning top that played 'Happy Birthday' in a synthesized twang as it twirled on the floor between us, and she let out high-pitched yaps of pleasure each time the tune repeated – until, at last, the train authorities deemed it bedtime and, with a resonant clang, all the lights went out. The top stopped spinning, and its grating cadence was replaced by the sonic boom of snoring from the man on the upper bunk.

7

Once Were Warriors

'Do you mean the Sheraton, the five-star hotel?' asked Helen.

I said yes. Helen looked disbelieving.

I was booked in for a much-needed night of luxury, thanks to Nancy and her Imperial Tours contacts. Helen was the guide whom Karen and Malcolm had hired for the day. They were travelling on to Shanghai that night on another sleeper train and had booked a guide with a car for the day as they'd have nowhere else to leave their luggage. Last night, as we'd cracked open our third bottle of beer, we had struck a deal: they could shower in my bathroom (and even help themselves to the free shampoo) and I, in return, would hitch a lift in their car to visit the terracotta warriors a little way out of town. As it was still only seven-thirty in the morning when Helen had met us at the station, we said we'd like to go to the hotel first for a shower and some breakfast.

There was a frown and a moment's silence from Helen.

'Sorry,' she said, 'but I want to be absolutely sure. Do you mean the *She-ra-ton*?'

She looked me up and down, examining my grubby jeans, my red jacket that had started to go black round the hem and cuffs, my sooty grey trainers, my tangled hair and my pallid unwashed face.

'Yes, that's right, the She-ra-ton,' I enunciated clearly.

There was a further silence. She began to blush.

'Do you mean the Sheraton spelt S-H-E-R-A-T-O-N?' she asked.

It was funny twice. Now she was making me nervous. I might not have been at my most glistening and sparkly, my anorak and trainers perhaps didn't scream of sartorial elegance, but did I look *that* bad?

I confirmed the spelling of the Sheraton.

'I'm sorry,' she began to blather. 'It's just that I have to be sure you don't mean a different hotel, one that sounds similar, just in case, um, I made a mistake with my English.'

She had a quick conference with the driver, then turned back to us.

'The Sheraton is thirty kilometres out of town,' she announced. 'It will take us a very long time to get there. I think it is better if we go to a different hotel for breakfast.'

This flummoxed us. Thirty kilometres was certainly much further than we'd expected – but I had booked a room there, and it was not even eight o'clock in the morning. We had time to kill. We said we'd go there anyway.

Helen and the driver seemed reluctant to take us, but in the end they had no choice. The driver fired up the engine and we joined the early-morning traffic of Xi'an. We took a couple of turnings – a right and perhaps a left – and a couple of minutes later we drew up in the forecourt of the Sheraton.

'That wasn't thirty kilometres!' we chorused. 'That was about two!'

'Oh, I don't know,' Helen muttered crossly. 'It's just what the driver told me.' And then, more plaintively, 'I am just a small potato. I must do as I'm told, or I will be in trouble.' And again, even more sorrowfully this time, 'I am just a small potato.'

It was a curious episode, small potatoes or otherwise. Clearly, Helen hadn't wanted us to go to the Sheraton. Perhaps she would have received some kind of commission from the hotel where she wanted us to have breakfast as payment for taking us there, and in going to the Sheraton we had deprived her of this easy money.

In contrast to Helen's obvious astonishment, the dark-suited man at the Sheraton's marble-clad reception didn't so much as raise an impeccably groomed eyebrow at my travel-worn look. Perhaps he was just eager that I should shower and change my clothes as quickly as possible, for the check-in process was painless and within minutes I was steaming off another Chinese journey under the shower. Downstairs, we ate a prodigious breakfast of sushi, fruit, bacon and eggs, muffins and Danish pastries, and then piled back into the car to visit the terracotta army.

As a concept, the terracotta warriors are mindblowing. It is incredible to think that this army of life-sized infantry soldiers, archers, officers, charioteers and horses was crafted two thousand years ago, and that we, today, can jump on an aeroplane and go and see them. They were created to guard the tomb of Emperor Qin Shihuang, the tyrannical First Emperor of China who also directed the creation of the Great Wall.

The First Emperor was concerned to protect himself

even in the afterlife. He therefore conscripted *seven hundred thousand* men over a period of thirty-eight years to build the army that he hoped would guard his tomb. The seven thousand warriors all lie to the east of the emperor's sepulchre, facing those states that Qin Shihuang had conquered. The scale of the project is astonishing, and the attention to detail phenomenal. Every statue is unique. Each warrior has a slightly different facial expression and posture. Their ranks are determined by painstakingly crafted clothing: foot soldiers in robes and puttees, officers in caps, and charioteers in their particular armour that reaches down over their wrists to prevent their arms from injury in battle.

I have no idea why it is, then, that both times I have been to see the warriors – for this was my second visit – I have found them faintly dull. They should be staggering, awe-inspiring, truly wonderful. And yet on both occasions I've had to fight hard to stifle a yawn.

Not everybody has the same reaction; some people really enjoy their visit. But I think the presentation is lacking. The warriors stand in a pit – which visitors must look down on over a Perspex fence – within a building that bears an uncanny resemblance to a railway terminus. There's no sense of history. The soldiers aren't placed in context for the visitor, they just stand in their lines looking grey, dusty, and remarkably similar to the fake terracotta warriors that you can buy in any street market in China. Only a fraction of the army has been uncovered to date, and many of the sculptures are broken, so there's a good quantity of muddy mounds and broken bits of pot. Am I a philistine? Maybe. But the only part of the tour that really did it for me was the video at the end in which actors recreated the building of the warriors.

Now we saw the back-breaking labour, the burning furnaces, the sweat and the toil as the workmen sculpted and painted these astonishing statues in vivid colours. We watched the subsequent looting of the tomb by vengeful peasants who despised the Qin emperor and his harsh, autocratic regime. At last, we had a sense of what the terracotta warriors were all about. But by the time I arrived at the video, I'd already been peering down into the warriors' pit for an hour or so too long.

Perversely, I found the terracotta warriors much more interesting once I was back at home, browsing through a book about them from my local library. Here, the photographs show the incredible detail of the statues in a way you can never see if you actually travel to Xi'an. Close-up shots picture elaborate belt buckles and astonishingly detailed hairstyles: elegantly entwined tendrils snake up the back of one head and are wound into a swaying topknot; a fine braid coils from temple to temple of another. Others wear their hair weaved into broad, knitted plaits fastened with intricately cast clips.

The Small Potato tried her best. She tried to point out a general from an infantry soldier, but she seemed a bland, starchy character. She didn't appear to be excited by the terracotta warriors either; she was just doing her job. Yet, possibly to pay us back for the breakfast incident, she talked us through the tiniest detail of every speck of clay in that building. Underneath her serious, wholesome, pastel-blue exterior, her neatly gathered ponytail and earnest expression, I reckoned Helen was revelling in her revenge.

'Ha-ha-ha-ha-ha,' her evil inner potato was probably chortling. 'After I've finished with this lot, they'll think Qin Shihuang was Father Christmas. By the time I've completed my desperately tedious descriptions of the footwear of every last soldier in this entire muddy hole, they'll be begging for a life sentence of hard labour just to escape. In the weeks to come, they'll have nightmares in which they're buried up to their necks in clay; thirty years from now, they'll turn pale at the merest mention of terracotta. Heck, am I going to punish them!'

Back in the city centre, I spent the afternoon walking. Xi'an was much more cosmopolitan than any of the Chinese cities I had visited so far, with the exception of Beijing. Noticeably, the people seemed to spit less here. Occasionally a passer-by would call out 'hello', but without the taunting tone that had grated in Datong. By late afternoon, the streets were filled with people strolling around the shops; their carrier bags contained CDs and clothes as well as food. They talked on mobile phones. These people were the burgeoning Chinese middle class; clearly they had disposable income, something I hadn't seen a great deal of lately.

By the bell tower in the middle of town I found a hypermarket selling flaky Chinese pastries, cubes of yellow sponge and mooncakes, which look deceptively like pork pies and can give the innocent glutton a very nasty shock when he or she eagerly takes a bite and finds them to be filled with a particularly unpleasant blend of lotus paste and egg yolk. On the meat counter row upon row of Chinese sausages lined up like skinny, fat-flecked salamis alongside cold roasted ducks, squashed flat with their legs splayed out to the sides.

I skirted past these sections and headed instead for the wine and junk foods departments. Having been presented with a set of scales in my Sheraton bathroom, I'd discovered that morning that I'd lost several pounds during my first week in China. I reckoned I had some bingeing to do.

With breezy abandon and calorific unconcern, I started out by selecting a suspiciously cheap bottle of 'Great Wall' wine. Moving round to the crisps and chocolate aisles, I chucked into my basket a large box of Pringles, a packet of chocolate chip cookies, a bar of Dairy Milk and two Snickers. It was the first time in a whole week that I had seen imported snacks for sale, and I seized upon them with a rabid joy that was frankly quite disturbing.

As night fell, the street-food stalls began to buzz. Narrow lanes leading off the main drag were suddenly filled with lights and lanterns. On flame burners, vats of noodle soup bubbled, onions and potatoes sizzled and filled the night air with their mouth-watering aroma. Men sold candied fruit from their carts. Others roasted chestnuts in woks, their sweet, mellow smell blending deliciously with the warm scent of glowing charcoal. The pavements were packed with low makeshift tables and coloured plastic stools where the people of Xi'an sat, gabbled and guzzled happily.

I contemplated joining them. I felt I ought to savour this vibrant scene. But then I remembered the bottle of wine I was carrying in my rucksack and thought of the rare pleasures of room service and HBO. I headed back to my hotel, put the wine in the fridge and ran a bath infused with lavender oil. Then I rang room service, ordered a 'Sheraton burger' and settled back in a comfy armchair with the remote control. For a brief but delicious moment, I entirely forgot that outside the window China was still festering.

8

Super Socks and Ancient Rocks

The train official was delighted with his super-strong, flameproof socks. He had come into our carriage a minute or two earlier with a green plastic shopping basket full of them, and had set up stage in the middle of the aisle from where he was very enthusiastically trying to sell them to the passengers. It was a fully interactive sales pitch.

'Now, madam,' he said to the woman to his left as he ripped one of the socks from its plastic packaging and dangled it for all to admire, 'if you would like to help me stretch the sock taut, I will demonstrate its incredible fireproof qualities.'

The woman looked about her, embarrassed, then chuckled and pulled the foot end of the rather unattractive, nylon sock as instructed; the train official grabbed the other. The rest of the passengers turned their heads from their tea jars and card games and looked on with amusement. It was show time. We all sat up a little straighter, grinned, and craned our necks to watch.

The train official flamboyantly whipped out a cigarette lighter. A titter of entertainment ran through the carriage. It was exciting stuff. Would the sock survive? With a flourish, the official ran the flame down the length of the taut sock. And . . . nothing happened! Despite the odds, *the sock had lived!* What a fantastic sock! It would have been just the sock for, oh, walking over burning coals, or running through a house on fire. How could we have lived this long without such a sock in our wardrobes?

The train official looked pleased with his display. He was young, probably in his mid-twenties, and had a face as round, smooth and hairless as a fine porcelain teapot. He stood a little taller in his pale-blue shirt and navy jacket with epaulettes.

'And for my next trick,' he seemed to be saying – for I couldn't understand his exact words, 'I will prove that this sock really can take a beating.'

He asked the man in the seat behind to hold the sock while he struck it repeatedly with a wire brush. The old man entered into the arena full of gusto. He stretched the sock as tight as he could between his hands, then the train official raised his sinewy young arm and bashed and thrashed the living daylights out of the sock – but still it didn't succumb. After that, a third man was enlisted to engage in a tug-of-war. Again, the valiant sock came through the brutality unscathed.

It was bizarre, really, the way the train officials sold things that had absolutely nothing to do with the railways. I never did work out whether the sock-selling display formed part of this man's designated duties, or whether he was just using his spare time at work to entrepreneurial effect. There was really no telling. Chinese companies seemed to do things in such extraordinary ways. Just that morning, on the way to the station in Xi'an, I had seen from my taxi window the entire staff of one restaurant out on a morning jog.

104

It was nine-forty-five on a Sunday and about twenty of them were running in formation, like an army platoon on a training exercise. At the front, all alone and barking orders, ran the front-of-house lady resplendent in her full-length red brocade cheongsam. Behind her in orderly lines the kitchen staff panted, perspiring in whites and aprons.

I was travelling today to Luoyang. As I was taking a daytime train and the journey was only six hours long, I hadn't booked a bed this time. Instead, I was in a soft-seat carriage. The seat itself wasn't at all soft, but the quality of the clientele seemed markedly superior to that of the hard-seat carriage I'd sat in from Taiyuan to Pingyao several days earlier.

They were an affable, humorous bunch. Some of them even bought socks when the demonstration was done. When I had boarded the train they had smiled at me in a welcoming way and helped me with my luggage. Across the aisle from where I sat were an elderly couple and a woman on her own, aged about sixty. She was neatly dressed in a red turtleneck, jeans and a black jacket; her hair was tied up in an immaculate, shiny black bun.

This trio watched me with some interest.

'Where do you think she's from?' I heard the old man ask the woman.

'America,' she replied with total conviction.

A few minutes later I took out my notebook and started to jot down some thoughts.

'She's writing!' exclaimed the woman with the bun.

I hadn't written more than a sentence or two when the hot-water lady came round filling up the tea jars. And then, to my surprise, the woman with the bun turned and spoke to me in carefully enunciated English.

'Would you like some water?'

'No thank you, I already have some.' I smiled and held up my bottle of mineral water.

The woman beamed with satisfaction, then moved over to sit by me. Her name, she said, was Mrs Qing. She had graduated from Xi'an Foreign Languages Institute in 1966 and had been an English teacher in a local middle (secondary) school. But then she had been sent to work in a factory, where she had stayed for the next twenty-five years.

'I have not spoken any English . . . at all . . . for more than twenty years,' she said, pausing every few words as her brain raced to retrieve the long-buried vocabulary. She was clearly happy to be speaking it now.

Concluding that the strange, pale creature across the aisle was relatively unthreatening, the old man moved over to join us. His name was Mr Liu; he had dark, crinkly skin and big, square, plastic-rimmed glasses. His shiny brown pate gleamed through his short, sparse hair. His head resembled the reflective, waterlogged fields that rolled by the window, punctuated by the spiky stubble of the harvested crops.

He told me, in faltering English, that he was seventy-three years old. He used to be a Russian translator; he graduated from the Chengdu Institute of Foreign Languages in 1953 then moved to the far north of China, near the Russian border, where he worked as a translator in the construction industry for twenty-five years. Then he had returned to his native Sichuan where he had taught in school.

'Very few teachers of foreign language in those days,' he said, and both he and Mrs Qing roared with laughter.

Until Deng Xiaoping's policy of Opening and Reform that followed Mao's death in 1976, it was unhealthy to show too great an interest in foreign languages in China. Intellectuals had been labelled the 'stinking ninth' category by Mao's Cultural Revolution and punished accordingly; schoolteachers were 'struggled against' by their students. Foreigners were reviled as bourgeois, capitalist and feudal. To be a teacher of foreign languages, then, must have been unfortunate in the extreme.

Mao's mistrust of foreigners arose in direct retaliation to the way European and American powers had been carving up China for their own trade purposes during the final decades of the Qing dynasty.

The relationship between the imperial government and the 'barbarians' had always been an uneasy one. The Chinese had historically seen themselves as superior, independent, and sitting contentedly in the middle of the world. Foreign travel was ruled against by Confucius as early as 600 BC as it interfered with his precepts of filial duty (a man obeys the emperor, a son obeys his father, and a wife obeys everyone – until she's lucky enough to acquire a daughter-in-law on whom she can vent her frustrations).

It was always the foreigners who courted China, eager for its tea, silks and porcelain. The Chinese did not look to the outside world. They didn't much want our wool. When in 1793 Lord Macartney arrived in Beijing as a representative of the British government and requested that he should be allowed to set up an embassy in the city, the Manchu sent him packing – apparently his refusal to kowtow to the emperor didn't help – and declared that they had no use for foreign goods. Trade was limited to a small area in Guangzhou (formerly Canton) and severe restrictions were exercised on foreigners' rights and movement. And so there was a trade imbalance: Chinese exports exceeded imports. As a result, the West found itself having to pay for Chinese goods in cold, hard silver.

Then, in the early nineteenth century, the British discovered a solution: opium. Although opium was illegal in China, the Chinese were partial to the poppy's effects. The British found they could profit from the Chinese propensity for opium consumption by importing Indian opium to China and selling it more cheaply than the home-grown seed. The opium traders achieved breathtaking success: opium consumption rocketed, and addiction coursed through China's weakening veins. The superior Middle Kingdom slid ever further into misery and degradation – and now it was the Chinese who were having to make up the trade imbalance in silver.

The Manchu tried to take a stand. Commissioner Lin, the viceroy of Hubei and Hunan provinces, ordered that smokers had a part of their top lip cut off so that they were quite simply unable to hold the pipe. He even wrote to Queen Victoria requesting her to put an end to the profiteering of the opium traders that was so damaging China. He implied that, should she ignore his request, he might bar the export to Britain of tea and, God help us, rhubarb, which the anally retentive British of those days apparently relied on to move their bowels.

The Queen may never have received the letter; in any case she did not reply. Tensions increased. The Western powers continued to insist their trading restrictions be lifted – not just on opium, but on merchandise in general – and the Chinese continued to desire self-sufficiency. Finally, when they were forbidden to trade, the British blockaded the port of

Guangzhou. When Lin protested, they opened fire and the First Opium War began.

'A war more unjust in its origin, a war more calculated in its progress to cover this country with disgrace, I do not know and I have not read of,' William Gladstone pronounced to Parliament in April 1840.

Still, whatever the concerns back home, the First Opium War blazed ahead and concluded with British victory. By the Treaty of Nanjing in 1842, the Chinese were forced to open five ports to foreign trade, to cede Hong Kong to Britain, and to pay substantial indemnities. The Treaty of Nanjing was followed by a series of further treaties that became collectively known as the 'unequal treaties' due to their bias in favour of the West. Still, the treaties were frequently not heeded, and relationships continued to be strained.

Then, in October 1856, Chinese authorities boarded a ship called the *Arrow* and arrested her entire crew. They claimed that a notorious pirate had been seen on board. The *Arrow* had been registered in Hong Kong (though its registration had expired); the Governor of Hong Kong, Sir John Bowring, together with a British consul in Guangzhou, Harry Parkes, deemed this an affront to Britain and attacked Guangzhou. The French, aggrieved by the recent murder of one of their missionaries, joined the fray. The allied forces seized Guangzhou, then moved north to Beijing. The subsequent Treaty of Tianjin, signed in 1858, allowed the opening of ten more treaty ports, permitted foreigners, including missionaries, to travel through China, legalized the opium trade and established the residence of a British minister in Beijing. The following year the allies returned to ratify the treaty and found their progress upriver blocked. They returned with an armed force; the Chinese captured and imprisoned

Harry Parkes and the allies burned down the Summer Palace. So much for cordiality.

The Manchu government that had ruled since 1644 was by now rotted with corruption and the Westerners seeped noxiously through China like an ever-diffusing coil of narcotic smoke. They set up their enclaves along China's lifeline, the Yangtze, and along its coastline and borders. In 1864, fourteen Chinese ports had Customs houses (run predominantly by the British, though officially administered by the Chinese government). By 1916 there were forty-one Customs 'ports' from Harbin in the frozen far north to steamy Simao near the Burmese border. In these pockets of land, the Westerners lived by the extraordinary laws of extra-territoriality, that is to say, they were governed by their own authorities and not by the Chinese. The Westerners – and some Chinese in their employ – grew rich and fat. And among the populace, resentment seethed and festered.

It's not entirely surprising, then, that when Mao Zedong finally succeeded in securing power over China he mistrusted the foreigners who had inspired such humiliation. Relations weren't set to improve. The Americans had sided with Chiang Kai-shek in the Civil War; after the Korean War they imposed on China a severe trade embargo. Diplomatic isolation meant that China was effectively closed off from the capitalist world for decades. It wasn't until 1972, shortly before Mao's death, that President Nixon visited China (hot on the heels of the American ping-pong team who had been invited the year before) and relationships started to thaw. So English, under Mao, wasn't much use to anyone.

It's all changed now. What with the Olympics coming to Beijing in 2008, and the general climate of expanding global business, the twenty-first-century Chinese government is so eager that the people should learn to speak English that they broadcast lessons daily on the radio and television. And this, it transpired, was how Mr Liu had learnt.

'I listen to the radio every morning between six-thirty and seven a.m.,' he told me proudly, his delicate, wrinkly skin crumpling into a wide, beaming smile. It was astonishing, really. He'd only been tuning in for the past year yet his English, though faltering, was remarkably good. This was the first time he had ever had a chance to have a proper conversation in the English language.

Mr Liu was an inquisitive character. What did I think about the situation in the Middle East? What did people in England think? He seemed to have a sharp and unrestrained curiosity about world affairs that contrasted starkly with Helen's robotic repetitions of yesterday. Admittedly, nothing he said differed from the line of the Chinese government but still, he seemed eager to hear an alternative view.

It was incredible to think of what this man had lived through – if he was born in 1930, he'd have known the Japanese invasion; the civil war and Communist victory; the mass starvation of the Great Leap Forward and the stark brutality of the Cultural Revolution that followed. He had worked for twenty-five years as a Russian translator on the construction sites of the north, places not renowned for their luxury and comfort. Yet his eyes leapt with life and a thirst for knowledge. I commented that he must have known many changes in his life.

'Oh yes, oh yes,' he said, and roared with laughter once more.

*   *   *

The train trundled on. The landscape through the window was, for the first couple of hours, flat and brown featuring mile after mile of arid, ploughed fields that stretched towards the distant, haze-enshrouded horizon. Occasional workers' dwellings flashed by, and every now and then a characterless town full of drab, boxy buildings.

Then the countryside became more dramatic. Sharply hewn gorges and dry riverbeds cut through the sandstone that rose up in extraordinarily shaped, weather-worn peaks on either side of the railway tracks. Clumps of tiny yellow flowers sprouted in abundance from the cliff walls. Sometimes dark, gaping holes gave way to caves within. Now the crops grew in tiny, steeply climbing terraces.

Then the ground flattened once more and orchards whose trees brimmed with bright red apples took root. Every so often, the countryside was sliced in two by a curiously empty, gleaming-new expressway.

The train passed through the station for Huashan. My mind slipped back to the time I'd visited the place a few years ago. Then, my Mandarin had been even more limited than it was now. In fact, I had only known two words: *xie xie*, thank you, and *pijiu*, beer. These were excellent words to know if I wanted to order a beer. In most other situations they were useless.

I had arrived at the station hoping to take a taxi to Huashan village about fifteen kilometres away. I had been staying with Guy and Nancy in Beijing. We'd visited Xi'an together, then I had spent a few days travelling across China on my own. I had stopped in Huashan in order to climb the Buddhist sacred mountain there. Nancy had rung ahead and booked a hotel for me; she'd written the name and address on a piece of paper in Chinese. All I had to do was get out of the train at the right stop, go to the taxi rank, and give the piece of paper to the driver.

The plan had seemed faultless – but when I arrived at Huashan station I found there were no taxis. What's more, I couldn't ask for one as I didn't know the word. I wandered round for a while looking lost. One kind soul offered me his bicycle. Seeing as I had no idea where I was going, I didn't think that would do.

Eventually, I ended up in a van with a man. The van was clearly not a taxi, and the man was certainly not a registered driver. As we set off into the distance, down a dusty road heading towards God knows where, I had to consider that things weren't looking good. I had shown my piece of paper to the man, but he hadn't given any sign of having been able to read it. Furthermore, he seemed not only not to understand what I said, but not even to comprehend the concept of foreign language. He just kept talking to me more and more loudly and became increasingly bemused at my failure to reply.

We drove for some minutes in this worrying way. Then we reached a cluster of houses and pulled over into a driveway. The man climbed out and shrieked something in voluble Chinese. From the buildings, a small horde of people scuttled. They gathered round the van, gawped, squawked, and pointed at the extraordinary creature within.

'Look what I've got in my van!' the driver seemed to exclaim. His friends were duly astonished.

After they'd all had a good long stare, and I had waved and smiled as best I knew how, we set off once more. When we reached the next village and pulled over into another driveway, I expected more of the same. But it wasn't to be. Instead, a plump, solitary

113

boy who looked about eight years old ran out of the house. He threw open the back door of the van, jumped in and, planting one elbow on the edge of the driver's seat and the other on mine, announced with supreme confidence, 'Hello! My name is David Jackson!'

Obviously David Jackson wasn't his real name; he just liked the sound of it and so had given himself an English name in addition to his Chinese one. It turned out that David Jackson was not eight years old, but thirteen – he explained in almost perfectly fluent English that he had a growth defect that made him short. What he lacked in height, he made up for in linguistic ability. In this remote part of China, where nobody seemed to speak any English at all, David Jackson latched onto every foreigner that passed through.

'My parents are peasants,' he told me proudly. It seemed a waste, really, that even given his obvious aptitude, he would probably never have the chance to continue his education much beyond a basic level as his parents would be unlikely to be able to pay the fees.

I told David Jackson that I lived in Hong Kong.

'Ah!' His face lit up. 'You know Jackie Chan?'

'You want to eat?' asked David Jackson a while later. 'We go to my uncle's restaurant!'

And so David Jackson stayed by my side for the couple of days I spent in the village. Whenever I came out of my hotel room, he would be sitting in reception. He ordered my food, made phone calls to find out train times, and bought my tickets. At the end, I tipped him some small amount that I hoped would please him but not destroy the harmony of his family, where his parents surely earned only a very paltry

114

sum each month. It was a bizarre episode, an odd encounter in a country that excels in peculiarity.

A part of me wanted to jump off in Huashan, to go and see if I could find David Jackson again – but this train didn't actually stop in the station. In any case, I had to continue my journey because, the day after tomorrow, I had booked into kung fu school in Shaolin and I wanted to see the ancient cave carvings in Luoyang first.

Fifteen hundred years ago, Luoyang was a glorious city. As the capital of the Northern Wei dynasty, which moved its base here from Datong in AD 494, it was home to half a million people. The Wei built magnificent palaces and mansions, and over a thousand Buddhist monasteries.

In an effort to evoke something of the town's glittering past, I checked into the Luoyang Grand Hotel. Its grandeur stopped at the lobby. The swimming pool, pictured glimmering and blue in the hotel's brochure, appeared not to exist. In the business centre, the internet connection ran so slowly that the computer crashed before I was able to retrieve a single email. I asked the receptionist about the gym. She looked worried.

'You want to go now?'

'Yes.' I didn't really. I was just curious to know whether the mysterious locked door marked 'Gymnasium' actually led anywhere.

Alarm spread across her face. She picked up the telephone receiver on the desk and jabbed frantically at buttons, jabbered into the mouthpiece, then told me to go to the sixteenth floor, where the gym was located. I went up there and waited by the locked door for a while, then gave up and went back to my room.

For supper, I went to the Chinese restaurant, but was hustled out before I'd managed even to cross the threshold and ushered into the Western restaurant downstairs. The only available food was a lukewarm buffet of unappetizing chunks of dark-brown meat, gelatinous noodles and greasy limp vegetables that seemed to have been laid out for some time. It looked at best revolting, at worst poisonous.

I went back to my room and dialled the number in the hotel's directory for room service. The woman on the other end of the telephone sounded confused.

'*Mei you*,' she said.

I sighed with great weariness and went back downstairs where I nibbled despondently on cold, crusty rice and dejected, flaccid vegetables from the buffet. When they saw me, the waitresses retreated into an agitated huddle. They seemed to reach some conclusion, then one of them marched over to the stereo and – oh yes – 'By the Rivers of Babylon' echoed out from the speakers once more, followed by the Carpenters. It was the same CD they'd had at the guesthouse in Pingyao. Perhaps every restaurant in China owns one so that they can whip it out in emergency situations, such as when a foreigner walks through the door.

But even Boney M couldn't soothe me tonight. I signed the bill at the counter, then left. The door attendant, who wore a full-length pink cheongsam and had lips like freshly boiled prawns, tried to block my way.

'You must sign the bill!' she squawked. Her plump, crustacean lips opened and closed, then pouted.

'I've already signed it,' I replied testily and walked off. It was time for bed.

*   *   *

I woke up the next morning with mild flu symptoms. Much as I'd have liked to blame the buffet from the night before, I couldn't think of any previous instance when bad food had brought on a slight fever, a headache and aching joints. It was the second time in three weeks that I'd felt under the weather. I'd had various worries before starting out on this trip. I had anticipated that in travelling round China by public transport I might at times be uncomfortable and cross. But I hadn't really contemplated that spending all those hours pressed up close against the Chinese populace would actually make me ill.

'This country is poisonous,' I wrote in my diary that day, cross and weak and far from home, 'and this even when I am washing my hands with a mania that makes Lady Macbeth look slightly scuzzy.'

I had a slow morning, sitting up in bed reading and drinking Lemsip, then forced myself out to look at the Longmen caves.

When the Northern Wei dynasty moved to Luoyang, carving Buddhas and their cohorts into cliff faces was still immensely fashionable. The devout therefore grasped their chisels once more and reverentially started to chip away at the limestone walls on either side of the River Feng, sixteen kilometres south of the city. Work on these caves continued for over three hundred years, right through till the end of the Tang dynasty in the ninth century.

The Longmen caves show a stronger Chinese influence than those at Yungang. The vast stone guardians with their ferocious expressions – bulging eyes and wide, grimacing mouths – and awesome physiques suggest the later Tang style. Lotuses continue to bloom, flying apsara glide across the ceiling, celestial musicians strum their strings, but the carvings are

117

considered to move away from the earlier Indian artistry and to take on a more specific Chinese character.

One towering Buddha here is supposed to be hewn in the image of Empress Wu herself. One of the most notorious characters of Chinese history, Empress Wu started her court life as a concubine of Emperor Taizong. After the emperor died, she began a liaison with his son and successor, Gaozong, and bore him a son. She proceeded, with quite dizzying haste, to secure the demotion of Gaozong's empress (she suffocated the empress's baby and made sure the empress herself was blamed) and usurped the throne for herself. When the emperor showed remorse for the way he had allowed his wife and another concubine to be treated, Empress Wu is said to have ordered that the two women's hands and feet be cut off and stewed into a broth that they were forced to drink. After Gaozong's death shortly afterwards, she successfully wrested control for herself, overthrowing all Chinese precepts of male lineage. She ruled – firmly and successfully – until AD 705 when, at the age of eighty, she abdicated in favour of her third son. She died a few months later.

The Longmen statue that is meant to resemble the empress has large, slanting eyes and round, full cheeks, a straight, commanding nose and a mouth set in stony determination. She neither looks nor sounds like a woman one would wish to annoy – let alone share a bowl of soup with. Modern historians, however, contend that tales of her gruesome deeds were exaggerated by subsequent Chinese generations who found the idea of having a woman in power so unnatural they felt obliged to demonize her by way of explanation.

Rather like Empress Wu's reputation, Buddhist art

in Luoyang has taken a battering over the years. As dynasties and belief systems rose and fell over the centuries, the caves were sporadically plundered. Earthquakes, landslips and water damage at the Longmen site took their toll; then, in the nineteenth and twentieth centuries, Westerners came along and hacked off every figurine they could fit in their clippers and sent them to the museums back home. Perhaps, with hindsight, they didn't do such a great disservice because then came the Cultural Revolution and the Chinese themselves desecrated much of what remained.

The result of all this pillage and plunder is that a disappointing number of the enclaves that line the rock walls at Longmen stand empty. After the Yungang caves, whose splendour I had never anticipated, I found these caves at Luoyang rather less mind-blowing. Still, the site was pretty and immaculately maintained – though the clearance of restaurants, shops and factories to create it incensed one peasant so greatly that he apparently tracked an official in charge to his home and stabbed him.

Back in Luoyang, I wandered the streets in search of food for tomorrow. It was going to be a long day. I had booked a car to leave the hotel at five-thirty a.m. to take me the three-hour journey to Shaolin, the cradle of kung fu. I'd spend the whole day learning to kick the life out of anyone who bothered me, then I'd jump back in the car at about five, in order to be in Zhengzhou, a few hours to the west, by seven-thirty. At that time I had to pick up my train ticket, then board a train for a nineteen-hour journey to Hangzhou.

I bought supplies, then, refusing to spend any further minutes of my life in the terrible hotel restaurant contemplating every sha-la-la-la, I headed for the one restaurant in Luoyang that my guidebook seemed to think worth visiting. I hadn't eaten properly all day. I'd had Lemsip for breakfast, just an apple and a few biscuits for lunch, and now I was starting to feel distinctly queasy. The restaurant didn't look far; I reckoned I could walk there.

Forty-five minutes passed, and still I was hiking along the main road of Luoyang. I contemplated flagging down a taxi but it hardly seemed worth it. Surely I must nearly be there. I trekked some more. Now I'd been walking for an hour. I was starving and tired. I seemed to be experiencing Chinese history and culture rather more closely than I'd hoped: this was the Long March and the Great Famine conveniently packaged into one tidy afternoon. Finally, after an hour and a quarter, I arrived at the restaurant. There was no English menu. But this time, I was not accepting defeat.

'Come with me,' I said to the waitress, and I stood up. The girl raised her eyebrows, then dropped them into a worried frown. She had no idea what to make of me. I started to tour the tables of other diners. Then she understood. Blushing slightly, she trotted along behind me with her pad. Together we peered at the vats of noodle soup, the piles of deep emerald Chinese spinach flecked with garlic, and the many other plates of strange brown substances.

At one table, an old man sat and dined with his wife. He jabbed his finger enthusiastically at a steaming bowl in the centre of their table and let out a loud smack of his lips.

'This one's very good,' he said, and laughed.

'Excellent, I'll have that one,' I told the waitress.

A while later, my own bowl appeared – a huge,

white porcelain cauldron brimming with an opaque soup from which steam rose with a tantalizing aroma. Salivating with anticipation, I plunged in my chopsticks and found lurking beneath the soup's surface convolutions of noodles entwined among generous hunks of white, fleshy crab, plump slices of tender pork and delicious fresh vegetables bursting with bright green goodness. With great satisfaction I ate and ate while a few metres away the old man, his wife, and the entire restaurant staff stood in a silent semicircle and gazed with rapt fascination at the foreigner who feasted.

9

A Good Kicking

Frankly, the six-year-olds were frightening. In perfect formation, they spun round on their little left feet. As their spindly right ankles flew up round their ears like the flick of a whip unfurled, they emitted high-pitched, death-defying shrieks. This was no half-hearted '*Pow!*' This was the bloodthirsty war cry of cut-throat combatants executing precisely co-ordinated kung fu kicks.

I sat safely in the car waiting for Miss Wong of the foreign students' section to come and collect me, and tried not to annoy anyone. There were seven thousand pupils at this school, the largest kung fu college in Shaolin. Even in the playground, where normal children would skulk or play football, these jumped and jousted, leapt and punched with power, precision and the kind of belligerent facial expressions that could inspire a nervous onlooker to tremble. Dressed in identical red tracksuit tops with black trousers and white pumps, they marched to class armed not with book bags but with swords and sticks.

Shaolin Temple, just down the road from this school, is where the art of kung fu threw its first punches. Back in the sixth century AD, an Indian priest named

123

Bodhidharma came to China to teach Buddhism. The story goes that he arrived at the Shaolin Temple where monks were translating scriptures from Sanskrit at the emperor's behest. The abbot at first refused to let Bodhidharma join them, so he went and meditated in a nearby cave. His gaze was apparently so intense that it bored a hole through the cave wall. The monks then appreciated Bodhidharma's religious zeal and invited him into the temple.

Once there, Bodhidharma found that the monks, who spent most of each day hunched over texts, were too weak to meditate effectively. He therefore devised a series of exercises to increase their strength and energy flow. Shaolin was a famous temple, and retired generals used to come here for contemplation. These generals were experts in the ancient Chinese arts of wrestling, boxing and martial arts techniques and they adapted Bodhidharma's exercises into more combative systems which have been passed down through the generations to these six-year-olds in the playground today.

I was looking forward to my day in kung fu school. It's not something I often confess to, but I secretly enjoy martial arts movies, not so much for the sadistic violence as for the grace and skill of the choreography. Somewhat worryingly, I laughed like a drain through *Kill Bill*, relishing every flying kick, severed limb and fountain of fake blood. More disturbingly still, I found myself coveting the yellow jumpsuit.

In all honesty, Uma Thurman can keep her samurai sword. But it would none the less be rather good, I thought, to be able to extricate myself from a sticky situation with a flying leap from a table and a couple of gut-busting kicks. Early signs in the playground were good: these kids looked as if they could finish off at least a handful of grown men each. I only had one day to learn my new art so I accepted that I might not advance all that far. It seemed unlikely that I would actually learn to bound up vertical walls as they did in *Crouching Tiger, Hidden Dragon*, or indeed to drop-kick a coffee cup with quite Uma's panache, but I harboured high hopes that I might at least learn how to give someone a slightly sore nose.

Miss Wong appeared and took me to meet my teacher.

'One day?' asked Shou-yan incredulously. 'You want to learn kung fu in *just one day*?'

'Just something very, very basic,' I told him. 'I just want to get an idea.'

Shou-yan frowned. He himself had been under-taking arduous training day in, day out for years – he was twenty years old and a former student of the school. He shrugged.

'OK. I teach you a basic sequence.'

We went to the foreign students' training hall. Two others were already there and well into their daily regimes. Up and down one side of the hall, a Japanese boy head-flipped in a most alarming manner across the mats and back again. By the window, a shaven-headed American man dressed in loose white pyjamas let out tortured screams as his teacher tried to inflict flexibility on his recalcitrant Western limbs. I wondered just what levels of pain my own basic sequence would involve.

'Run in circles round the room,' commanded Shou-yan.

On the scale of things, running round in circles seemed like an easy option. I therefore kept it up, uncomplaining, for quite some time. Shou-yan limbered up in the middle of the room, thrusting his legs into unlikely contortions as he lunged low, then stood and nonchalantly lifted his foot so that his ankle tickled his ear. Beneath his baggy blue trousers and navy T-shirt, he looked spectacularly lean. He was of slight stature, almost skinny, in fact. As he twisted his legs about his torso, it was hard to make out a muscle upon him – yet there was something about the steady expression of his eyes and the determined set of his mouth that suggested this was a highly trained individual one wouldn't want to fight with.

The American was still howling by the window; as he lay on the floor on his back, his po-faced, implacable teacher was pushing his up-stretched legs towards his face with the full force of his body weight. Some small part of me started to hope that if I didn't make a fuss and just kept jogging quietly round the room, Shou-yan might forget my existence altogether.

He didn't. After about ten or fifteen minutes he told me to stop and took me to the side. It was my turn for torture by stretching. This was no gentle yogic surrender. The kung fu fraternity didn't seem to believe in such softness. This was a full-on, ligament-snapping assault. When my chest didn't reach my thigh, Shou-yan gave my back a mighty shove until it did.

'My hips don't do that,' I yelped as he made a good show of trying to dislocate my joints. Shou-yan furrowed his brows. He looked disconcerted and heaved all his weight against my leg once more. He seemed to find it difficult to accept that, really, truthfully, my hips just wouldn't bend. *Real* students are forced into the splits. But, to my great relief, Shou-yan just regarded my feeble legs with a doubtful expression, and suggested we move on instead to the basic stances.

I was to learn a very simple routine of lunges, kicks,

punches and blocks. It was a short enough piece to learn – and I had the whole day to master it – but immediately it transpired I had severe problems. My eyes were not spirited enough; my wrist was too high; my arm was too low. Kung fu was a precise art, even on day one. My forward lunge was a disaster because my hips just didn't extend that way.

'Again!' commanded Shou-yan.

I tried again.

'No! Leg too low! Again! From the beginning.'

I stood once more, face front, hands pulled back into fists at my waist, expression fierce. I glared hard and, eyeballs bulging in as frightening a way as I could muster, lunged forward and punched as if I wanted to send my imaginary assailant's nose to the back of his head, through the earth's core and into some distant continent.

'No! Wrist too high! Again!' Shou-yan barked.

'Again!' he shouted again, and, 'Again!' – again, and again, and again.

To be quite honest, it was starting to become a little tedious. I'd been there for a couple of hours now, and I seemed entirely incapable of progressing past the first three postures. Worse even than my body's failure to garner even the faintest of praise, my mind was turning to porridge. With every rallying call of 'Again!' the less I seemed to remember. It wasn't too long before I wasn't just failing to improve; I was actually becoming worse. I was blocking instead of punching, lunging instead of leaping, spinning, snapping and sinking amid a flurry of confusion and malcoordinated limbs. Shou-yan looked despondent.

'I think,' I said to him, 'we will take a ten-minute break.'

In the course of normal kung fu instruction, were a

127

student to dictate such a concept as a rest to a teacher, terrible punishment would ensue for this was heinous insubordination. Kung fu schools are nothing if not disciplined. Stories abound of small children forced to hold difficult postures for long periods with bowls balanced on their heads and severe beatings if they fail – though I have to say I saw no such thing that day. But when I demanded my break, Shou-yan just looked momentarily surprised, then agreed that it was a good idea. Even he could see that I was a hopeless case. I was only going to be there for one day and it seemed pointless to waste too much effort.

I sat on a bench by the wall and talked to the American student. He had been there for two months so far. The Japanese boy, he told me, wanted to be a kung fu movie star. According to the American, I was having a pretty easy ride. *He* had spent the first two weeks, four hours a day, repeating just two postures. The problem, we agreed, was that our poor Western brains just hadn't been trained for this kind of rote learning. The Chinese are conditioned almost from birth, it seems, to repeat their lessons until they have learnt them perfectly, and not to question. Our own upbringings had forced us to develop in different ways. Where a Chinese student might find herself panic-stricken when asked to break the mould with independent thought, my own brain had hurtled into full retreat and battened down the hatches after just two hours of learning by mind-numbing repetition.

Across the room, the Japanese boy seemed to be doing rather better. He hurtled up and down in a series of flying leaps, skull-splitting chops and blood-curdling screeches. Outside the window, formations of students spun round with nimble high kicks and lethally potent punches. The older students lifted weights; a group of boys aged about seven learned to box. Others stretched their limbs into eye-watering contortions or slid gracefully into the splits without so much as a whimper.

Perhaps they were grateful for the sacrifice their families were making to send them to such a prestigious establishment. The school costs about eight to ten thousand yuan a year, Shou-yan explained. For most Chinese families that constitutes a hefty sum. The children split their time evenly between kung fu and academic lessons. When they graduate, the best students may be taken on as teachers at the school; others go on to be bodyguards or policemen, or simply return home to help their families farm. Those who actually succeed in becoming the next Bruce Lee or Jackie Chan are of course few and far between. Even Shou-yan, who had succeeded in being taken on as a teacher, didn't seem to think much of this life.

'There's more to the world than kung fu,' he said as his sat on the bench and stared morosely at the wooden training-hall floor. He originally came from a town in Anhui, about a seven-hour journey from here. Now he lived in one of the cramped, untidy bunk rooms that lined the foreign students' training hall. The pay was poor but, he said, he was qualified to do little else.

After a good lunch of rice and vegetables in the school canteen, I returned to the training hall and paraded up and down countless times practising various high kicks – swinging in from the outside, kicking out from within, and the so-called cross crescent and outside crescent kicks. And then we returned to the dreaded routine, the lunges, punches and kicks that form the basic stances of kung fu. Again and again and again.

According to popular myth, ridiculously flexible monks aren't the only warriors the Shaolin Temple has spawned. The temple is also the birthplace of another infamous fighting force – one that has over the years substituted high kicks and knock-out punches with the rather more gory technique of chopping an opponent with a robust kitchen cleaver. For three hundred years ago the forebears of today's monks became the first Chinese Triads – or so they say.

Legend has it that during the early eighteenth century, some Mongolian tribes were rising up against the Qing emperor. The monks at Shaolin were experts in martial combat. Keen to get in a spot of sparring practice, they offered their services to the emperor and when after a few months they had quite literally given the rebels a good kicking, they returned to the emperor victorious. The emperor offered them titles and government posts to reward them but the monks turned the honours down as they preferred their monastic existence to the high jinks of court life.

They didn't leave, however, without managing to annoy one of the emperor's officials. Jealous because the monks had found such favour with the Son of Heaven (and probably envious of their abdominal six-packs too), the official convinced the emperor that the monks' superior fighting skill was a threat to his authority. They had only declined the positions offered because they meant to overthrow him, the official maintained. And so he persuaded the emperor to send his troops to the monastery. Given that if they tried to fight the monks the emperor's troops might go the same way as the Mongols, they instead burned the monastery to the ground.

Only a handful of monks escaped the inferno. Hunted down by the Qing army, soon there were only five of them left. They decided they would be less conspicuous if they disbanded so they went their separate ways, each consumed by a burning hatred of the Qing. Travelling individually through the land, the five monks set up secret societies, taught martial arts, and fomented revenge against the dynasty that had destroyed their monastery. These men became the legendary First Five Ancestors of Triad mythology, and to this day the societies repeat the motto *fan Qing fuk Ming* – overthrow the Qing, restore the Ming.

The years progressed, the Qing dynasty fell and back in Shaolin, the temple was rebuilt and repopulated, then burned down again during the 1920s and outlawed altogether during the Cultural Revolution. As the monks came and went, the Triads' political affiliations became diluted by their members' desire to turn a quick buck through illicit means. The religious and political symbolism they use in their ceremonies became purely ritual as their main concerns began to revolve instead around the lucrative industries of extortion, money laundering, drug trafficking, counterfeiting and prostitution. By the early twentieth century, when the Qing dynasty fell and chaos reigned in its place, the Triads enjoyed unprecedented power. In Shanghai, bosses such as Pock-Marked Huang and Big-Eared Du acquired almost mythical status.

'Baltic ears, cold cruel lips uncovering big, yellow decayed teeth, the sickly complexion of an addict . . . I had never seen such eyes before. Eyes so dark that they seemed to have no pupils, blurred and dull – dead, impenetrable eyes . . . he gave me his limp, cold hand. A huge, bony hand with two-inches long, brown, opium-stained claws,' wrote Ilona Ralf Sues in her book *Shark's Fin and Millet* after meeting Big-Eared Du in the 1930s.

In *The Soong Dynasty* Sterling Seagrave describes the same man:

> [Du's] outstanding features were a big shaved head and ears that stood out like tree mushrooms. His face was lumpy and irregular, like a sack of potatoes – the result of childhood beatings. His lips were stretched taut over his protuberant teeth in a perpetual smirk, and his left eyelid drooped in a permanent wink, giving him a lascivious air. There was always fresh gravy on his gown.'

W. H. Auden and Christopher Isherwood met Du when they travelled to China in the 1930s. 'Peculiarly and inexplicably terrifying were his feet, in their silk socks and smart pointed European boots, emerging from beneath the long silken gown,' they reported in their subsequent book *Journey to a War*.

The Triads penetrated every aspect of life and politics in Nationalist-controlled China during the first half of the twentieth century. Sun Yat-sen himself – the man who is credited with overthrowing the Manchu and, briefly, became the first President of the Republic of China – was a member. Indeed, Sun's failed coup of October 1895 was manned predominantly by conscripted Triad rank and file.

Chiang Kai-shek – the Nationalist leader who attempted to govern a very fragmented China from Sun's death in 1925 until the Communists finally took control in 1949 – was deeply involved in organized crime. His funds came not only from the Communist-phobic American government of the day, but from opium dealing, extortion and money laundering. It wasn't until the Communists came to power that business in China became too dangerous for the Triads. They evacuated in their droves to Hong Kong, which already had a well-established Triad network, or followed Chiang and his retinue to exile in Taiwan.

Nowadays, with wealth and big business drawing them like hungry sharks to freshly chopped flesh, the Triads are moving back into China, as well as infiltrating every aspect of the Chinese diaspora. It's estimated that approximately sixty million Chinese live overseas, and the Triads run their empires in London and Sydney, New York and Auckland.

I wasn't really very surprised that the Triads had given up on kung fu and relied instead on frighteningly sharp knives with which to lash their opponents to death – although they're not always so vicious. When they just want to warn somebody that they're not reaching their performance target, they merely chop off his little finger, or limit themselves to lacerating his arms. Kung fu probably wasn't for me, either, I decided as I limped back to the relative comfort of my car and driver at half-past four, clutching a photograph that Shou-yan had given me of himself – a keepsake of that painful day, perhaps. The picture had been taken just the previous weekend: Shou-yan and his kung fu buddies had hiked up one of the mountains that overlooked Shaolin. On the summit of the hill, Shou-yan stands in the photo against the clear blue sky with the peaks of the surrounding mountains at his feet. Dressed in purple silk pyjamas, he balances perfectly on one white plimsolled foot. He holds the other foot high over his head with his opposite hand; his legs are in perfectly straight, upright splits. With his free hand, he extends his palm outwards in the Buddhist symbol of protection. His face is serene, calm and concentrated. The posture looks effortless, relaxed, easy even. But how many years of torturous discipline lay behind that pose?

We drove out of the school and through the local town of Dengfeng on the way to Zhengzhou where I would catch my train. School was ending for the day. Kung fu kids swarmed in the streets from the many schools that have been set up in the town, all drawing on the fame of the nearby Shaolin Temple.

There must be easier ways of becoming a star, I reckoned as we clattered along yet another bumpy road. Kung fu school made the *Pop Idol* route look quite benign. Why would anyone want to spend years getting up at dawn, having one's limbs agonizingly contorted and generally being battered and beaten to a pulp in order to be the next Jackie Chan when one could just fill out an entry form and have one's ego shattered by a panel of bored judges instead? At least the latter path would be short.

When we arrived in Zhengzhou we headed straight for the China International Travel Service office where a man called Mr Li had very kindly acquired a ticket for me for that night's sleeper train to Hangzhou. He was waiting in his office till seven-thirty p.m. so that I could go and collect it. It was really incredibly helpful of him. I'm not sure how many administrative workers you'd find in England willing to spend an extra couple of hours in the office at night just so they could help a random foreign traveller. The Chinese were like that, often. The driver that morning had gone out of his way to wander round the school yard trying to locate Miss Wong on my behalf; that evening, when I went for dinner before catching the train, the waitresses rushed around, helped me with my luggage, and even stood guard by it while I went to the loo. Once I had left the more downtrodden areas where

134

the people, quite simply, were less educated, many of the Chinese seemed genuinely to care that outsiders went away with a good impression of their country. They honestly appeared to want to help.

After dinner, I went to the train station and sat, once again, on a hard plastic seat in the waiting hall while hordes of Chinese pushed and shoved around me. I was travelling tonight to Hangzhou, on China's east coast. A friend of mine from Hong Kong, Clive, was on business there for a couple of days and we'd arranged to meet for a drink the following evening. It may seem a little desperate to travel for nineteen hours on a Chinese train just to go for a beer with a friend – indeed, it probably is – but I had been looking forward to it for days.

A girl came and sat next to me. She was a student, she said, glad of the chance to practise her English. She too was making the nineteen-hour journey to Hangzhou, where she had been invited to a job interview. And then? I asked. Would she come straight back to Zhengzhou again? Probably, she said. It seemed a long way to go for a job interview, and the idea of doing this same, long journey in reverse just a day or two later seemed to me quite terrible. But we had no more time to discuss the intricacies of long-haul train travel: our train was ready and we jostled through the ticket barriers.

'Your carriage is that way,' said the girl, pointing towards the sleepers. And then she headed off in the opposite direction.

Good Lord, I thought, she's travelling in a hard-seat carriage. She's going to perch for *nineteen hours* amid the fruit skins, egg shells and half-eaten noodle boxes. She's going to spend the whole night, and then most of tomorrow, in that hawking, squawking, suffocating fug. Then, when she emerged, smutty and sleepless grey, she'd go to a job interview. And then she'd do the whole journey over again, but in reverse.

I climbed into my upper bunk feeling deeply grateful, for the first time, for the hard, narrow bed and pillow whose cover had probably been washed at some point in the last year, at least. On the bottom bunks two businessmen were preparing themselves for the night. They took off their trousers to reveal ankle-length white Y-fronts. The one in the bunk diagonally opposite then unbuttoned and took off his shirt. He was clearly a prosperous man who had plenty to eat – tyres of pale dimpled flesh cascaded down and over the elasticated waist of his underwear. He then extracted from his bag a neatly pressed white T-shirt and put that on over the Y-fronts. Now he was ready for bed.

It was strange the way these sleeping carriages completely redrew the lines of socially acceptable behaviour, I mused. It was unlikely that, in any other circumstances, a group of Chinese businessmen would strip down to their profoundly unattractive underwear in front of me, but here they all did so without a second thought, as if they were in their bedroom at home and nobody at all could see them. The women on the trains, on the other hand, always slept fully dressed, taking off just their shoes and jackets.

The Man of Substance lolled on the bunk below, his legs splayed, his bloated belly hanging free. Then he took out a great, fat cigar and lit it.

It was a simple issue of survival. If I was going to spend the next nineteen hours sitting in a cloud of cigar smoke, my continued existence – certainly in the sane and smiling form I knew and loved – was far from assured. The carriage window was closed and I couldn't reach to open it from my bunk.

I couldn't think how to say in Chinese, 'Please could you open the window a little,' so I used sign language instead. I stared hard at the man till I caught his eye, then screwed up my nose and wafted my hand in front of my nose. Then I pointed at the window.

He missed the bit when I pointed to the window. It was, after all, against the rules to smoke in the carriages on Chinese trains, and the Man of Substance thought I had asked him to smoke outside. He wasn't pleased. He tried to laugh, to brush off the humiliating loss of face inflicted upon him by a foreign woman telling him what to do, but his laughter was hollow and short-lived. Glowering, he raised his corpulent, Y-front-clad form from the bed, and stormed from the carriage, gesticulating wildly and muttering tersely as he went.

'*Waiguoren* . . . jabber jabber . . . *waiguoren* . . . jabber jabber . . . *waiguoren*,' I heard him smouldering down the corridor. I had a feeling that in between the repetitions of the one word I understood might have been some ripe vocabulary that we never would have covered in my Chinese class. Indeed, given the fact that I hadn't had a chance to shower since the rigours of my kung fu class, he might well have been saying, 'Stinking bloody *waiguoren*. Comes into the carriage smelling like a road builder's singlet and when I discreetly light my cigar to cover up the stench . . . *Baaahh*. Filthy bloody *waiguoren*.' He might have had a point.

After that little episode, nobody in the carriage much wanted to speak to me. But to be honest, it wasn't a bad feeling. I was sorry to have upset the Man of Substance, but happy to be rid of his cigar smoke. Also, it was rather nice to think that as I was now *persona non grata* among the company, nobody would be coming to me for English practice and I could spend the journey sleeping and reading in peace. And so I lay on my bed with my book while the men down below played cards and ate noodles. It was becoming a familiar scene. Then – *vroom!* – the lights went out and the snoring began.

It would have been good, on such a long journey, to have been permitted a lie-in the next morning, but at six-thirty the lights duly glared into action, and the carriage-dwellers leapt eagerly from their bunks to greet a new day. With extraordinary energy, they washed at the cold-water taps that furnished the end of each carriage, attacking their faces and necks with flannels in the vigorous way one might scrub at a particularly obstinate stain. Then they ate more noodles, played cards, ate nuts, drank tea from their jam jars, and the train trundled on. I ate some Oreos and dried apricots for breakfast, and read some more of my book.

At midday, I went to the dining car for lunch. The waitress was kind. She waited patiently while I tried to work out how to order, then smiled sympathetically when I reverted to my usual trick of pointing at other diners' food. I ordered rice and vegetables with some kind of meat. The tables had blue-and-white checked paper cloths, each covered by a very worn piece of once see-through plastic. There was a strange attempt at decoration: aluminium wine racks on each table held dusty bottles of beer. At many of the tables, groups of men downed bottle after bottle, their faces growing steadily redder as they tried to dull the pain of the long journey.

The food I had ordered had looked quite edible when I had seen it on other people's plates. On closer inspection, though, the rice was grey and congealed.

The vegetables swam limply in a blackish slop, like seaweed gasping for life in an oil spill, and the meat was nothing but fat. I forced myself to eat – I couldn't leave the table until I'd eaten a quarter of the rice and half of the vegetable concoction, I told myself. I picked up a glob of gunky rice on my chopsticks, and shovelled it into my mouth, then with great determination chewed and swallowed. The waitress was still waltzing up and down taking orders, smilingly distributing plates of unspeakable slop onto tables as she went. I courageously tackled a mouthful of oily vegetables, chewed and swallowed. I turned my attention back to the rice, piled up my chopsticks and was just about to eat when . . . '*Pphhhhhkkkooooow*' – the most extraordinary noise came from the table across the aisle. I looked up just in time to see the man sitting there pinch the tops of his nostrils and, with a mighty exhalation, blast two great jets of snot from his nose. With a gooey, sonorous splat, his mucus slammed into his bowl among his leftover rice and vegetables.

It was hard to finish my meal after that. I went back to my bunk and consoled myself with more Oreos. I roused myself to go to the loo. The woman in the queue before me took her turn, leaving her small son outside the door to wait for her. He was a very little creature, walking but not yet old enough to talk. As he waited for his mother to finish, he turned his head and saw me towering behind him. His tiny eyes opened incredibly wide and bulged so that they dominated his minuscule features like huge, shiny black bowling balls. An expression of absolute terror contorted his face. Panic-stricken, he fled towards the nearest Chinese man, an innocent bystander who was standing peacefully between the carriages smoking a cigarette, and flung his chubby arms round the smoking man's long, lean thighs. The man looked down in surprise – after all, he'd never laid eyes on this child before – and as they made eye contact, the child raised its pudgy fist, pointed at my monstrous head and let out a full-throated, terror-crazed scream.

The man laughed a little, embarrassed. I shrugged in a way that was meant to say, 'Who? Me?' The little boy continued to bellow as though he had seen the bogeyman.

'I don't know what you are,' his petrified shrieks rang clear, 'but you are big and white and ugly and I don't like you one bit.'

I tried to smile in a friendly manner. 'I know I haven't taken a shower in a while,' my beaming countenance was meant to say. 'And I appreciate my hair's not looking great. And yes, I'm hungry. But don't worry. I won't start eating small children until at least dinnertime.'

But by now the child was becoming quite breathless in his hysteria and, to save him from psychological payback later in life, I felt obliged to hide round the corner in the next carriage, out of sight of the child, until his mother emerged to collect him.

10

New Message

'When I was here a month ago,' said Clive as we settled into our second beer, 'that whole area round the northeast side of the lake wasn't there. All the flowers and trees and grass are brand-new. They told me they were going to finish it for National Day on October the first, but then it was still a building site. I didn't think they stood a chance of completing it in time. But they did.'

Clive has been travelling round this part of China for many years working for Swire, which holds the Coca-Cola franchise here. Hangzhou, he reckoned, was one of the nicer places on his patch.

Hangzhou is a cosmopolitan city. It has gleaming shopping malls with shops selling designer clothes and cosmetics. It has Häagen-Dazs and Starbucks.

The growth of Starbucks itself is an indication of the way China's younger generation is seizing hold of the Western consumer lifestyle. The first Starbucks store opened in Beijing in 1999. By the time of my visit in October 2003 there were 119 branches on the Chinese mainland. Meanwhile the Chinese were wolfing down Big Macs and Coke at a rate that would have blown the minds of the previous generation who, during China's famine years, would have rejoiced at the sight of a bowl of plain rice and a jar of tea. The volume of Coca-Cola consumed in China rose from 5.7 million litres in 1983 to ten times that amount a decade later. Another ten years down the line, and the volume was three and a half *billion* litres – that's to say that in 2003 the Chinese drank more than ten billion cans' worth of Coke. McDonald's first restaurant opened in 1990; they expect to have a thousand branches in China by 2008. Interestingly, though, the Chinese don't seem to see this trend as an invasion of foreign brands, but rather as a sign of their own country's development. According to an article in the *New York Times* in February 2002, nearly half of all Chinese children under the age of twelve thought that McDonald's was a Chinese brand.

Given all this, I felt it would be remiss of me not to taste something of American restaurant culture during my visit to Hangzhou. The next morning, therefore, I valiantly eschewed the hotel breakfast buffet of suspicious-looking dumplings and went instead to Starbucks. It's tragic, I know, but as I sat back in my armchair, clutching my mug of coffee, guzzling a strangely stale apricot Danish and listening to the sounds of sultry jazz that strummed gently in the background, I was quite ecstatic. I'd only been away a couple of weeks, my hardships had been paltry, and here I was in raptures at the first sight of Starbucks. It doesn't say much for my abilities as a traveller, really. It doesn't exactly scream 'fearless cultural experimentation'. Indeed, my excessively exuberant reaction suggests that I should score from my list of possible future journeys anything such as a sled-trip to the South Pole or a rafting expedition down the

Amazon, neither of which would feature Starbucks at all. But I enjoyed my breakfast a lot, anyway.

Buzzing with caffeine, I walked for two or three hours round the lake. The West Lake is the big attraction in Hangzhou. It was originally dredged in the eighth century. Ever since then, painters have painted and poets have pined by it – and, more recently, international five-star hotel chains have set their tills tringing joyously on its banks.

The brand-new grass, trees and flowers that lined the water's edge were immaculately landscaped. The pathways were sparklingly clean. The willows wept, the blossoms bloomed, the fishing boats chugged, and the birds in the trees duly chirruped – except that, on closer inspection, I found that they didn't. When I peered up among the perfectly formed leaves to watch the little feathery creatures throw open their beaks and clamour their exuberance at being alive in such a spotless place as this, I found that there were no actual birds in the trees at all, just large, metallic-grey loudspeakers strapped with aluminium bands to the branches. Scattered along the waterfront, 'ancient' pagodas built circa three weeks ago provided a helpful reminder that I was, remarkably, still in China.

Nestled in the grass were more speakers, this time in a decorative mushroom shape, that crooned synthesized versions of popular tunes. As 'Don't Cry For Me Argentina' filled the air, I had to concede that Hangzhou was broadcasting a confusing political message. Here I was, in a Communist country, but in a city that seemed to be exuberantly embracing capitalism in the form of tourism, department stores and American fast-food franchises, while being serenaded by a tune in which Andrew Lloyd Webber meets Peronism.

I wandered back from the lake into the city itself. I was astonished by Hangzhou. It seemed nothing like the China I'd seen over the last couple of weeks, where I'd had to learn quickly to leap out of the way of flying phlegm and to wash my hands with paranoid regularity. Hangzhou was clean; there were shops with things that I wanted to buy. There was a foreign languages bookshop. Admittedly, its stock was extraordinarily dusty and limited to last April's edition of *Vogue* (well thumbed), a few shelves of classics – the Brontës, Austen, Thackeray and Shakespeare – and a paltry smattering of foil-embossed romantic sagas. But it was encouraging to think that if I needed to refresh my reading matter, here was an opportunity, albeit a limited one.

The people were fashionably dressed. Chinese women that autumn were wearing their jeans drainpipe-tight, their bottoms turned up into huge cuffs so that the trouser legs ended halfway down the shin. Beneath the turn-ups they wore calf-length boots with pointed toes and stiletto heels. Any woman of any standing seemed to have her hair dyed, streaked with shades of blonde, or tiger-striped orange against the original black. Others went for red or purple tints. Clearly colouring one's hair was all the rage.

I studied the clothes for sale in the window displays of one, glistening mall. I observed the stylish women who strutted and sauntered in their finery. Then I paid a visit to the mall's loos. They were Western-style – but the seat of one cubicle was anointed on each side with muddy footprints where one bemused customer had climbed up to squat. I wondered how one would manage such a feat in stilettos. Perhaps the woman in question possessed remarkable flexibility and balance due to many years' training in kung fu.

I'd decided that the following night I'd take the ferry from here to Suzhou by means of the Grand Canal. The Canal stretches all the way from Hangzhou to Beijing, though large sections of it are no longer navigable. I needed to find the ticket office. I walked to the north end of the city, from where the Grand Canal flows, crossing many terrifying roads as I went. The great disadvantage of Hangzhou's prosperity was that walking through the city was fraught with even greater danger than in Beijing. In Beijing, at least, the traffic had moved so slowly round intersections that the perils of having one's brains dashed out onto the tarmac were marginally reduced. Here the gloriously wide roads, newly built to accommodate that most modish of accessories, the private car, were six or eight lanes across and the traffic for the most part moved fluidly. The locals just ambled slowly into the onslaught of blasting horns and revving engines without so much as glancing right or left. It was more than my nerves could handle. I would wait by the side of the road until a few people had amassed to cross, then shuffle out with them, making sure I kept the others between myself and the galloping, honking assault. When we arrived at the middle of the road the cars charged from the opposite direction and I'd have to scuttle round to the other side of the group.

After half an hour or so of such nerve-racking negotiations, I arrived on the far side of the vast, fast Tianmushan Road where I found a narrow, brown, dirty stream. It didn't look very grand. Rusting pipes were piled up on the canal bank; beyond, rundown high-rise blocks stretched as far as the eye could see. Two men dressed in shabby suits were standing by the water's edge. I asked them where I could buy tickets for the boat.

'Boat?' they asked incredulously.

'Yes, the boat to Suzhou.'

'*Mei you.*'

'There's no boat?'

'No. Maybe you should take the bus.'

I arrived back at the lakefront in the early evening. It was dark now, and the walkways were packed full of domestic tourists who had gathered to watch the daily fountain display. Beyond the crowds, illuminated jets of water spouted purple, blue, yellow and red to the tune of 'O Sole Mio'. Vendors sold balloons and toys on strings that flashed and flickered pink and neon green. Nestled in the lush, emerald grass, tiny spotlights shone up into the newly planted trees so that their leaves glowed the colour of freshly waxed limes. The pagodas shimmered across the lake. Candles glimmered on the outdoor tables of the waterfront cafés. I sat down at a table, ordered a beer, and watched the new, affluent China on holiday.

There was a large tour group staying in my hotel that evening. After they'd finished dinner, when their schedule decreed that they return to the hotel to rest, they ran up and down the corridor, hopping from one room to another, jabbering loudly, giggling and slamming doors like teenagers on a school trip.

At nine-forty-five, the phone rang. I'd talked to Clive last night about the calls I'd been receiving. Having stayed in rather a lot of Asian business hotels himself, he was alarmingly knowledgeable on the subject. Apparently, in different countries they use different euphemisms.

'In Taiwan they ask if you would like any hot water,' he explained.

It's confusing, really, and most important to know

the terminology. If somebody phoned me and asked if I'd like any hot water, I might well say yes, thinking it would make a nice cup of tea. There's a whole new language out there.

'The thing is,' Clive went on, 'you've got a foreign name, so when they look at the hotel guest list they don't know if you're a man or a woman.'

Remembering this conversation, I picked up the receiver and then, in the deepest, hoarsest voice I could muster, grunted, 'Hello?'

There was a moment's silence, then a throaty female voice chattered hesitantly in Chinese.

'I'm sorry?' I said in my normal voice, and the line went dead.

On Clive's recommendation I got up early the next day and by seven o'clock I was walking round the lake.

It was misty that morning. There was scarcely a shift in tone between the steely-grey water and the slate of the sky above. On the far side of the lake, the faint outline of hills rose and fell in a fractionally deeper hue. A fishing boat paddled by silently, propelled by its boatman's single oar, leaving blue-black ripples in its wake.

On a concrete walkway that jutted out over the lake, an elderly man dressed in a black tracksuit swayed gracefully through his t'ai chi. His movements were slow and seemingly effortless, his expression serene. Holding his arms at shoulder height, he swept his hands before him as though he were manipulating string puppets that leapt and glided across the ground.

A group of perhaps ten people stood under a pagoda at the end of a stone jetty. Its six pillars were topped by a hexagonal roof whose corners curled up into long, shapely talons. The figures stood and chatted, their black silhouettes contrasting sharply with the hazy blue beyond.

Others took up their place in the landscaped gardens around the lake's edge. Here, every few metres, a different group was engaged in some activity. Six women lunged to the music of their portable cassette player, their left hands pushing down and away, their right hands beckoning upwards. One of the women was dressed in a loose jade-silk suit; the others wore ordinary trousers, sweaters and jackets for their morning routine. A slightly larger group of women practised aerobics to jauntier tunes while one of their number stood out in front and issued instruction.

Two men in their sixties brandished silver-coloured swords from whose handles dangled lush red tassels. They swept their weapons through graceful arcs as they executed their fluid, deliberate dance. An elderly man practised all alone, brandishing a long stick. A few metres away, a girl aged perhaps thirty performed her solitary t'ai chi movements. She was an elegant creature, with her hair tied back in a neat ponytail and dressed in lilac silk trousers and a matching collarless shirt.

On one path a man clad in black hunched his shoulders with concentration as he etched Chinese calligraphy onto the paving slabs with a long-handled brush. But his words – poetry or protestations, I couldn't tell – were daubed only in water and within minutes they were gone.

I went back to Starbucks for breakfast, ordered another coffee, and was just mulling over the pastries when the girl behind the counter stepped in to help me with my decision.

'These ones,' she said in English, with a proud

flourish towards a small tray on the second row, 'are new!'

It was as though they were the next season's line of clothing fresh from the catwalks of Milan rather than a tray full of cinnamon twists.

'New today?' I asked.

'Today!' she affirmed, and glowed.

I walked that afternoon onto the island in the middle of the lake. It's connected by road but, still, it's a peaceful spot. I strolled through the woods and came upon a pagoda where a couple played flute and *erhu*, a two-stringed fiddle, while a woman sang.

Coming out on the other side of the island, I sat on a bench and watched rows of brides and grooms having their photographs taken against the background of West Lake. They weren't really wedding photographs: these couples weren't actually getting married that Tuesday afternoon. This was just the photograph, a prestigious adornment for display rather than a memento of the happy day itself.

Each couple seemed to have to wait for hours. The white satin of the brides' dresses gleamed as their shiny faces perspired beneath their immobile layers of foundation and rouge. They sat stiffly: a mere shift in posture could crinkle the slick bridal fabric; the slightest rub of the eye could dislodge the mascara that caked their lashes. In contrast, their grooms flapped uncomfortably in their unfamiliar suits, like desperate fish on a wet market stall.

Still they waited. None of the couples appeared to speak to each other. They looked grumpy, bored and rigidly unromantic. Then at last their turn would come. The appointed couple would carefully rise and move beneath the trees whose autumn leaves were turning from saffron-yellow to rich fiery red. Before a backdrop of water lilies and the lake beyond they would, for the briefest moment, clasp each other and smile – and then the photograph was done.

My mind slipped back to a Saturday evening in Hong Kong, shortly after I'd started living there. A British friend was marrying a Chinese girl and a group of us had been invited to the wedding party in the evening. We ate a suckling pig which had glacé cherries inserted into its eye sockets. Under each cherry a tiny bulb flashed, illuminating the fruit in sporadic bursts of garish pink. Instead of making speeches, the happy couple stood on a platform and carried out little challenges. First of all, the bride had to get down on her knees and, using only her mouth, push an apple up one of her husband's trouser legs, over the groin, and down the other side. He had to eat two buns that were tied with string round her neck so that they lay over each breast. It seemed an excruciating performance to go through in front of one's granny.

I checked out of my hotel. Despite my failure to find a ticket office on the waterfront the previous day, it had transpired that there was, after all, a night boat to Suzhou. The hotel's business centre had booked a ticket for me with no problem. I might have started by asking there. Would I like a four-bed cabin or a two-bed one, the woman had asked. I had wondered whether the boat would be full. I'd rather have booked a two-bed room if there was a chance of having the place to myself; on the other hand, I didn't much fancy being stuck in a room alone with a single, strange man.

'Oh, the boat won't be full,' said the business centre

woman, and laughed uncomfortably. Clearly the boat wasn't a fashionable mode of transport for travel to Suzhou. Why, after all, would any self-respecting person journey for thirteen hours on a clanking, rusty boat when they could get there in five hours in an air-conditioned bus on the shiny new expressway?

'I'll tell them to give you a room on your own,' she said confidently.

I took a taxi to the ferry pier which, it turned out, was a short distance away from the tumbledown canal bank I'd been to yesterday. After a couple of days in Hangzhou, several good meals and numerous cups of coffee, I was feeling much more relaxed. Cheerfully, I paid the driver and made my way to the waiting room. I was in high spirits, and greatly looking forward to my cruise in my private room on a peaceful, pottering old canal boat.

11

A Night With Two Soldiers

A jowly, bovine man stumbled into my cabin and dumped his bag on the lower bunk. He had pouchy eyes and slack, pudgy cheeks. I looked up in alarm. This hadn't been part of my plan. I'd arrived, found my cabin, and taken the top bunk, then installed myself in a chair on the other side of the room and started to read. I hadn't wanted a companion.

'*Ni hao.*' The man smiled at me nervously. He took off his shoes, stowed them neatly under the bed and put on over his dark grey socks the white terry-towelling slippers he had ferreted from his bag.

'*Ni hao.*' I sighed. The slipper-clad man looked anxious and disappeared through the door. A few minutes later he returned with his friend.

'*Ni hao,*' said the friend.

'*Ni hao,*' I replied.

The friend was dressed in olive-green military uniform. He sat on the lower bunk while my fleshy-faced companion took the other chair.

'My friend,' said my cabin mate, 'is a soldier in the PLA.' He spoke in faltering English, pointed at the uniform, and smiled self-consciously.

'I can see.' I grinned. The friend was short and round and had a flat, slightly upturned nose, little round glasses, and spiky crew-cut hair. His green army trousers were several sizes too big for him and were gathered in round his waist by a black, plastic belt.

'What is your name?' asked the soldier.

'Polly,' I said.

'What is the meaning?'

'No meaning.'

'*No meaning?*' They seemed astonished that one could have a name with no meaning and discussed the wonderful conundrum between themselves in Chinese.

'What is your name?' I asked my companion.

'My name in English means Ox,' he said. 'And my friend in English is called Hero. We are both soldiers in the PLA.'

My anxiety at having to share my accomodation with Ox began to dissipate. In the next-door cabin he had a friend with a wife. For some reason, this made it seem less likely that during the night he would pummel me to death with his tea jar. Furthermore, he was beginning to entertain me: he had an amusing name which suited him strangely well, and a friend in military uniform called Hero.

Ox and Hero lived in Beijing; they had come to Hangzhou on holiday, and now were travelling to Suzhou.

'Why are you wearing your uniform when you are on holiday with your wife and your friend?' I asked Hero. There was some discussion between the two men. At last Hero replied.

'Today I have been working,' he said. It seemed that Hero had a better command of English than Ox.

'And why are you travelling by boat when it is faster to take the expressway?' I asked.

Hero smiled patiently and said in a tone one might use to explain something to a slow child with a very small brain, 'Because the Grand Canal has a very important history.' He paused and gazed out beatifically at the brown sludgy water. 'Do you know when this canal was built?'

'Um,' I said. I had read a potted history in my guidebook, but the facts had slipped easily from my mind.

'The Grand Canal of China is the oldest and longest canal in the world.' Hero nodded to himself with satisfaction. 'The earliest part was built in . . .' he paused to think, 'five hundred BC. Then it was made bigger by the Emperor Yangdi of the Sui dynasty.'

I had seen a painting of this emperor who reigned nearly fifteen hundred years ago. He was a stern, determined-looking individual dressed in black robes. His face appeared curiously flat; the handlebars of his moustache descended gloomily down each side of his mouth. He was flanked in this portrait by two courtiers who looked entirely miserable.

What Hero didn't tell me was that Emperor Yangdi was a decadent man with a great fondness for alcohol and women. When he travelled on the water, his boat was apparently drawn by beautiful young girls attached to the vessel by silken cords.

Neither did Hero reveal that – as Chinese legend has it – one of the canal's overseers, Ma Shu-mou, ate a steamed two-year-old child each day that he worked on the canal's construction. Whether that's true or not, the building of the Grand Canal certainly took great toll on the emperor's subjects. He conscripted *five million* men to work on the project. The hardships that his grandiose schemes engendered, combined with a series of disastrous military campaigns, meant that

Yangdi was not a popular man. In 618, when he was fifty years old, his own attendants murdered him. He might have done well to pay a little more attention to their grumpy expressions in that portrait.

During the early years of the twentieth century, missionary families used to travel along the Grand Canal as the first leg of their journey to the resort town of Mogan Shan, which lies in the hills about sixty kilometres north of Hangzhou. Their memoirs tell of the breezy peace of the journey, of trailing their feet in the cool waters of the canal as their lackeys rowed past lush paddy fields and fishermen with cormorants.

Times had changed.

A heavy fog descended during the night. Unfortunately, the cabin I was sharing with Ox was the one closest to the driver – and to the fog horn.

'BLAAAAHHH.' The horn sliced into my sleep, brash, blaring and extraordinarily loud. I leapt awake; then, as the boat rocked back to silence, fell to sleep once more.

'BLAAAAAAAAHHH.' The noise cleaved open my consciousness a few minutes later. The volume was really quite phenomenal as it cut through the dead-of-night tranquillity. Across the water others echoed back their own warnings with ear-splitting discord.

Then there was quiet, just the unwavering thrum of the engine. I seemed to have drifted off again only for a minute or two when—

'BLAAAHHH-BLAAAAH-BLAAAAAAAAH.'

The next morning, the canal was thick with traffic chugging through the fog. When darkness had fallen last night, we had been the only boat in sight. Now the wide waterway was steaming, snorting, coughing and choking with long, flat goods vehicles. Many were painted bright colours – turquoise and yellow, or olive-green and orange. They were battered old boats, their paint peeling and stained, their long, low front sections laden with freight, while at the back ramshackle cabins housed the family. Occasionally, sparse, spiky potted plants attempted to give an impression of home.

Some vessels carried countless crates of bottles; others ferried coal or coils of rope. Sometimes as many as twenty boats were tied together tip to tail and, as one, they made their way upstream like a long, slow goods train of many carriages. Often, a solitary man or woman stood on the stern dressed in thick jumpers and a warm jacket and stared out into the murky blue morning. Others squatted and drank tea from bowls, or went about their morning chores.

'These families spend all their lives on their boats,' Hero explained. 'There are whole communities living on the water.'

He was still wearing his uniform, I observed. Presumably he hadn't slept in it all night, so the fact that he had chosen to wear it today – when he definitely wasn't working – cast into some doubt his excuse of yesterday. It seemed odd to me. It couldn't have been because he didn't have any other clothes. If he could afford to take a holiday, and to pay for a private sleeping cabin for himself and his wife, he could surely afford a pair of trousers. Maybe his wife had a weakness for men in uniform.

As we neared the city, the water, that life-blood of the canal families, took on a powerful pong. It stank strangely like school cabbage. Hero sighed.

'The people, they throw in their rubbish.' He looked forlorn. 'In London, the river does not smell, does it?'

I conceded that usually it didn't smell quite as bad as this.

Hero went on. 'And the water is beautiful, blue and clear, no?'

When I told him that the Thames was much the same murky brown colour as the Grand Canal, his face fell dramatically as though his one, last waterborne fantasy had been cruelly crushed.

We arrived in Suzhou four hours late: the fog delayed our arrival from seven o'clock till eleven. Still, that gave me plenty of time to check into my hotel before heading out into the tiny tree-lined lanes of the city. In contrast to the youthful boughs hanging over Hangzhou, these branches were ancient, knobbly with contortions and contusions. The birds that chirruped were real. I sat in a small café where the eager, smiling staff brought me a sizzling tray of perfectly fresh dumplings filled with spinach and pork, and several cups of steaming green tea.

I had decided that I wanted to take home teapots from China – and the most famous teapots in the country come from Yixing, just a hundred kilometres from Suzhou. They say that you can merely add hot water to an aged Yixing pot, and still you'll pour out a delicious cup of tea. I was determined, therefore, to buy good ones. Not for me the mass-produced, tourist teapots of the city – I was going to travel right to the very heart of teapot land, and buy my wares in Yixing itself.

Legend has it that tea was first drunk in China about five thousand years ago. The story goes that the emperor Shen Nong was an observant and intelligent man who had proclaimed that all drinking water was to be boiled as a health precaution. One day, while travelling, he stopped with his entourage for refreshment. The servants began to boil water to drink, and a few dried leaves from the tree overhead fell into the pot to create a yellow liquid. The emperor was interested in this new infusion, drank some, and found it marvellously energizing.

Another story – neither as pretty nor as credible – relates that the Buddhist Master Bodhidharma (the same one who went to Shaolin Temple and bored a hole through the cave wall with his gaze) cut his eyelids off so that he couldn't fall asleep while meditating – or, presumably, at any other time. His eyelids fell on the ground and from them the first tea bushes sprouted.

However it was discovered, over the centuries the popularity of tea spread and became known in China as *cha*. As early as the eighth century AD a man called Lu Yu wrote the first definitive book of tea, the *Cha Ching*, which covered three volumes.

England didn't hear of the new drink until many centuries later, in the mid 1600s, but the subsequent British addiction to tea was to play a significant role in Sino-British relations: it was the importation of copious chests of tea that led to the trade imbalance that, in turn, gave rise to the Opium Wars. That innocent, dried-up little leaf that fell into Emperor Shen Nong's pot all those years ago eventually wreaked havoc on a scale that the emperor could never have imagined. And, on a somewhat lesser scale, it was to bring turmoil to my day too. I hadn't been back on a Chinese bus since that dreadful first ride out of Wutai Shan – but today I was to take *five* (and that's not to mention the taxis) all in the name of a nice cup of tea.

The first bus from Suzhou to Wuxi was huge, comfortable and air-conditioned. My spirits rose. Perhaps I had just been unlucky the first time, I thought. Maybe the Wutai Shan to Taiyuan experience had just been a dreadful aberration and, in reality, most Chinese buses had suspension and ventilation. Could it be that *Sam Hong the Happy Ghost with Supernatural Powers* had merely been the lurid hallucinations of a nicotine-drugged mind? For two hours or so, I zoomed luxuriously down the highway and, still feeling chipper, arrived in Wuxi.

From Wuxi, it all went downhill – though not in such a catastrophic manner as it might have done had a kindly fellow passenger not rushed up to me as I boarded the wrong bus, grabbed my arm and prevented me from spiriting myself away to the very ends of the earth, never to be seen again. The right bus was cramped and clattering and the journey lasted another two hours. I still wasn't in teapot town proper, though. To buy teapots, I had to travel a short distance further to Dingshan. I walked out of the station, looking for the third bus. I was hounded by touts.

'*Mei you, mei you*,' they responded to my enquiries about public transport. 'You'll have to come in my car.' And then they quoted some ludicrous price.

'*Mei you, mei you*,' leered the layabouts squatting by the side of the road. They seemed eager to join in the fun and tease the foreigner.

The touts were sticking to me with irritating persistence. One was a man who looked to be in his forties. He was frighteningly skinny. His collarbones stuck out through his thin, taut, mole-spotted skin like two chopsticks splayed at a careless angle across a plate upon which drops of soy sauce had spattered. His gaunt head with its angular, jutting cheekbones was shaped like an inverted triangle descending to a bony point at his chin. He bellowed reams of unintelligible Chinese at high volume, his mouth uncomfortably close to my ear.

I tried to edge discreetly away from him. A second tout, a woman who looked decidedly plump in comparison to her friend, laughed uproariously and tried to steer me in her direction by grabbing hold of my arm and pulling hard. I broke free, abandoned the idea of the bus, and escaped somewhat limply into a licensed taxi parked at the side of the road. A short while later, four and a half hours after leaving Suzhou, I arrived in Dingshan.

Dingshan, I was less than enchanted to discover after all that trouble, was a dusty hellhole sprawled out on two sides of a beige, characterless highway. There were, however, piles, heaps, perhaps even small mountains of pottery. Brown clay teapots lined row after row of shelves. There were tea sets in boxes, pots on their own, and little thimbles of cups. There were minuscule pots, tiny pots and pots that were merely small. When drinking high-class tea, one is obviously not meant to binge.

Just off the highway lay a huge, unkempt yard flanked on three sides by shops and stalls selling ceramics of every colour and creed. There were great glazed planters, sprawling crockery sets, and shelves packed tight with brightly coloured mugs, crackle-glazed vases, coffee pots, dishes and bowls. For about an hour I wandered around looking at them all. I seemed to be the only tourist silly enough to have come to Dingshan that day. There were no coach loads in matching baseball caps here. The occasional solitary soul wandered through the odd shop, but nobody was buying.

I'd have thought, in that case, the shopkeepers would have been happy to see me, but instead they seemed somewhat disdainful. Either that, or they were so astonished that any foreigner was mad enough to come here that they were stunned into silence. Even if that was the case, though, their surprise wasn't sufficient to put them off their noodles, which they slurped wordlessly while I browsed.

It took me about an hour to select my teapots. I paid careful attention to the depth and fit of the lid, and made sure that they were suitably brown and unglazed – for this is vital in a good teapot, I had read. And then, that was that. My mission was completed. There seemed to be absolutely nothing else whatsoever to do in Dingshan. And so I climbed on yet another rickety old bus, this time heading back to Yixing.

At Yixing station, I didn't have to wait in the hall with the other passengers. Perhaps the station official had been in Wuxi that morning when I had nearly boarded the wrong bus. Whatever the reason, he wasn't taking any chances. Before the barrier in the waiting hall had even opened to allow my fellow passengers through, I was personally escorted onto the bus and into a preferential window seat. The uniformed official said something to the driver, who smiled and nodded in a friendly, welcoming way. I didn't understand exactly what he said, but took it to be something along the lines of: 'It's another one of those pale-faced, directionally incompetent creatures that kick up such a fuss when they end up in the back end of beyond with nothing but a bowl of rice and a lump of coal for sustenance. Just keep an eye on it, would you?'

Really, everyone was being immensely helpful, and with the combined aid of the uniformed man and the driver I arrived safely back in Wuxi where I boarded the last bus of the day back to Suzhou. This vehicle, again, was smelly and smoky and stopped every minute or two to pick up passengers or set them down.

About half an hour into the journey, two women, one of whom looked to be at least in her eighties, climbed aboard hauling hulking cloth-wrapped bundles behind them. There were no seats so they sat on a metal platform at the front of the bus and from there engaged the conductress in a lusty, full-throated row.

They were shrieking, I think, over the fare. I couldn't understand the words, but from the proffering of small notes and aggravated, arm-waving refusals on the part of the conductress, I concluded that the two women were offering only to pay half the fare each, seeing as they had to sit on the floor. The other passengers were loving it. Enthusiastically they joined in the row, calling out with clamorous ripostes and robustly casting their own opinions into the fray. Every now and then, the argument would die down and there would be a few minutes' disgruntled silence. Then, from somewhere in the middle of the bus, a little voice would pipe up.

'She's eighty-four, you know, and sitting on the floor! It's a disgrace!' I imagined the jaunty, wizened old man in the third row to be saying.

Or maybe, 'Just think, she might never get up again. She might be stuck there on the bus floor for the rest of her days, knees bent up round her ears, piles of fag ends and rubbish heaped up round her hips. And you want her to pay the full fare! You ought to be ashamed of yourself!'

And then the other passengers would screech with laughter and the trio would kick back into their rambunctious hullabaloo.

My return journey took five and a half hours. Added to the four and a half hours of the outward journey, I had that day spent *ten hours* on Chinese buses just to buy a few small, brown teapots. By the time I arrived back in Suzhou, I was utterly exhausted. What was most disappointing of all, though, was that I now realized that the teapots in every tourist shop in the city were exactly the same as those I had bought in Dingshan. There was nothing special about mine at all.

I had intended the next day to visit Zhouzhuang, a pretty little town criss-crossed with canals, bridges and cobbled lanes. Hero had positively insisted that I go there. But after the previous day's marathon, I'd frankly had my fill of buses. And so, instead, I spent the day strolling quietly in Suzhou's famous gardens.

The gardens were built by scholars, officials and merchants who first took up residence in the city when the Southern Song dynasty moved its capital to nearby Hangzhou in AD 1127 and again, a couple of hundred years later, when the Ming set up court in Nanjing. In addition to its proximity to these two capitals, Suzhou was considered an attractive residence for a merchant keen to turn a tidy profit as it was the centre for silk production in China. While impoverished workers perspired in cavernous sweatshops, the privileged classes that employed them pottered elegantly around their perfectly mellifluent retreats.

The gardens were meant to be harmonious combinations of elements. Rocks, water, trees and flowers were meticulously arranged. Pavilions were built so that the view was perfect from whichever side one sat; intricately latticed walkways ensured that a scholar in need of inspiration could stroll in the gardens even in rain and snow without fear of dampening his silken slippers.

I wandered round the Garden of the Master of Nets,

a tiny area said to be designed to technical perfection, and the much larger Humble Administrator's Garden. The blue sky reflected as deep azure in the carefully modelled rock pools; the swooping upturned roofs of the pavilions and the overhanging trees shone from the water's surface with a shimmering intensity. Walking along the cobbled pathways past streams and ponds, bamboo and bonsai, pagodas and stone bridges, I thought about the poets who used to come here to compose their lines and concluded that they must have soon had very sore bottoms. These gardens were fantastically pretty, but they weren't comfortable. The stone stools and sculpted outcrops of rock provided the only seating. I thought that my own creativity might quickly have become stifled by the practical consideration that I might contract haemorrhoids. But maybe writers were made of sterner stuff in those days – or maybe they came armed with cushions.

Despite their stony seats, I was entranced by the gardens. In the Humble Administrator's Garden, huge blue-and-white porcelain urns housed goldfish who swam around in green, scummy water. One such bowl was labelled in English, 'Goldfish swimming joyfully.' I wondered how they knew. A little further down the cobbled pathway talking myna birds perched in cages.

'*Ni hao*,' one squawked as I walked by. And then, 'Hello!' chirped another.

Good heavens, I thought, even the birds are welcoming.

I strolled home via the tiny side lanes of the city, along the banks of narrow, winding canals onto which backed a ramshackle collection of houses with haphazard balconies and laden washing lines. It was a tranquil world, a far cry from the main, traffic-clogged roads and shiny new shopping malls that lay just a block or two away.

In one lane, under a wooden chair on a pavement, huddled a small white dog whose owners had taken the Chinese propensity for dying things perhaps one step too far. Its ears and tail had been coloured in pink.

12

Sea and Sun

When trying to eat a fried egg with chopsticks, it is vital to ensure that the egg is well cooked. A hard-yolked egg is a solid enough object, something you can easily pincer and grip. If, on the other hand, you opt for a lightly cooked, oil-drizzled sunny side up version, all kinds of trouble ensues.

I sat at breakfast the next morning and considered the conundrum. I had thought it would be a good idea to fuel up with something nutritious before embarking on the next leg of my journey – the bus to Nanjing – but each time I tried to pick the egg up with my chopsticks, the soft, slippery white just slithered out of my grasp and smacked back down onto the plate. I considered holding the plate up to my mouth and scooping the whole shebang straight down my throat with no further ado, but had to conclude that the egg was just too big. In the end, I hacked away at it with my porcelain soup spoon and, with the help of my fingers, managed to negotiate its safe passage into my mouth. And then, just when I had finished, the waitress appeared with a knife and fork.

Eating a fried egg with chopsticks, I thought as I

sat on the bus to Nanjing some hours later, bears small-scale similarities to the greater trials of travelling round China as a foreigner. It is frustrating and frequently ludicrous. Sometimes it is funny. Small tasks take infinitely longer than they ought. You look ridiculous, often. But in the end, pride shattered, patience tried and seemingly against all odds, you do in fact arrive. And then somebody comes along smiling and points out the easier route you should have taken.

Still, the gods of humiliation, whoever they are, satisfied themselves sufficiently early that day to leave me alone once breakfast was done. The bus to Nanjing provided, in contrast, an experience of sheer, unadulterated pleasure. The large, comfortable, air-conditioned bus roared voraciously up the expressway with just one stop, and that was for the loo. For once, I actually travelled along one of those brand-new shiny roads that the Chinese have been building with such gay abandon, instead of staring at it forlornly from a parallel pot-holed track. The expressway was gleaming black tarmac, its white lines still bright, yet, despite its devastating good looks, it had managed to attract very little other traffic. And so, just a couple of hours later, with no incidents or rumpuses whatsoever, I arrived in Nanjing.

Nanjing translates as Southern Capital – and the capital it was for several chunks of history as dynasties came and went, moving their power bases as they did so. When the Ming came to power in 1368 they established their capital here and it was from Nanjing that one of the more colourful chapters of Chinese history set sail.

The southern Chinese had, in ancient times, been seafaring people. Confucius, however, had preached against foreign journeys as they interfered with his prescribed notions of family duty. As his teachings took hold from the second century BC, travel went out of fashion for several hundred years. (Confucius, a philosopher rather than a divine presence, was born in 551 BC, but was largely unknown during his lifetime. He spent many years wandering about China preaching his ideas on social order to anyone who would listen – to no very great effect. It wasn't until his Analects – that is, his sayings – were published many years after his death that Confucian ideas came to form the basis of all education in China.) Still, despite Confucius's objections from beyond the grave, by the time of the Tang (AD 618–907) overseas trade was roaring once more. By the ninth century, there were African slaves in China and Persian-style veils became de rigueur among the women of the court.

It was at the beginning of the fifteenth century, though, that China's naval exploration reached its apogee under the auspices of the Ming emperor Zhu Di. Ignoring the anguished cries of his Confucian advisers, Zhu Di ordered from his court in Nanjing the construction of a vast fleet of trading vessels and warships. The armada became known as the treasure fleet.

During the first decade of the fifteenth century, nearly two thousand ships were built under the emperor's instructions. Their commander-in-chief was the eunuch Zheng He, nicknamed 'San Bao', Three Treasures. He left Nanjing and ventured over the seas to south-east Asia, India, the Middle East and Africa. Through his fabled journeys, he entered Western literature as the legendary Sinbad the Sailor. More recently, he's even been accredited – somewhat controversially – with the discovery of America by retired Royal Navy commander Gavin Menzies who, in his book *1421*, claims that Zheng He landed in the New World seventy-one years before Columbus did.

Eunuchs were employed by the Chinese imperial families for more than two thousand years until the last dynasty, the Qing, was overthrown by revolutionaries in 1911. Their popularity arose on account of the dynastical bigwigs' concern for the emperor's bloodline. The emperor, the Son of Heaven, was considered to be chosen by divinity and he was required to perform the necessary rites of ancestor worship to ensure harmony between the heavens and earth. It was vital that his son and heir was really his own. The employment of eunuchs, therefore, was principally a very draconian way of ensuring that the emperor's wife didn't play around with the servants.

By the end of China's succession of dynasties, most eunuchs were volunteers. Due to their close relationships with those in power, eunuchs had access to bribes and royal favours; if they exploited these successfully (and some eagerly offered themselves to their masters as sexual objects to ensure that they did) they could become wealthy and influential.

In general, eunuchs were castrated as young boys – they were considered especially pure if the operation was performed before they reached the age of ten. The boy's family received money for their son, but in addition they hoped that he would acquire influence at court and pass wealth to them. Goodness knows why: being a eunuch wasn't much fun and it seems optimistic to hope that one's son would thank his family for allowing a man with a knife to lop his bits off. Eunuchs frequently suffered from an inability to control their bladders, and things didn't look up for them in the next life as they had no sons to make offerings for their souls after they died.

The process itself was a grisly one. On the fateful day, the boy's family would escort him to a so-called 'knifer'. The boy was placed on a low bed and, after being asked one last time if he was happy to be castrated, had bandages tied round his lower belly and upper thighs to act as tourniquets. He was drugged with opium and, in what sounds like a sadistic attempt at anaesthesia, his genitalia were anointed with chilli sauce. Then, with one fell swoop of a small, curved knife, the knifer chopped off both testicles and penis as close as possible to the body, in order not to leave any kind of stump. He then inserted a metal plug into the urethra, bandaged the wound, and forced the boy to walk around for two or three hours. Finally, the boy was allowed to lie down, but was forbidden either from drinking or urinating for *three days* during which time he quite understandably was said to suffer excruciating pain. After three days, the plug was removed and, with a bit of luck, a jet of urine shot out. This was a good sign and implied that danger for the boy's health had passed. If, on the other hand, the urethra had closed up, the boy died an agonizing death.

The penis and testicles (known in Chinese parlance as the 'three treasures') were then stored in a jar and the eunuch kept his shrivelled genitals for life so that when he died his body could be buried whole.

According to Sterling Seagrave in his book *Dragon Lady*, one Ming-dynasty eunuch kept a concubine 'whom he savoured in other ways' and desperately wanted a son. After a long search to find a way to reverse his situation, he found a doctor who told him that if he ate the brains of seven living men, his penis and testicles would grow back. The eunuch therefore obtained seven criminals, had their heads split open and consumed the pulsating mass within. It was not recorded whether or not this treatment worked.

Zheng He, however, was not a voluntary eunuch. He was a Muslim, born just south of Kunming in Yunnan province. As a boy, he was taken prisoner by the Ming army which invaded Yunnan in 1382. Zheng was castrated by the invaders: this was customary treatment of the young sons of prisoners. He was then placed in the household of Zhu Di, the fourth son of the emperor.

Zhu Di was a military man and Zheng He was raised in army camps, gradually becoming a trusted friend of Zhu Di and going on to become an able commander in his own right. Eunuchs who had been castrated during their boyhood usually grew up with effeminate tendencies and high-pitched voices. Zheng He broke the mould. He was said to be seven feet tall and immensely broad, with glaring eyes, bright white teeth and a booming voice. By the time Zhu Di seized the throne in 1402, his eunuch commander held a position of considerable influence.

In 1405, the first treasure fleet set sail under Zheng He's command. Its boats were laden with gold, silver, silk and porcelain. Over the next several years, the sailors jousted with pirates and battled with storms to trade these goods for spices – cardamom, cinnamon, pepper and turmeric from India, mahogany from Siam (now Thailand), ebony and aloes from Malacca, and from Sumatra resins such as frankincense and camphor, and healing volcanic sulphur.

From Bengal (now largely Bangladesh) the treasure fleet brought back to China a creature with a long neck that the Chinese believed met the description of

172

a *qilin*, one of the four divine creatures of Chinese legend that was supposed to appear only at times of great fortune and prosperity. It was, in fact, a giraffe. When the heavenly creature was presented to the court in Nanjing in 1414, the officials were enraptured. The giraffe was soon joined by 'celestial horses' (zebras) and 'celestial stags' (presumed to be oryx), elephants, tigers, leopards, parrots and peacocks, who took up residence in Zhu Di's imperial zoo.

The sailors also brought back to China incredible tales of other cultures. In India, they saw Hindu women burn themselves on their husbands' funeral pyres. In Siam, Zheng's men noted with some astonishment, the women ran the show. As for the upper-class men, they had peculiar tastes in personal adornment: when they walked, an unusual tinkling noise emanated from their genital regions. It transpired that this was because they considered it fashionable to insert a collection of tiny metal balls into their scrotums, which jingled like bells as they moved.

As well as fabulous riches and wondrous tales, the ships brought back with them foreign dignitaries who journeyed to Nanjing to pay homage to the Dragon Throne. The foreigners were housed in a special compound where four hundred servants prepared their food and answered to their needs, and from where they were allowed to trade, within strict limits, with the public.

Zheng He departed from Nanjing on his final, seventh voyage in 1431, now under the patronage of Zhu Di's grandson, Zhu Zhanji (Zhu Di had died seven years earlier). The fleet sailed round south-east Asia to Calicut and then to Africa but during the voyage home Zheng He died aged sixty-two. As it turned out, this was also the last voyage of the fabled treasure fleet. In 1435, Zhu Zhanji himself died and his successor concluded that the enormous resources required by these expeditions placed too great a burden on the people.

Attitudes towards boats didn't seem to have improved much in the intervening years if my next administrative conundrum was anything to judge by. I wanted to travel along the Yangtze River from Nanjing to Shanghai. I was learning by now that it was wise to make my arrangements for leaving a town almost as soon as I arrived, as there was frequently a delay of days before I could buy the correct train ticket or, indeed, unearth the boat.

No sooner had I arrived, then, than I asked the concierge at my hotel how I could book a boat ticket to Shanghai. She tittered and giggled and suggested I took the train. I then walked to the spot where my guidebook told me the ferry's booking office was located. Where the office ought to have stood there was a vacant lot. The office appeared to have been pulled down. I asked in the hotel business centre, where the woman snorted derisively and told me the boat no longer existed.

The thing was, I had now been in China for long enough to realize that '*Mei you*', there isn't one, doesn't necessarily mean there isn't one. Chinese face-saving etiquette – or simply a desire for an easy life – frequently dictates that their answers to questions are not what we in the West would always term strictly truthful. And while, when foreigners first arrive in China, we find this intensely aggravating, the Chinese for their part find us outrageously rude when we are blunt and tactlessly to the point.

In this instance, there was something about the way

they were telling me there was no boat that made me suspicious. There was too much giggling and foot-shuffling. Nobody had said in an authoritative tone, 'Ah no, that service was stopped in 2002 when the last ferry finally broke into tiny pieces and sank.'

I had therefore not given up even when I found the booking office razed to the ground, but had instead phoned two different travel agencies. I had received from them much the same response: why would you want to float slowly down a stinking, sewage-filled river in a crumbling bit of old tin when you can take a nice new train and arrive in a quarter of the time?

The answer was a simple one: a boat journey on the Yangtze evoked history. The longest river in China, and the third longest in the world after the Amazon and the Nile, it slices through the middle of the country from Tibet in the west to just above Shanghai on the east coast. Despite its sometimes tortuous navigation, the Yangtze has always been China's vital, pulsating main artery, one of its major transport links that has allowed food to be carried to and from the inland regions. The Yangtze has always held powerful political symbolism, too. In 1956, Mao took a swim in the river that was to reach mythological status. He wasn't just going for a dip. He was using the surging, swelling, untamed river to proclaim his own infallibility as the Great Helmsman, his Party's conquering of China – and at the same time, he tacitly threw down the gauntlet to his bickering cadres. (Despite the danger, his aides emerged more happily from this swim than from Mao's spin down the Pearl River at Guangzhou earlier that year. Then, the Chairman had decided to bathe without warning, and the guards and Party leaders were forced to strip off and join him in the water wearing only their underwear.)

175

In recent years, the Yangtze has garnered not just column inches but feet, yards, perhaps even miles thanks to the controversial Three Gorges Dam project that will create a reservoir four hundred miles long.

Enthusiasts point out that the dam will allow the Chinese to harvest enormous hydroelectric energy, which in this country choked with coal smog has to be a cause for celebration. It will dramatically improve the opportunities for navigation along the river: supporters say that ten-thousand-tonne freighters will be able to sail straight from the ocean and into the middle of China for six months of the year. And it will prevent flooding, which has killed more than a million people in the last hundred years.

Others are considerably less excited. Environmental organizations say that the ecological and social damage will be catastrophic: the dam will lead to an accumulation of toxins as the flow of the river will no longer wash away untreated waste from the communities and industries around it. One and a half million people have had to be relocated; more than a thousand historical sites will be submerged. If the dam breaks, the loss of life will be cataclysmic. In his book *The River at the Centre of the World* Simon Winchester even suggests that the stories of flooding have been exaggerated by the Chinese authorities simply to justify the dam. The year he travelled along the river he listened to reports of devastation on the radio while observing no such thing with his own eyes.

In any case, I wasn't proposing to take a boat all the way to the Three Gorges. I just wanted to travel down the very last section of the river. It would be neatly symbolic, I thought, to arrive in Shanghai by boat as did the notorious import-export merchants of yore, and then to leave on the Maglev, the high-speed magnetic levitation train that is the gem in China's technological crown.

I took a taxi to the port. If the boat existed, I thought, I would surely find some sign of it there. The driver dropped me off in a deserted street on the outskirts of town. It looked dank and disused. There were a couple of fruit vendors, and a handful of bored old men who called out, 'Hello.'

I walked up and down for some time trying to locate dock number six, from where my guidebook claimed the passenger ferries left. Numbers one to five were clearly marked. The road turned a bend, there was nothing for while, and then I came upon a huge concrete car park with a large building at the far end. Perhaps this was the passenger dock.

I started across the car park. A group of five labourers heckled: 'Hell-oo-oo!'

I stopped and turned round.

'*You mei you duchuan qu Shanghai?*' Are there any ferries that go to Shanghai? I asked.

Their astonishment that the odd creature had spoken was matched only by my great surprise that they had understood what I had said, for these labourers were surely less experienced at interpreting the grating tones of foreigners than the concierges on hotel desks with whom I usually communicated.

There was a brief, shocked silence while we stared at each other. Then four of the workmen quickly dropped their heads like puppets whose strings have run slack and stared, startled, at the flimsy plimsolls on their feet. The most confident of the men broke away from the group and strolled towards me. His face was ruddy, rough and pockmarked, like the skin of a giant lychee.

177

'*Mei you*,' he said in a rasping voice husky with cigarette smoke. He shook his mottled head vigorously and gesticulated forcefully in an upstream direction. 'The only ferries go the other way, to Wuhan.'

To be honest, I was secretly relieved. I still wasn't entirely convinced I was being told the whole truth, but I felt I'd put sufficient effort into taking the boat. I really had tried quite hard. And now, great joy, I could take the nice, fast, clean train to Shanghai, instead of the stinking old ferry. The extra time this would afford me meant I could first spend a couple of days in Huang Shan, the fabled mountain resort. But before that, I had a few days to check out the historical city of Nanjing – for even when it hasn't been China's capital, Nanjing has frequently seen a slice of the action.

The treaty of 1842 was signed here, ceding Hong Kong to Britain and opening up China to the foreigners. It was in Nanjing, too, that the Taiping set up their base just a few years later. The city fell to the Heavenly Kingdom of the Taiping in March 1853 and remained under its control for eleven years. The conquerors were led by a character named Hong Xiuquan who believed that he was the younger brother of Jesus Christ and the son of God: he had had a dream featuring an old man with golden hair and a younger man who addressed him as brother and told him to go and annihilate demons. His mission was to overthrow the corrupt Manchu and to rule a fanatically pure and spartan China in which there would be no opium or alcohol, no foot-binding or prostitution, no idolatry or ancestral offerings. His uprising spread to sixteen provinces and is reckoned to have resulted in the deaths of twenty million people before the Qing regained authority in the mid-1860s.

As if that weren't violence enough, Nanjing was also the site of one of the most appalling atrocities of the Japanese invasion. In the early 1930s, China was still in political turmoil and the Japanese took advantage, occupying increasing swaths of China until they were routed at the end of the Second World War. In Nanjing, they are reckoned to have slaughtered three hundred thousand civilians and soldiers in a matter of weeks. They exercised breathtaking brutality, using live Chinese prisoners for bayonet practice and subjecting women to repeated rape and sexual torture. In the Nanjing Massacre Memorial Hall skeletons lie in piles and photographs depict corpses littering the main roads of Nanjing, where today glittering department stores stand. There is even clothing stained with blood on display. It was almost impossible to marry in my mind the unspeakable violence that the Japanese had meted out on these streets in 1937 with the prosperous city today.

It's in Nanjing, too, that the remains of Sun Yat-sen lie. His mausoleum sits square and stony on a high hill in the city's park.

Sun had been plotting revolution against the Qing dynasty for years, but in the end the event was not quite the heroic execution of a watertight master plan that he and his cohorts had hoped for. In fact, the revolution was started by accident: in October 1911, a group of discontented army officers in the city of Wuhan, who were planning their own uprising, set off a bomb by mistake. They could either face arrest and brutal punishment or attempt to see the insurrection through. They chose the latter option and the next day took control of the city. It was the tenth day of the tenth month, the auspicious 'double tenth' that is still celebrated in Taiwan today. Within days, surrounding provinces joined the rebels and the centuries-old Qing dynasty was toppled.

Sun Yat-sen wasn't even in the country at the time. He was in the United States and is said only to have learned of the uprising from a newspaper report. He also read that he was considered one of the contenders for the role of president of the new regime. He travelled to Washington, London and Paris in an attempt to garner support; he failed in all three. He arrived in Nanjing in December to find the Republicans unable to agree on a president; he was elected as a compromise.

A month later his position became untenable and amid chaotic power-broking he resigned. When, two years later, his successor Yuan Shikai ordered his arrest and execution following an unsuccessful revolt, Sun fled to Japan. He returned to China a few years after that and was elected head of the self-proclaimed national government at Guangzhou in southern China. Realistically, though, China was not governed by any single body at this time, but by competing factions and warlords. After Sun's death in 1925, his followers split into two opposing groups: the Kuomintang Nationalists under Chiang Kai-shek and the Communists. The Kuomintang ruled to begin with but, after they massacred five thousand Shanghai Communists in 1927, the Communists gathered their forces and began to rise. There followed more than two decades of bloodshed in which Communists and Nationalists fought both each other and the occupying Japanese. Following the Japanese departure at the end of the Second World War, the Communists finally secured victory in 1949. The Kuomintang retreated to the island of Taiwan; the Communists have been in power in mainland China ever since.

Still, despite the fact that Sun never ruled a united country, he is considered by both the mainland Chinese and the Taiwanese to be the father of modern China. Both claim his Three Principles of the People have formed the basis of their government though their interpretation of these principles – nationalism (as in freedom from imperialism), democracy and socialism – differ wildly.

A tablet inscribed with the Three Principles hangs over the threshold to Sun's memorial chamber. This inner sanctum is decorated with blue and white tiles that mirror the colours of the Kuomintang who, during their tempestuous reign before the Communist take-over, were determined to claim the recently deceased Sun as their own. This mausoleum, then, was much more than a final resting place for a revolutionary who had never really ruled. It was an attempt by the governing elite of the day to somehow extricate approval for their own policies from Sun despite the – perhaps convenient – fact that the great man himself was dead.

I climbed many, many steps up a vast stone stairway to reach it. It was an imposing but ugly place, eighty thousand square metres of cold, unyielding marble. In the first hall, a statue of Sun sat stonily on a chair surrounded by the complete text of his *Outline of Principles for the Establishment of the Nation*, which were carved into the walls. In the next room lay the tomb itself, a marble coffin featuring another statue of a supine Sun. There was no ghoulish corpse on display, although the cadaver was re-embalmed when it was moved here in 1929. At the same time, the authorities gave Sun a change of outfit, removing his Western-style suit and dressing him instead in a Chinese blue satin gown with a black silk jacket and black satin boots. Still, one can only suppose that the preservation process, which took place half a century before even that of Mao's corpse, must have been insufficiently effective to allow visitors to gaze upon the body today. Sun's remains instead lie sealed in the marble box to which, each day, thousands of Chinese troop in pilgrimage.

My favourite discovery of Nanjing, though, was neither a mausoleum nor a museum, but the little green men at the pedestrian crossings. In most cities, these illuminated characters stand in an upright, controlled walking pose. Sometimes they flash to tell you to get a move on. In New York, there's no little green man but a command to 'Walk'. Not in Nanjing. In Nanjing, the tiny light bulbs flash furiously to create not a walking movement but an all-out sprint. The little green men hunker their heads down in a hurried, harried posture; their arms pump frantically. This is no indication to walk. This is a Chinese road, and the implication is that you should run for your life.

I spent the whole of the following morning sending my teapots home in two boxes. I had very proudly succeeded in acquiring boxes from the post office in Suzhou. I'd even managed to enact sign language for 'little polystyrene bobbly bits' and enjoyed a positive outcome. I'd packed the boxes and brought them with me to Nanjing. All that remained was to despatch them.

The hotel concierge sent me off down the road with directions to the post office. I soon took a wrong turning and, during the course of my very indirect route, I asked 'Where is the post office?' so many times that, by the time I actually found it, I had more or less perfected the phrase.

I joined a queue and battled my way to the front. In China, this is not simply a matter of waiting your turn. It involves judicious jabs of the elbow, shifty use of the shoulders, and above all a very loud voice so that you can shout your request to the cashier even if you're somewhere beneath the crowd and not physically visible to her.

Finally, I struggled to the top of the scrum in front of the first counter. The woman sitting behind it in a neat uniform gabbled something I didn't understand, then waved her arms over to a second counter. I had been in the wrong queue. I was to go to the back of another line over to the left.

On arrival at the correct counter – again having lost my place several times to zealous Chinese not disposed to wait for hours for a foreigner to muddle through in front of them – I was given a form to fill in. Then I was told to join queue number one once more and was pushed, shoved and barged for a while longer until finally the first uniformed woman took pity and relieved me of my boxes.

I ate that evening in a pizza restaurant that seemed to survive on the patronage of the foreign exchange students at the university. They played that seventies CD again. At the next table a German man with a straggly blond goatee tackled a great plate of spaghetti that was strangely similar in appearance to his beard. We started talking: he was a teacher at the Technical University, where he tried to instil the German language into engineering students. The students learnt engineering for the first two years of their course; in the third year they studied exclusively German. They took German classes all morning, six days a week, and then had three full afternoons of German conversation. After that, they went to Germany on an exchange programme. It seemed a very Chinese approach – hard, intensive and guaranteed to bear results. I asked if the students were easy to teach.

'Yes, as long as I set an exact task,' said the teacher. 'If I give them any choice at all in what to do, they get very upset and worried.'

The following morning I visited one final historical site before I boarded the night train to Huang Shan. I had decided to pay homage to the Yangtze River Bridge. This stop isn't on most tourists' agenda, but it was an engineering feat of which the Communists were proud. It's a double-decker bridge – cars on top, trains below – and was constructed entirely by the Chinese after their relationship with the Russians soured in the 1960s and the Russians hot-footed it out of China, taking the original designs for the bridge with them.

The taxi driver seemed very unsure of where to take me – or, perhaps, he was just at a loss to understand why I might want to go there. According to my guidebook, the easiest way to get up onto the bridge was to go through Daqiao Gongyuan, Big Bridge Park. We drove and drove, out of the city centre, into the suburbs and along backstreets. In the end, the driver pulled up doubtfully in front of a kiosk at a grubby gateway. Across the road, monumental concrete pillars supported an elevated expressway. It looked like a gargantuan, monolithic grey dinosaur with lumbering great columns for legs and a voracious, capacious body through which tiny specks of cars and lorries ran like multicoloured blood cells up its veins. It seemed to be the right place.

I paid my entrance fee and walked through the scrubby, deserted park towards a towering building.

There was a solitary tourist coach parked outside. I wandered around for a while, trying to work out how to get up onto the bridge. There was nobody to direct me. In the end I found my way through the shop and into a lift with about four Chinese tourists. Up we went and finally we found ourselves on the viewing platform.

Nanjing being a Chinese city, of course, the smog was so thick that I couldn't actually see to the other side of the river. The bridge stretched out wide and long and vanished into the haze. But somehow, on this occasion, the pollution enhanced the scene of chaotic industry. The four traffic lanes were choked with cars, vans, trucks and buses, all clattering slowly across the great river that divides the south of China from the north.

Looking in the opposite direction, tremendous socialist realist sculptures dominated the approach to the bridge. Gigantic statues of men and women stood glorious and revolutionary, back to back, on a giant plinth. Some raised their hands in triumphant, air-punching salutes like goal-scoring footballers; others held rifles ready to gun down insurgents. Their chests were puffed out, their shoulders thrown back, their postures tall, patriotic and proud. They each stood with one foot slightly in front of the other, perpetually prepared for action, ever ready to lead China forward into a great Communist Utopia.

There was something uplifting about these statues standing firm in the smog, never wavering from their decades-old optimism. Somehow it seemed to me as I studied the scene that this was contemporary China – a chaotic blend of the wonderful idealism of the Communist past with the lung-choking problems of the present; the terrific determination and self-esteem that fuelled such great construction projects standing shoulder to shoulder with practical limitations; the unity of China both north and south – and that ubiquitous smoggy, concrete, overwhelming sense of grey.

And then I took the lift back down to earth.

13

The Sun Doesn't Rise

It was a week since I'd taken an overnight train and, arriving at the station that evening, I felt little joy at the prospect of the night ahead. I sat on my blue plastic seat in the waiting hall under a dull, dingy fluorescent light. The people looked squalid. I was hardly a vision of high-class refinement myself, but still, I didn't want to be among them.

When the boarding gate opened, I fought my way through the surging, shoving ruckus. I found my carriage and my berth. A woman sitting by the window stared up at me and then started tapping frenziedly at the window and mouthing eagerly to her friends on the platform.

'Look, look!' she seemed to be saying as she pointed in my direction, her face lit up and beaming with excitement. 'Look what's in my carriage! A foreigner!'

I scowled at her. She blushed and looked down.

I climbed into my upper bunk and lay down. Really, I reflected, I shouldn't have shot that poor woman such a homicidal glare. She was just pleased to see me. I ought to have had sufficient self-control to keep my bad mood to myself. This trip round China didn't seem to be doing much for my tolerance. It was as though the constant battle for survival – the fact that *everything*, from eating to sleeping to sending a parcel, was difficult for me here – had propelled me into a defensive mood of almost perpetual irritation. I worried how far this descent into grumpiness would take me. After a few weeks of snarls and hissing, to what levels might I then sink? Ineptly executed kung-fu kicks? Samurai swords? Kitchen cleavers?

As if an hour or so of self-reflection weren't punishment enough, I then couldn't sleep. Usually on these journeys the combination of the train's movement with my aeroplane sleeping mask and ear plugs lulled me off almost immediately – but not tonight. The train stopped and started, juddering violently at every station. My fellow passengers snored and snorted creating an extraordinary symphony of rattling, roaring, moaning and groaning. The man in the bunk opposite was doing a good imitation of a slowly expiring farmyard animal.

I lay in the darkness plagued by the disconcerting, unfamiliar chorus that sang out around me. My body began to ache with a desperate weariness but my eyes stayed wide awake. I turned again and again on the hard, narrow pallet, but no position was comfortable. I finally dropped off for an hour or two but had little real rest. Then – *boom!* – the lights glared, the tannoy blared, and at six-twenty we arrived in Tunxi, the nearest town to the Huang Shan mountains.

I was hustled immediately by a tout into an almost full minibus which left a few minutes later for the mountains. We drove up, up into the hills – and into the clouds that engulfed them. As we rose through the winding bends of this legendary beauty spot, one of the most talked-of scenic landscapes in China, we could suddenly see nothing at all. All that surrounded us was frothy whiteness. It was as if the world had been suddenly and unexpectedly submerged in steamed milk.

I had booked a room on the summit of the mountain. From here, it was just a short walk to the best point for viewing the sunrise. The sight of the dawn breaking over the misted peaks and wooded valleys of Huang Shan was supposed to be truly spectacular.

Another time, I'll leave my luggage in some sensible spot – the train station left-luggage room, for example – and walk to the top carrying little more than my toothbrush. Lacking hindsight, sadly, I had decided to keep all twenty kilos or so of my luggage with me, take the cable car to the top, check into my hotel, and walk from there.

The cable car queue didn't look too bad. Little did I know, however, that a car arrived only once every five or ten minutes and few people could fit inside. The queue was not orderly. The people shoved, shouted and pushed. They jostled and jabbed their elbows. Every time a slight movement could be seen at the front of the crowd, they pressed forward, bruising and bludgeoning all those around them, as though they were fighting over the last sunrise photo in the world. My lungs felt horribly constricted as the swarm crushed in hard, tight and choking. The feeling was similar, I should imagine, to that of being constricted and swallowed whole by an anaconda. This went on for two interminable hours.

For some strange reason, however, the Chinese found the queue funny. Senses of humour differ from culture to culture, to be sure, but the American failure to understand irony is nothing compared to the hilarity the Chinese apparently find in being crushed alive. As the herd surged forward and the air was pressed from their bodies, they screeched and screamed with breathless rapture and then, when the pressure eased slightly, shrieked with exuberant laughter.

At last, with all the joy and humour I might eke from the funeral of a close family member, I reached the front of the queue. Finally, the cable car ascended into the clouds. All around there was nothing but white. I couldn't see so much as a couple of metres. For a second or two, through a chink in the cloud, a couple of trees appeared on the mountainside below us.

'*Waaaaaaah!* Look! How pretty!' my fellow passengers squealed. They were still high on the delights of the very exciting queue. Then the clouds closed in once more and even they were silent.

On the summit it was raining. I checked into my hotel. My room was freezing cold. There was no heating. I put on my walking boots and waterproofs. On my way out, I stopped at reception.

'Excuse me, could you tell me what time the sunrise is in the morning?' I asked.

'Tomorrow no sunrise,' the manager replied in a matter-of-fact tone.

'No sunrise?' I was mildly incredulous. I had known that my foray into China was going to be full of surprises but I had fully expected that the sun would rise each morning, at least.

'Tomorrow no sunrise,' he repeated. 'Tomorrow raining.'

So low were my spirits that I briefly toyed with the idea of leaving there and then, of loading my luggage onto my back and stomping back down the mountain in a temper. Fortunately, the small dram of sanity that was left to me prevailed and I set out instead to see what little I could of Huang Shan in the rain.

The drizzle was soothingly cool. It was pleasant, at last, to be in open, unpolluted air high up in the mountains even if the craggy peaks and soaring rock columns were rendered invisible by a thick curtain of white.

Every now and then, I passed a porter carrying goods in baskets that hung from either end of a long bamboo pole balanced on his shoulder. Each of these men was dressed almost identically in a thin yellow cotton singlet, electric-blue tracksuit bottoms, and those olive-green army-issue plimsolls that were popular among the poorer Chinese as they were both durable and very, very cheap. The loads they carried up the steep steps that lined the mountain were staggering: whole crates of Coca-Cola and beer, prodigious sacks of potatoes, baskets bursting with fruit, massive vats of bottled gas. They were tiny, wiry men who sweated profusely as they climbed. They looked exhausted.

As I climbed lower the pathways became crammed with increasingly dense crowds. Mostly the people swarmed in organized groups, distinguishable from one another by their matching baseball caps in different shades. One tribe sported red headwear, another yellow, a third white, and then there was a gaggle of navy. Beneath their caps they were smartly dressed, the men in suits with a shirt and tie and, as a nod to their hiking expedition, trainers on their feet. Most were carrying identical, brand-new walking sticks which they had bought from the souvenir stall at the bottom of the mountain. Each babbling little party was headed by a woman bearing a flag and a megaphone. Every now and then, she would stop and the troop would huddle round.

'Over there,' she would point with great conviction into the milky abyss, 'you can see the magnificent leaping dragon rock.' Or laying chicken. Or lounging lion. Or whatever. Except of course, they couldn't see it at all. Her charges dutifully stared into the whiteness and took photographs of each other standing grinning in front of the wall of fog. What would they tell their friends and family when they showed them the photographs later, I wondered. Would they square their scrawny shoulders and with confidence proclaim, 'And this is Young Feng, standing in front of the magnificent Swan Hatching Eggs rock'? Or would they giggle good-humouredly at the realization that they had spent an entire film taking photographs of each other in the mist?

I climbed back up towards the summit. Disembodied megaphone voices emanated upwards from the cloud below. I was still strangely cross. I felt pretty sure that when Marco Polo made his fabled expedition, he wasn't almost crushed to death in a Chinese cable car queue, nor trampled underfoot by hordes of pilgrims in matching baseball caps. The eunuch commander Zheng He didn't have his reveries interrupted by amplified explanations of rock formations. So why, then, were all these people in *my* way? Oh yes, and what was up with the weather? I was in one of the most famous scenic spots in China, and I couldn't see beyond the end of my nose. Really, I was feeling very grumpy. Indeed, with the blissful calm of hindsight, one might even say I was being unreasonable.

As I strode peevishly along, I was stopped by a group of four French hikers who asked me for directions. We talked for a minute or two – there had been clear blue skies yesterday but never mind, they laughed, I could always look at the postcards – and went on our separate ways.

Suddenly, I felt better. Just a few minutes of conversation, and I no longer felt the desire to hurl innocent tourists from rocky precipices into the cotton-wool clouds below. I cast my mind back to the last time I had had a normal, social conversation. There had been the German man in the pizza restaurant in Nanjing, but that had been cursory and fleeting. Really, the last proper face to face chat I'd had with anyone had been with Clive in Hangzhou ten days ago. Perhaps the solitude was getting to me.

That evening, I made two new friends in the hotel dining room. Newly aware of my self-destructive loneliness, I had decided I needed to become more sociable. If necessary, I would just accost total strangers and attempt to become their friend – for the hour or so that our paths collided, at least. It was unfortunate for them, I accepted, but they would get over it in time.

I walked into the restaurant where a revolting buffet of cold, congealed noodles and greasy vegetables was laid out. There, sitting at one of the big round tables, was a Western couple. They looked about my age. They would do nicely as my first victims, I thought.

'Do you mind if I join you?' I asked as I approached their table wielding a small pile of limp stir-fried lettuce and a couple of undernourished prawns.

My new friends were French. They lived in Shanghai and had been there for the last six months. They'd flown to Tunxi; the airport there was apparently so tiny that they'd never even stepped inside. Their luggage had been dumped straight from the plane onto the tarmac.

The buffet food was execrable but the beer was free

so we drank plenty and discussed the troublesome issue of how to build a large hotel on the top of a mountain. There were no roads leading up here, just the cable car and the pathways. The hotel, though, laid on not only food and drink, but kitchens, beds, and television sets. Then there was the building itself: the bricks, the paint and the roof tiles. Were all these things brought up by cable car, or by porter?

I was firmly of the opinion that the hotel must have come to some arrangement with the cable car company which, for a price, laid on extra runs early in the morning before the tourists arrived. Bernard and his wife, who knew China better, looked doubtful.

'No,' said Bernard. 'The cable car would be too expensive. The porters would be cheaper. I wouldn't be surprised . . .'

I cleared the matter up by asking the manager later that evening.

'Everything comes up with the porters,' he said. 'All the fruit, vegetables, meat, everything.'

'And what about the furniture?'

He gave me a blank look. He hadn't understood.

'The beds, the televisions, the chairs, the tables.'

'Yes, yes, the porters bring them.' The manager was starting to smile now. He was amused by my astonishment. The reception girls had started to gather round to join in the fun.

'So how many rooms does this hotel have?'

'Two hundred.' Each room was a twin; that meant the porters had carried four hundred beds up the mountain – plus, presumably, extras for the staff to sleep on and a couple to hold in reserve.

'What about the doors?' I pointed to the huge, plate-glass double doors at the reception's entrance. 'And the floor?' I nodded towards the weighty slabs of marble that we stood upon. 'And this enormous granite reception counter?'

'Yes, yes! The porters!'

The porters were paid forty yuan per load, and each man made one trip up the mountain per day, then ran back down again carrying the rubbish that the hotel and its tourists had generated. And I had been feeling sorry for myself.

I set my alarm for six the following morning just to be absolutely sure that the manager was right and there was to be no sunrise. The clock bleeped; I rolled out of bed, shuffled to the window and pulled back the curtain. Outside there lay a thick white wall of fog. I went back to bed.

A couple of hours later I resurfaced and went for another walk. I meant to head down the west steps as the mist seemed to be lifting slightly and that route was supposed to have the best views. But somehow I took the wrong turning and went somewhere else altogether.

My new, unintended route was wonderfully free from fellow tourists. As I walked along the deserted track, the cloud started to thin and then to swirl up and around. I stopped and gazed over a precipice as dark shapes began to take form amid the billowing mists. A peak of rough-hewn rock rose up in the foreground with pine trees protruding at improbable angles from its sides. Then, suddenly, the brume beyond lifted and revealed in the abyss a far-flung range of crags and peaks that stood immutable above a sea of eddying, undulating white. Sky and land were indeterminate. Both the bed below and the canopy above blended in flurrying alabaster; but between them, as paradisiacal islands rising from a heavenly sea, the mountains magically materialized. And then, a minute later, they were gone.

I walked back down the mountain. That one minute of incredible, otherworldly beauty had instilled in me a sense of wonder and calm. It had been fleeting, but just for a moment I had witnessed the very spectacle that has brought hopeful crowds to Huang Shan over all these years – for although the mountains are reputedly pretty on a clear day, it is the vision of the peaks rising out of the clouds that has really inspired the aesthetes. I didn't want my spirits crushed once more in the cable car. It was only a couple of hours' walk to the bottom of the mountain. It was all down-hill. And twenty-odd kilos wasn't so very much to carry – was it?

The walk was hard work. The going was steep and I hadn't really packed all those books and toiletries with a view to taking them hiking, but that day I enjoyed the exercise. The path led through a wooded valley. The damp mist that had upset me yesterday now seemed soothing. The woods took on that nostalgic smell of wet foliage and bark. Autumn was approach-ing and the trees' leaves were dandelion-yellow and rusty red. Every now and then a bird would flit and dive between the branches, or a squirrel would dart across the path. The squirrels here, I noticed, moved with remarkable pace. They were much nimbler on their paws than their cousins back west.

As I descended I passed perhaps thirty or forty porters on their trek up the mountain with their in-credible loads: watermelons and pomelos, tomatoes and carrots, and litre upon litre of wine. They stopped frequently to rest, their faces haggard with exertion. This was the shorter, steeper route up the eastern steps, but even this ascent must take them three or four hours, I calculated, for I was walking for two with almost no breaks, and I was going downhill.

From the foot of the mountain, I took a taxi to Tangkou, the tiny amalgamation of buildings that serves the mountain's tourist trade, then a bus back to Tunxi where I was to spend the night.

Tunxi is not a spectacular town, but it has one fabulous street. Old Street, as its name implies, is old. In fact, it is ancient – its buildings date back to the Song dynasty, which ruled China from the turn of the first millennium until the thirteenth century. That means that even the youngest Song buildings are three or four hundred years older than most of the historic houses in Stratford. Other buildings here are newer Ming and Qing dynasty constructions but even these have known several hundred years of activity. The upper storeys of the rickety wooden buildings jut out, overhanging the worn flagstone street. Ornate lattice-work adorns the carved windows and balconies of these living quarters; below, heavy calligraphy sign-boards swing over shop fronts. These premises are now, needless to say, dedicated entirely to the tourist trade, but here the transformation has been made in a tasteful way with an emphasis on history.

The pharmacist stood in her white coat behind a heavy, dark-wood counter that stretched the length of her shop. The entire back wall was occupied by a colossal wooden medicine chest. Its hundreds of tiny drawers, each with a neat, white label affixed, glimmered with the patina of decades, perhaps even centuries, of attentive polishing. Above the drawers stretched a single, tall shelf. Within its delicate latticed compartments stood a row of shapely grey urns.

Next door was a shop dedicated to calligraphy

brushes. By the sign that hung above the doorway a single, enormous brush, the height of a grown man, was suspended like a bushy, upside-down tree. Inside, row upon row of brushes of every size and breadth hung in haphazard lines along the mirrored walls. On the counters smaller brushes were displayed in porcelain pots. Still others dangled from carved wooden stands. There were thin brushes and thick, brushes with soft, plump, white bristles, and others with firmer, tapered, brown tips. Some had black lacquer handles, some pale bamboo.

Along the street, other shopkeepers sold teapots, furniture, porcelain, paintings and souvenirs. I browsed happily for an hour or so, and then went into a large, lively restaurant at the end of the street. I was told I'd have to wait twenty minutes for a table and was given a number. It was the first time this had happened to me in China; if there was a queue, I decided, the place had to be good. If I actually had to wait for a table, I was definitely staying here.

A short while later, I was led by a man in a full-length purple silk robe and matching skullcap up a flight of stone steps guarded by carved lions. He took me to my table in a private alcove decorated with red lanterns; the furniture was polished black wood.

Down on the lower ground floor, the food was displayed on a long counter in front of the open kitchen. A woman with an electronic handheld gadget appeared at my side, I pointed at a greater number of tasty-looking dishes than I would ever be able to eat, then returned to my table to sip my chrysanthemum tea and await the onslaught on my stomach. I had just started on the fabulously difficult task of consuming a large urn of delicious noodle soup, a platter of succulent fried dumplings packed with pork and vegetables, and a bowl of crispy spring rolls when two familiar faces popped around the latticework. It was the French couple from last night, armed now with packages wrapped in newspaper. I had friends in the place!

They joined me at my table and ordered their own insurmountable feast – half a chicken in soup, a dish of stewed, spicy fish, yet more dumplings and a couple of plates of vegetables. They were catching a late flight back to Shanghai and had time to kill. We ordered a couple of beers and idled the hours away.

The next morning, I asked the woman at my hotel's tourism desk to organize a car to take me to the nearby Ming-dynasty villages of Xidi and Hongcun, where *Crouching Tiger, Hidden Dragon* was filmed. Before I could go, however, I needed a special permit from the Public Security Bureau, China's police force, as entry is restricted to foreigners.

The woman from the hotel instructed the driver to take me to the PSB and to obtain the necessary papers. It seemed really to be a simple ruse to extract a little extra cash from foreigners rather than a genuine attempt to monitor one's movements or control access. The taxi driver pulled up on the pavement outside the police station and we went in. I filled out the necessary forms, allowed the policeman on duty to photocopy various parts of my passport, paid some money and we were on our way.

The villages were well worth this half hour of bureaucracy. They're unusual because their architecture and layout have remained virtually unchanged for hundreds of years. And, whereas most towns with ancient architecture have turned to tourism, these villages seemed to continue very much as before. Yes, the families were selling trinkets from their front rooms, in Hongcun there was a market that was definitely geared to the tourist trade, and there were plenty of coaches parked outside the imposing stone gates. But somehow this had little impact on the villages' character.

My first stop was Hongcun. It was a cold day and the village was enshrouded in mist. Most of the houses had two storeys, and their flat whitewashed fronts were stained with the blotchy grey mildew of time. Over the rigidly rectangular windows and doorways jutted sloping, grey-tiled awnings that curled up at the corners while domed archways led within. Down the side of each thin street ran a babbling stream of water. Women crouched by these rippling canals and washed dishes, scrubbed clothes and cleaned vegetables. One was gutting a chicken whose spiky feet poked up from her pot towards the sky. No refuse littered these waterways, though. There was no stagnant smell of rotting giblets, no decomposing cabbage leaves or scum from the laundry suds. This water was clear, clean and fast-flowing.

The streets were cobbled with small, round stones. They created a path too bumpy for a bicycle or a moped and too narrow for a car. As a result, the village streets were idyllically tranquil. In the middle of the settlement lay the very pond across which Michelle Yeoh leapt so gracefully in *Crouching Tiger, Hidden Dragon*. That day, though, it was perfectly still except for the circular ripples that eddied outwards from one point on the edge where a woman squatted as she scrubbed carrots. The houses that encircled the water were mirrored on its surface with a rhythmically undulating symmetry. That tiny spot of China was perfectly silent. There was scarcely a sign of the modern world.

Given that my own kung fu wasn't quite up to the standards of Michelle Yeoh's (and I didn't have an invisible bungee cord to help me bound with such fluid elegance) I chose to walk round the pond rather than glide across its surface, then spent an hour or so exploring the rest of the village. I bought some pretty porcelain bowls from one woman, and an engraved bamboo pot from an elderly man who was carving calligraphy into the wood from his seat on the street side. I was just making my way back out towards the car park when my driver appeared from a doorway.

'*Ni e ma?*' Are you hungry? he asked.

I was. I had just been wondering where I was going to find some lunch; breakfast had consisted of a packet of Oreos gobbled in the back of the car as the hotel buffet had ended by the time I'd finished making my travel arrangements that morning.

The driver beckoned me through the doorway and into a room of four or five small square tables. There were no other customers, just two men and a woman who seemed to be friends of my driver, and who ran this tiny eatery. I couldn't read the menu, so I just asked for some vegetables and rice.

'And tofu?' asked the older of the two men. His body was somewhat bent. From a mole beneath his mouth grew one extraordinarily long, grey hair.

'Yes, good. And some tofu.'

Two large dishes of food arrived, and then a bowl of rice. I had just started to eat when the woman, plump and smiling, brought out a plate of pork and chilli for her family.

'You want some?' she said, nodding at the plate.

'Well, yes, OK, yes please.'

She gave me that plate and brought out another for the men. The bent old man noticed that my teacup was half empty and tottered on his creaking legs to refill it with enthusiastic hospitality.

After all that food, it was all I could do to stay awake in the car to Xidi. Along the road, boys led water buffalo and donkeys. These were the first donkeys I'd seen in weeks. In Datong and Pingyao there had been many, but on the more affluent east coast I had seen none.

Xidi was similar to Hongcun, except that the alleys were paved with slabs of black slate instead of cobbles. They were glistening and slippery in the rain. Art students sat in secluded corners and painted the tranquil old buildings. I peered through one archway onto a cobbled path lined by trees and pink and red flowers. At the end of the path a traditional circular portal gave onto a bridge that crossed a canal, and led into the family's home. The owners were smiling and friendly and beckoned me to come in and take a look.

I went out through the magnificent village gateway and stood for a moment to admire the soaring mountains in whose shadow these people lived their simple lives. To the side of the gateway a river ran cold and clear. This was another world from the clogged towns and cities I'd visited so far. The air out here was fresh, crisp and clean. Somehow, in this tiny corner of China, away from the express trains and the factories, they seemed to have escaped modernity. Indeed it was as if, here, they had stopped the clocks altogether.

14

Gathering Speed

The other passengers waiting to board the Shanghai train that night were not the usual crowd. There were no dark-skinned chain-smokers lugging bundles the size of their grandmother. Nobody hawked or spat. Instead, smart young urbanites stood in an orderly line, each towing a neat wheelie suitcase.

As an additional treat, the train wasn't full. In fact, less than half of my carriage was occupied. In my section, only the two lower bunks were taken, the other by a Korean student; all the upper berths were empty. Announcements were made in both Chinese and English. An official came round serving coffee.

We arrived in Shanghai at seven-fifteen in the morning. I was ridiculously excited. I had been to Shanghai twice before, and loved it both times. Shanghai has energy and atmosphere, imposing colonial architecture along the glorious waterfront Bund and crumbling, shuttered houses in its shadow. There are restaurants and bars, glittering department stores and roughshod street markets. It is almost as if the ghosts of the past, with all their glamour and gall, still haunt the old streets steeped in history. But best of all, I had a list of names and telephone numbers of friends of friends to look up in the city. After weeks of solitude, I had the beginnings of a social life.

It wasn't just Shanghai itself I was looking forward to. It was also the hotel – for thanks to Nancy and Guy's contacts, here I was staying in the Grand Hyatt. This hotel *starts* on the fifty-sixth floor of the tallest building in the city. It's on the Pudong side – the new development across the river from colonial Shanghai – which means that it has sensational views across the water and onto the buildings of the Bund embankment. The rooms are not just decorated, they are furnished with tasteful *objets* – a bronze by the bathtub; an ornamental plate displayed above the television cabinet. After all those nights in characterless Chinese business hotels where the carpet was matted by hair and the drains regurgitated other people's fluids, I was ecstatic. I was spending four days here – four whole days of sleeping in comfort, of being able to eat easily in a range of restaurants. I had four days in a hotel where the hotel staff spoke impeccable English and would help me solve life's little complexities. From Shanghai, I was flying west to the Tibetan border where I was meeting up with Guy for a further four days' trekking in the mountains. So for more than a week, now, I wasn't going to have to battle to solve my journey's challenges with my incompetent Chinese. I felt burden-free, as though I had just broken away from a choking motorway traffic jam and struck out onto empty country lanes surrounded by fields of green.

I checked in, took a shower, and checked out my room. From my window, I could see the slate-grey Whangpoo River which slices through the new city and serves as a constant reminder of the foreign trade that created the Shanghai of old, that creature of stark contrasts with its bejewelled, glittering head and its fetid, feculent tail.

A hundred years ago, Shanghai was the most opulent and bewitching of China's treaty ports – for the well-shod, at least. To those down at the heel, it was merciless and cruel. For a whole century – from 1842 when the Treaty of Nanjing ended the First Opium War and opened Shanghai to international trade, until 1943 when extraterritoriality was formally abolished and foreign concessions were returned to China – Shanghai was home to British and French, Americans and Russians, Japanese and Koreans. Sikh policemen in scarlet turbans patrolled the streets of the International Settlement. The city was a heaven for those wanting to make money through trade – in the 1920s, it was home to half of China's factories and one third of the country's foreign investment – and a sanctuary for the dispossessed, for one needed neither passport nor visa to settle in extraterritorial Shanghai.

'At one point, if you fell ill, you could choose your doctor from twenty-eight nationalities including two Romanians, one Armenian, one Egyptian, one Mexican and ten exceptionally competent Hungarians,' wrote Harriet Sergeant in her book *Shanghai*.

Shanghai, the foreigners fervently believed, was a model of international co-operation which other great cities would follow. No longer must a city belong to one nation alone: in the spirit of trade and profit, each country could build its own 'concession' and from there conduct dealings with the world.

Wily merchants built their godowns by the waterfront and filled them with tea, silk, rubber, opium and silver. The British owned the largest bank and the biggest trading firms. They built the Bund (from the Hindustani word meaning embankment) whose huge, imposing edifices boomed of immutability and power. Pale-faced youths arrived from Britain on P & O liners and crafted themselves into 'old China hands'.

They did everything they could to recreate 'home'. They bought stout, bad-tempered Mongolian ponies that were driven down once a year from the grasslands to be sold at horse fairs. They were wild, shaggy creatures and the first month – the period considered necessary to break them in – was a bruising time. After they had been somewhat tamed, the horses were ridden by their owners on Shanghai's brand-new race-course, or on hunts where a trail of paper stood in for the fox. Those gentlemen deemed sufficiently superior drank at the Long Bar of the Shanghai Club along whose length they took their place according to their rank.

Where they couldn't mimic the lives they had left behind, they attempted to improve on them. They kept servants to whom they spoke in pidgin, that peculiar dialect that had to be learned by both native English speaker and Chinese alike. Harriet Sergeant quotes an old Shanghai cartoon, in which a Chinese servant of the Shanghai Club answers the telephone to a woman speaking pidgin:

'That belong Hall Porter? Well, my wantie savvy s'pose my husband have got, no got?' (Is that the Hall Porter, I want to know if my husband is there?)

The Hall Porter replies: 'No missy, husband no got.'

The wife says angrily: 'How fashion you savvy no got, s'pose my no talkee name?' (How do you

206

know he is not there when I haven't told you his name?)

To which the Porter says, 'Maskee name, missy any husband no got this side anytime.' (The name doesn't matter, madam, nobody's husband is ever here, at any time.)

This was the time that world cruises were becoming fashionable. P & O steam liners set sail for Hong Kong from 1845 and were travelling round the world just a few years later. Anyone who was anyone travelled by P & O.

'If you are ever shipwrecked, my dearest Laura – do contrive to get the catastrophe conducted by the Peninsular and Oriental Company,' wrote a Mrs Dulcimer to a friend in 1863. 'I believe other companies drown you sometimes, and drowning is a very prosaic arrangement fit only for seafaring people and second-class passengers. I have just been shipwrecked under the auspices of P & O and I assure you that it is the pleasantest thing imaginable. It has its little hardships to be sure, but so has a picnic, and the wreck was one of the most agreeable picnics you can imagine.'

The great, the good and the not-so-good set out to see the empire, and Shanghai was a compulsory stop on any self-respecting tourist's agenda. Noël Coward came here in the 1920s and caught the flu. From his sickbed in the Cathay Hotel, he wrote *Private Lives* in just four days. Aldous Huxley and Somerset Maugham, Bertrand Russell and George Bernard Shaw all made the trip to China.

Outside the very British auspices of the Shanghai Club and their ilk, the White Russians sprinkled glitz and glamour with their dazzling nightclubs and restaurants, their beauty salons and dress shops. These were upper and middle-class Russians who had been forced to flee from home when their loyalty to the Tsar would have assured their deaths under the Bolsheviks. Those who could escaped to Europe. Those who couldn't undertook extraordinarily arduous journeys through Siberia and into China. Deprived of citizenship in revolutionary Russia, the White Russians belonged to no country. Extraterritorial Shanghai provided refuge – but the White Russians were always slightly despised. They were considered unsuitable for either marriage or business and their livelihood, so superficially flamboyant, was never secure.

There was, of course, a sadder, seedier side. Shanghai seethed with gangsters and warlords, opium dens and brothels. It was estimated that, in the 1920s, nearly one per cent of the female population of Shanghai was involved in prostitution. Twelve-year-old girls entranced their customers with their tiny, bound feet.

The Chinese were binding women's feet as far back as the tenth century. It was apparently the influence of foreign dancers in the Tang dynasty court that inspired the practice. The Tang were said to be impressed by the newcomers' dancing skills and admired the way they could totter about on the tips of their toes. They decided to imitate their moves by binding their feet as these foreigners did. To begin with, only the court dancers indulged, and even they only bound their feet just enough to enable them to stand on their points.

As the centuries passed, however, fully bound feet became the norm. On her tiny, crippled feet a woman couldn't stray too far, which fitted nicely with Confucian values that dictated wives and daughters should be kept in their place. But bound feet were also considered by the Chinese to be fantastically sexually alluring. To walk on her deformed limbs, a woman had to adopt a mincing posture that apparently strengthened her vaginal muscles and buttocks to sensational levels.

The girls' feet were bound from about the age of four or five. With the big toe – the Gold Lotus – protruding, bandages were wrapped tightly around the remaining four toes, forcing them down under the foot, towards the sole. Each day the bandages were tightened to bring the toes as close as possible to the heel so that, when the process was complete, a woman walked on her knuckles and heel. Bones broke, flesh rotted, and pus oozed. Sometimes a couple of toes would drop off. After about two years, the process was complete: the crippled feet were just a few inches long and an object of great lust for a Chinese man.

In Shanghai's brothels, the men would smoke opium and play mahjong, and the girls would preside over drinking games. Placing a wine glass in one of her minute silk shoes, the girl would invite the men to throw almond seeds into it. She would then dish out penalties according to their performance, requiring them to drink from the glass that sat inside the slipper so that they inhaled the deliciously exciting perfume of her crippled foot as they imbibed.

'In a private chamber, it was customary to linger over the girl's feet, stroking, sniffing, and licking them, and even dipping them in tea before drinking it. A favourite indulgence was to eat almonds from between her crushed toes. When mounting passion could be contained no longer, the gasping customer would at last drive his jade spear into her jade gate and, raising her tiny feet to his shoulders, insert her Gold Lotus entirely into his mouth and suck noisily till the moment of "Clouds and Rain",' Sterling Seagrave explains in *The Soong Dynasty*.

Often these girls had been sold to brothel owners by poverty-stricken parents. Their brothers and sisters probably enjoyed no happier fate. In Shanghai's silk factories, small children plunged their hands into boiling water as they soaked the cocoons; babies lay swaddled at their mothers' feet amid the steam.

'In the accumulator factories, half the children have already the blue line in their gums which is a symptom of lead poisoning. Few of them will survive longer than a year or eighteen months,' wrote Isherwood and Auden in *Journey to a War*.

Out on the street, rickshaw men tried to scrape a living in equally uncertain circumstances. They were mostly farmers who had been driven from their land: in the early twentieth century, between seventy and eighty thousand of them lived and worked in Shanghai. They didn't own their rickshaws – they had to hire them at a cost of one Shanghai dollar for twenty-four hours. Two men usually shared this in two twelve-hour shifts during which they could expect to make sixty or seventy cents each. That left almost nothing for food and rent. If they were forced to borrow, the usual annual rate of interest was 120 per cent. One rich Chinese woman summed up the attitude with the comment, 'Our rickshaw men are so strong, we treat them like machines.' Most of these machines had expired by the age of forty.

Dead bodies of the destitute and the tiny corpses of abandoned girl babies littered the streets. In the final decades before the Communist takeover, it was reckoned that up to thirty thousand cadavers a year were cleaned up from Shanghai's streets and water-ways. The rivers and canals were filled with rubbish and excrement. They were so filthy that Shanghai-landers, as the expatriate population called themselves, found their laundry stank. Their 'clean' clothes gave them eczema or even made them ill. The problem was so bad that some people used to send their laundry on a two-week round trip to Japan for washing.

I walked to the Metro and took a train to the former French concession. The old three-storey houses with their dormer windows and shutters still stood, though their magnolia walls were now stained and the rust-coloured paint on the window frames was peeling.

In bygone times, it wasn't just the French who lived in the French Concession (nor just British and Americans who had homes in their International Settlement). In the 1920s, half a million people resided in this part of town and only 1,400 of them were French. The majority were rich Chinese, the wealthiest of whom bought large mansions with leafy gardens. Sun Yat-sen lived in this area with his wife Soong Ching-ling. A few streets away was the house of Zhou Enlai, who would later become one of Communist China's most influential leaders. Ornate wrought-iron railings separated the pavement from the gardens of the larger buildings that now housed restaurants and pubs with wide-screen TVs instead of the families of rich compradors (the Chinese middlemen who made tremendous profits working for foreign trading houses). Bottle-green lamp posts sprouted five white globes of light; beneath them pink and white busy lizzies tumbled from hanging baskets.

I wandered off the main road and down the back-streets where laundry lines looped between the buildings. Well-worn shirts, trousers and children's split-bottom pants dangled overhead. Below, at street level, fruit shops dotted the pavements. In a wet market, a tangle of eels slithered in the shallow water of a plastic washing-up bowl. A woman sat behind a wooden table chopping up a pig with mighty slices of her cleaver. A pure white cat with piercing blue eyes gazed fixedly at a turtle in a pale green plastic bowl. The cat's nose twitched, its neck craned forward towards the strange-looking, sweet-smelling creature that tried to scramble up the sides of the bowl, slithered backwards, and tried again in vain to find a grip on the unyielding plastic walls that imprisoned it. The cat raised one paw and made tiny swiping movements towards the turtle but was unable quite to work up the courage to pounce. In the end, it sat back on its haunches at a safe distance and chose just to sit and stare.

I walked for an hour or so, then ate some lunch. And then I made my way down Hengshan Road where I had a most important appointment to keep. I was going to have my hair cut.

One evening, all those weeks ago in Beijing, I'd sat round a table eating sushi with a group of Guy and Nancy's friends and asked if anyone knew of a good hairdresser in Shanghai. I'd calculated that by the time I arrived here my mane would be in need of a trim. When I asked my question, the men around the table had stared at me in total astonishment. An American woman sitting opposite me, Paige, had looked back at them, raised her eyebrows to the heavens with an expression that said, 'Men!' and replied straight away and with no nonsense whatsoever, 'In Shanghai, you go to Laurent at Eric's. I'll email you the details.'

And so, on my first afternoon in Shanghai, I presented myself at Laurent's swivel chair. Laurent was a lean, olive-skinned Frenchman dressed in a tight black shirt and trousers; his lustrous, long black hair was swept back under sunglasses. He was from Marseilles and had been working in China for six years.

I told him about my trip and how happy I was to have arrived in Shanghai. The last few weeks, I told him, had sometimes been arduous. It wasn't just the endless train journeys and the clattering, smoky buses. It was that everything was complicated for me. It had taken me half a day to post a parcel.

'It's incredible how quickly mealtimes come round when ordering food is so tricky. I look at my watch and see it's lunchtime, and I think, "Oh no, not again, I've only just dealt with breakfast,"' I told him.

Laurent seemed to agree. 'Business here is good, but everything is difficult. Even the smallest thing is difficult here,' he said, shaking his head and exhaling in a mighty sigh as he snipped and styled.

And then, taking one small step to make my life easier, he gave me directions to the nearby Xiangyang market.

'It's the fakes market,' he said. 'It's not the best quality in the world, but . . .'

He gave a very Gallic shrug. Newly coiffed I went there and spent a fabulous hour fighting off over-zealous hawkers and browsing through bags and shoes, cashmere and clothing, silk tableware and outdoor gear.

I had dinner that night with Luc and Lily who run a literary agency in Shanghai. Lily is Chinese, Luc, her husband, is from Belgium but has lived in China for many years. They put me straight on a number of issues that had been troubling me. For example, the reason Hero, the soldier on the Grand Canal ferry, was wearing his uniform while on holiday with his wife was that PLA soldiers enjoy many advantages while travelling round the country. They are allowed to jump queues and they don't have to pay at all for some amenities.

Second, one *can* travel by boat between Nanjing and Shanghai, as I had wanted to, but foreigners are forcefully discouraged from doing so. Lily and Luc had made the journey as they had booked under their Chinese names but – and at this point they started to laugh – it hadn't been a very luxurious trip. The boat, they said, is the way the migrants travel. On the lower level the people are packed in among their chickens and pigs who urinate and defecate and generally create a terrible stench. Lily and Luc had travelled on the upper level which, they said, was little better. Foreigners are actively encouraged to take the air-conditioned bus along the gleaming new expressway instead.

The next morning, I walked through the tangled lanes of the old Chinese quarter. The buildings here were grey brick with the same rust-red woodwork as I had seen in the French Concession yesterday. It was as if the Shanghai authorities had bought a very substantial job lot of that particular shade of emulsion. Overhead, criss-crossing electricity cables vied with laundry lines. Red-painted French windows gave onto balconies where pot plants were scattered haphazardly among up-ended bicycles, buckets, unwanted furniture and yet more laundry.

Among the chaos lay the tiny details of that elegance important to architects of years past. Domed windows with ornamental red-brick arches stood out against the grey walls; decorative cornicing and shapely stone awnings peeped through rows of washing. At street level, bicycles weaved around fruit vendors. Old men sat and smoked in doorways, their songbirds in cages suspended from the guttering above. As the afternoon progressed, a yellow evening light cast a mellowness on the chaotic scene. The red of the shutters and doors grew in richness and depth as the cyclists stopped at a fruit stall for a pomelo or a bag of apples and then pedalled home.

That evening I met up with Pascoe, one of Guy's friends who lives and works in Shanghai. He picked me up in his car and drove me off for a tour of Shanghai at night. We started off in a stylish bar in an old French villa. A pint of beer here cost sixty-six yuan – not far off double the daily wage of those porters at Huang Shan – and the place was so packed that we had to perch at the bar, which just goes to show how Shanghai is booming once more. Then we went to a jazz bar, and then to the 'Buddha Bar', all of which rivalled London or any other city on the hip-ometer.

The next day I visited the Shanghai Museum, where the old pots on display were *seven thousand* years old. That means that these carefully crafted bowls were two thousand years older than Stonehenge. The Chinese were of course ahead of the game as far as ceramics were concerned. It was their porcelain bowls and plates, originally imported to the West only to provide ballast for the tea clippers, that gave rise to the English word 'china'. Until the eighteenth century, the Chinese had the monopoly on this translucent clay ware (as opposed to pottery, which is opaque) as the Europeans hadn't figured out how to make it yet. To confuse the matter, when the English finally worked out the recipe, they started adding animal bone ash to the pot and created 'bone china' which is never from China, but always from England.

I continued over to Dongtai Lu where rather less ancient 'antiques' stalls lined the streets. In reality, there are very few real antiques for sale in China: many were destroyed during the Cultural Revolution, others were smuggled out of the country, and most of those that remain reside either in museums or are still sealed in tombs. There are, however, plenty of fabulous replicas crafted circa 2003 which can be snapped up for the price of a round of drinks.

I bought a large Tibetan painted box – and from that point forward, everything went downhill. There was no way I could carry it round China with me – and why ship home one small carton when I could send two large ones? So then I bought a gilded Buddhist statue with blue hair to keep the box company. And then, I considered, it would be silly to pay for the weight added by wrapping them in newspaper when I could pick a few select pieces of cashmere and silk and pad my purchases with those instead, so I had to visit the Xiangyang market once more. By then, I was so heavily laden that I had to take a taxi back to the hotel.

I took a walk along the Bund that evening. The august, colonial buildings were set back some way from the waterfront: the Chinese had decreed that no foreign building could be constructed within thirty feet of the shoreline as the coolies needed space to track their grain boats along the river. As darkness fell, floodlighting cast an orange luminosity on those towering edifices of Shanghai's gloriously inglorious past. The green pyramid atop the Cathay Hotel glowed emerald bright. The twelve-storey hotel was once the epitome of Shanghai glamour. It was built by Victor Sassoon (cousin of Siegfried, the poet), the founder of Sassoon & Co. through whose auspices he had accumulated considerable wealth from the trading of opium. The hotel was the shiniest gem in his jewel box. Silver taps delivered purified water into its marble bathtubs. Sassoon threw lavish parties in his own penthouse suite.

A little further down, the former Shanghai Customs House rose tall and splendid from its square, colonnaded base into a majestic clock tower. Its chimes were said to mimic Big Ben; Shanghailanders called it Big Ching. Next door the old offices of the Hong Kong and Shanghai Bank stretched wide on either side of its sumptuous portals; 'Spare no expense but dominate the Bund,' the bank's head office had instructed its architects. Above, a great round dome gleamed in the floodlight beams like an outsized golden bauble. From the many flagpoles fluttered the red flag of the People's Republic that had, at last, routed the foreigners.

On the opposite bank of the river, new Shanghai rose phoenix-like from the reclaimed mudflats. The towering high-rises of Pudong, Shanghai's business district, glimmered behind the searing bright lights of the Oriental Pearl Tower that shot like a giant, gaudy, upturned syringe towards the stratosphere. There were no red flags here. This was not a conquered land but the bright face of a brash, rejuvenated China, the glittering showpiece of the economic miracle that the modern-day mandarins were so very determined to realize.

My last morning in the city, I sailed on the flagship of the avant-garde Shanghai. I had failed to arrive by boat down the Yangtze as planned, but I still nurtured high hopes for a classy departure on the high-tech, futuristic magnetic levitation train that connects Pudong with its airport. I was flying out of Shanghai to the Tibetan border; I had thought this means of travelling to the airport should work well. But then I discovered: I was leaving from the domestic airport and the Maglev serves only international flights. And so, on Saturday morning, I got up early, took a round-trip journey on the Maglev to the wrong airport, returned to my hotel where I picked up my luggage, checked out, and then took a taxi to the other airport. It wasn't quite such a sleek operation as I'd had in mind but, none the less, for a whole sixteen minutes I rode on the fastest train in the world.

While we in the West still battle with leaves on the track, in Shanghai they've done away with the track altogether. Propelled and positioned by powerful magnets, the Maglev glides about ten millimetres above a 'guideway'. Because no friction is generated, it can accelerate much more quickly than a conventional train, reaching 430 kilometres an hour in just two minutes.

Shanghai seems to be an auspicious spot for railway innovation: it was here that China's first steam locomotive ran for five kilometres from the city to Woosung at the mouth of the Yangtze river. It was built by the British in the second half of the nineteenth century. The local people were tremendously excited by the 'fire-wheeled carriage' – a name which sticks to this day: the Chinese for train translates as 'fire carriage'. The Manchu were less impressed, however. They feared that the roaring, belching monstrosity would upset the gods and destroy the *qi*, the energy force, of the surrounding landscape and thereby provoke natural disasters. Just a year after the train's maiden journey, the imperial court bought the railway, tore it up and dumped it in Taiwan.

Nearly twenty years passed before the Manchu government approved an official railways policy. Then they held concessions for their construction up for grabs, and the foreigners leapt at the chance to improve transport links to those parts of the country in which they had built trading centres. The French, with their interests in Indo-China, built a line from Kunming to Hanoi; the British built the Beijing–Tianjin line; the Russians constructed tracks in the north, the Germans in Shandong and the Japanese in Manchuria.

Since 1949, of course, the railways have been an all-Chinese affair. When the Communists came to power they standardized the hotchpotch and gradually moved from steam to diesel to electrically powered locomotives. Since the 1990s, the government has entered into railway building with renewed zeal; today, workers are frantically laying down and upgrading tracks in a fervent attempt to meet the transportation demands of an ever more productive China.

Of all the industry's projects, the Maglev is the most ambitious by far. I was looking forward to riding on it. I'd been schlepping round for weeks on those regular trains that stopped and shuddered at every station; I'd endured the cranky local minibuses. Now it was time to experience the other face of Chinese transport.

The Maglev was, at the time of my visit, only running at weekends on 'joy rides' for tourists; its regular, working schedule would not start for a couple of months yet. I went to the station and bought my ticket from the gleaming new booth, then took my place in line with about a hundred very excited camera-wielding Chinese. I examined my ticket. 'Admittance to the station or to the train is declined for those who are unneatly dressed. Drunken. Seriously infected patients or mentally disabled,' it said.

The station was eerily empty; its gleaming white

tiles gave it a ghostly air. The turnstile gates were cordoned off and each was presided over by an officious uniformed woman. I stood in line – for once, all the Chinese were standing in an orderly manner, with none daring even to think about jumping ahead. We waited for some minutes. One of the officious women came up to tell me I was holding my ticket the wrong way round. In keeping with the disciplined spirit of the place, and a little nervous she might deem me mentally disabled, I turned it round.

We waited some more. After ten or fifteen minutes, to our immense relief, we were finally allowed to pass through the turnstiles and to proceed to the platform itself. There, we waited a while longer – this time we were required to stand punctiliously at the correct distance from yellow painted lines on the ground. By now, I was starting to question whether I really wanted to travel on the Maglev after all. Despite my overwhelming desire in past weeks to see the Chinese queue in a less life-threatening way, now that I was required to be obedient too I was finding it rather a chore.

But then, with scarcely a whirr, the wait was over. A collective sigh whispered its way along the platform as, pure, celestial and perfect, the futuristic locomotive glided stealthily into the station like a white-clad rocket from heaven. Being careful to keep our toes in the designated position, we craned our heads to admire its sleek bodywork, its super-fast angular nose, its beatific, hyper-modern beauty. Such was the glory of the moment, one almost expected high-tech angels to emerge from the doors that purred as they slid open. And then, finally, we were allowed on board.

There were no angels. Instead, as the train pulled out of the station, a beaming uniformed woman made a little speech that I didn't understand. She glistened in much the same way as the train. Her cheeks glowed with goodwill, her eyes shone with pleasure, her hair gleamed like a poster girl's. Her blithe smile was painted unswervingly across her face. It could, possibly, have been fastened there by cutting-edge surgery. On the other hand, perhaps she was genuinely entranced to be here, to be the mouthpiece of the showpiece of the brave new China, dressed in her perfectly pressed uniform and making pert little speeches to transfixed passengers.

When she had finished her rapturous little recital, everyone clapped. Then she came over to me and, blushing like a sun-kissed peach, she delivered my own personal rendition in English. 'Good morning passengers,' she started, smiling cheerfully at me alone, 'and welcome to the Maglev.'

At the end of the carriage, above the doorway, a digital display recorded our scorching speed and – yes! – within a couple of minutes we reached 431 kilometres an hour. Really, it was quite exhilarating. But best of all, the train line followed the route of the highway below and it was terrifically empowering, for once, to be flying past those superciliously speedy cars on the tarmac instead of gazing wistfully at their progress from the scratched windows of a dirty old bus. For just a few transitory minutes, I travelled faster than a fleck of flying phlegm – and I liked it a lot.

15

Pilgrims' Progress

The man sitting next to me on the cramped China Eastern Airlines flight hawked into his air sickness bag and farted liberally. I was flying across the breadth of China, from Shanghai on the east coast into the wild recesses of the west. My final destination was Zhongdian in the far north of Yunnan, near the border of the Tibet Autonomous Region. To reach Zhongdian, however, I had to change planes in Kunming – and, as my flight from Shanghai arrived in the evening and the connecting flight didn't depart till the next day, I had to spend the night there.

I checked into the hotel I had pre-booked, went to my room and examined its array of personal hygiene products. The sachets on the bathroom counter were labelled 'Only For Man' and 'Only For Woman'.

'This product is specially designed for washing man's genitals,' explained the Only For Man packet. Again, it was 'uncomplimentary'. I wondered what would happen if a woman inadvertently cleaned herself with the 'Only For Man' lotion, or vice versa. Boils? Unsightly rashes? Peculiar smells?

I decided not to experiment and headed out instead

to find something to eat. It was getting late and I didn't want to wander too far, so I walked into the first place that looked clean and had a good number of customers. I couldn't read the Chinese menu, but by now I was becoming used to this.

'Come with me,' I said to the waitress as I stood up from my chair. She looked momentarily confused as I took off on a tour of the other diners' tables, peering at their provisions as I went. The other customers weren't fazed, though. I was beginning to discover that the Chinese loved this game and tended to join in, shouting out their recommendations like exuberant stallholders flaunting their wares. The problem was, I had no idea what they were saying. For all I knew, as they jabbed their fingers vehemently at certain dishes and hollered, they could have been saying, 'The civet cat is super!' Or, 'Whatever you do, don't have the fish. It's come fresh from the Yangtze and has two heads and three tails!'

I played it safe.

'This,' I said, pointing at a large plate of vegetables.

'And would you like some gobbledy-gobbledy-gook?' asked the waitress. She too seemed to be enjoying this innovative ordering technique now she was getting the hang of it.

My confidence was increasing.

'Yes, that too,' I said, though I had no idea what it might be. And so I ended up with a cast-iron skillet piled high with fabulously tender slices of beef and sizzling peppers, onions and chillies bubbling in a potent sauce, a large plate of green vegetables, a bowl of rice and a big bottle of beer, all for twenty yuan. I went back to my hotel feeling full and pleased with myself. At last, I seemed to be mastering restaurant survival techniques, if nothing else.

Zhongdian is a city with many names. As well as its Chinese appellation, it is called Gyalthang in Tibetan. The airport, for some reason, is known as Diqing. And in brave new tourism speak, the area has been re-named Shangri-La.

I had bought a copy of James Hilton's *Lost Horizon* in the Foreign Languages Bookshop in Shanghai and had started reading it on the plane. Hilton was the British author who first came up with the name Shangri-La for the lamasery in the Tibetan mountains where his characters end up after their plane is hijacked and crashes. The passengers are taken to Shangri-La against their will, but the lamasery turns out to be an idyllic refuge from the turbulent world beyond the mountains. In Shangri-La, the ageing process slows; the lamas live for hundreds of years in a land of clean air, lush green valleys and snow-capped mountains.

Ever since Hilton's book was published in the 1930s, debate has raged as to the location of the paradise that inspired him. Hilton himself didn't venture further than the perilous enclaves of the British Library reading room in his research, but he is said to have been influenced by the magazine articles of the botanist Dr Joseph Rock who lived for many years in the west of China. Wherever James Hilton took his ideas from, in 2002 the Chinese government declared that they had figured out the conundrum and unveiled a massive spending scheme to bring tourism to the area. Zhongdian County was renamed Shangri-La.

The greyness and filth of some of the Chinese cities I'd visited in recent weeks hadn't led me to think of an earthly Eden, so it was with a delightful sense of anticipation that I stepped off the plane at Diqing airport against a backdrop of deep blue sky and mountains, breathed in the chill, clean air, and felt secure in the knowledge that I had arrived at last in Utopia.

In the arrivals hall, Guy was waiting with an entourage. He had flown in from Beijing the night before and met up with our guides. From the airport, we were leaving directly on our journey west.

We were going to trek along the inner *kora*, or shorter circuit, of the Khawakarpo pilgrimage route. Real pilgrims journey for several days and complete the whole *kora* that loops round the sacred peak. We were just going to do a small section of it – in fact, the majority of our four-day 'trek' would be spent in the minibus. From Zhongdian it was a whole day's drive to the border town of Deqin where we would spend that night. The following day we'd walk, then camp in the mountains before returning to Deqin for a third night. We'd then spend the last day driving back to Zhongdian. Our journey wouldn't take us into the Tibet Autonomous Region itself; we would be close to the border, but would stay in the Chinese province of Yunnan. This, our guides explained, was a better option. Inside Tibet proper, regulations are much more stringent. Foreigners can't easily talk to locals; guiding companies have to follow strict and pre-determined routes. Here, just the other side of the border, we'd be free to move as we chose.

Our group's head honcho was Yeshi. With his black felt cowboy hat, longish black hair, goatee beard and olive-green fleece, he looked every part the hip, twenty-first-century Tibetan. Actually, he would have blended well in any old Wild West. He looked just the type to gallop hell for leather into a Californian gold-mining town amid a flurry of dust. But he didn't have any pistols in holsters. Or indeed a horse. Maybe it was just the hat.

Yeshi is co-owner of Khampa Caravan, a trekking company that aims to recreate the traditional Tibetan spirit of adventure, be that in retracing journeys of the Tibetan mule caravans or by following Buddhist pilgrimage routes. Yeshi comes from authentic wandering stock. His grandfather was originally a muleteer who used to make the five-month journey between Darjeeling and Tibet carrying tea and textiles; he later set up the biggest family trading enterprise in the Gyalthang area with branches in Lhasa, Kunming and Darjeeling. Yeshi himself grew up in India, though. His parents went into exile there in the 1950s following the Chinese occupation of Tibet and he spoke with a lovely, soft Indian lilt. He then went to university in the States and worked as a rug salesman in Manhattan and a banker in Switzerland before returning to his native Tibet to set up his company.

He had brought with him a guide, Thupten, who was once, Yeshi told us, a Buddhist monk. This revelation provoked considerable hilarity among the rest of the group. Clearly Thupten had fallen from the righteous path – as indeed he had tumbled from his motorbike just yesterday. Now he wore a terrible, deep gash across his forehead and his bandages seemed to be doing little to stem the blood that was still seeping. There was also a cook called Adro, a driver and yak-butter-teacup-washer named Numey (Tibetan for 'younger brother'), and a very knowledgeable librarian named Ah-ping. Ah-ping was Bai – one of the ethnic minorities whose land lies just south of where we were now. He imparted his gems of wisdom to Guy in Mandarin; indeed, he explained, he frequently had to speak even to other Bai people in Mandarin rather than Bai because the dialect differed so greatly even between nearby villages that the people couldn't understand each other. If Ah-ping wanted to talk to his own relatives who lived just fifty miles away, Mandarin was their only possible means of communication.

We drove through town. Black yaks with tousled hairy coats clopped across traffic junctions; floppy-eared pigs trotted along the edge of the tarmac. Countless donkeys trundled by carrying their loads. This was another world from the China of the east. Gone was the grey of the past weeks. The skies here were deep, brilliant blue, the air was crisp and clear. The tiny shop fronts were coloured in bright reds, pinks and blues. Even the meanest little shacks seemed to be intricately decorated: pink lotus flowers, green leaves, orange and yellow fruits were painted amid Tibetan cloud designs and geometric lines.

One feature that had reached these mountains, though, was China's mania for building roads. The surface we drove along was excellent: the road was apparently only two years old. We wound up through the hills to a village where the people made wooden pots for a living. We parked the minibus and made our way over a rickety swing bridge. Below, the water ran turquoise with glacial silt. On the banks, the branches of orange trees were laden with ripe, knobbly-skinned fruit. Deep green bushes sprouted huge, pink flowers.

On the far bank huddled a dozen flat-roofed, white-washed houses. They were rudimentary, rectangular buildings that ran either side of a single mud track along which people, yaks and cows ambled. The ground floor of each had a doorway but no windows. This was where the animals lived. The family rooms were located on the second storey and decorated with rows of carved and painted wooden windows. The top storey of each house extended only half the width of the building; the other half formed a flat roof over the storey below. Fastened to the upper reaches of several houses, satellite dishes beamed in news of the faraway world.

We were invited into one of the houses. We sat at red lacquer tables and ate fruit – pomelos and the bitter, knobbly oranges that were growing on the trees outside – and walnuts that were presented to us on red-and-gold lacquer trays. In one corner lay piles of round wooden bowls, with stepped, domed lids. These were the traditional containers in which the Tibetans kept tsampa, their staple food of ground roasted barley. I thought it would be courteous to buy one and so I selected a dish embellished with decoration in gold paint and asked how much it cost. They seemed pleased that I liked it and gave it to me as a gift.

Back in the bus, we continued to climb. As we drove, Yeshi pointed out the teetering old tracks along the mountain's edge where his grandfather would have led his caravans.

At about six o'clock in the evening, we arrived in Deqin. This was a real border town, the last stop before the Tibet Autonomous Region. A hairy-faced yak ambled down the main street snuffling at piles of rubbish. Everywhere there swarmed groups of pilgrims who poured in from the surrounding country-side at this time of year when the harvest was over to complete the *kora* of Khawakarpo.

A boy aged about fourteen stood and stared at us, his long, narrow eyes gleaming in shy surprise above his high, angular cheekbones. His lips, wide and full, parted slightly in astonishment; his head, wrapped in a yellow woollen scarf, sat quizzically askew. In his ear lobes he wore small baubles of turquoise.

A gaggle of women stood in the entrance to a shop

229

selling felt hats and thick woollen clothing and giggled as we walked by. Their heads were adorned with long striped scarves in reds, greens and yellows. Around their necks hung strings of multicoloured beads and golden chains strung with nuggets of turquoise. Their teeth glistened bright white against their dark, weather-worn faces. Their noses were long and flat, and their wind-bruised cheeks stained red and purple as though handfuls of ripe summer fruits had been crushed against their skin.

One girl wore no covering on her head. Her hair was black, dull and matted, and sticking out at extraordinary angles. It almost perfectly echoed the tousled coat of the yak that trotted past. Under her coarse, grey outer robe she wore a bright red cotton top, fastened under the shoulder. Her feet were clad in the ubiquitous green army plimsolls.

Parked on the side of the street sat monstrously large open-backed lorries which arrived in town with more than a hundred people crammed tightly into each. On the front of the lorry, above the cabin, hung a dusty Buddhist swastika of peace.

'That must be an uncomfortable way to travel,' I said to Yeshi as I looked at pilgrims packed in and piled high.

'Actually, I think they would find a car more uncomfortable,' Yeshi said. 'They're not used to travelling that way. They get carsick.'

We browsed for an hour or so in the open-fronted shops that lined the streets selling nomadic necessities such as clothing, horses' saddles, and tin kettles and pans. In a weak attempt to look as cool as Yeshi, Guy and I bought cowboy hats, and I went overboard by acquiring a bright blue woollen Tibetan nomad's coat. It was floor-length, decorated with gold, pink and yellow brocade and a fur trim. The salesman was tiny and camp. He minced up and down his poky establishment, his tight little bottom swaying from side to side with a pert elegance, like the sashay of a sleek, black-haired cat. He had a curiously high-pitched voice in which he crossly refused to bargain. It seemed wonderful that this character, more effeminate by far than any of the women he served, should survive in this rugged land.

We ate yak meat, rice and vegetables for dinner in a small restaurant on the main street, then Guy and I retired to the Tibetan Cowboy Bar where we drank extraordinarily cheap beer. Outside, an ever-burgeoning group of pilgrims pressed their long red noses against the glass and created little misty circles as they breathed. Huddled in a tight group, the shy ones sheltering behind the more confident, they stared in unblinking fascination at the whey-faced aliens who had landed in their midst. These were rural people who had probably never seen a foreigner before in their lives. They didn't smile or attempt to communicate; they simply gazed steadily, unwavering, their eyes shining through the glass like a row of tiny, unflickering lights.

The first bottle of beer we ordered was so revolting we deemed it undrinkable. As it had only cost a few yuan, we pushed our glasses to one side and tried a different brand. Before long, a wayward pilgrim rolled through the door. His courage that night had been boosted by something stronger than yak butter tea. He stumbled towards our table, his full lips red and glistening with spittle, his narrow eyes pink and rheumy with drink. He pointed at the rejected glasses and slurred some words we didn't understand. His meaning was clear, though; we said he could have them. Without wasting a second, he picked up one almost-full glass and, vigorously throwing back his matted head like a yogi saluting the sun, he poured the amber liquid down his throat in a single gulp. He blinked, burped loudly and wiped his drooling mouth on his sleeve. The bargirl was unhappy. We were attracting too much attention and she asked us to leave.

The pilgrims slept rough on the pavements. Small groups bedded down on the tarmac around the fires that lined the edges of the street. We, on the other hand, were softer by far. We spent the night in the best of the town's hotels and so were able to enjoy a good sleep and a hot shower before setting off at dawn the next day.

Our first stop was the monastery on the hilltop where we were to offer incense before embarking on our own, much curtailed pilgrimage. A row of chortens, or stupas, lined the approach. In the dusky morning light, their square whitewashed bases and tapering steps that symbolized the ascent to enlightenment stood strong against the dark mountains beyond.

We climbed out of our bus and shivered in the cold dawn air as we bought sprays of juniper, then warmed ourselves as we placed them inside the burning furnaces whose smoke rose in clouds around us and created a rich aroma of bonfires and pine.

Yeshi presented us each with a bunch of pink incense sticks. We held their tips in the flames until they caught alight, then planted them deep in the soft ash so their burning ends fell out into a smouldering, orange fan that glowed in the pewter light. From each fine, lucent tip a delicate wisp of smoke curled and spiralled along a meandering path to heaven.

232

The smoke from the furnaces billowed outwards in swirling eddies, engulfing the hundreds of strings of multicoloured prayer flags that fluttered from the columns of a pagoda, and were tied, layer upon layer, between the branches of trees and bamboo poles planted in the ground. Beyond lay the snowy peaks of the Khawakarpo range towards which we were heading. As we stood and gazed, the sun started to rise. The sky became infused with a creeping pink that seeped into purple then a watery blue behind the mountains' jagged forms. Then, suddenly, their snow-capped peaks caught the light and shone with brilliant intensity.

Having made our offerings, we retreated to the warmth of one of the low buildings on the side of the road where we ate eggs, home-baked flat bread and tsampa and drank yak butter tea to fortify us for the day ahead.

'I've had this before,' said Guy as Numey graciously filled his bowl with the opaque, yellowish liquid: it resembled a watery, sour-smelling béchamel sauce. There was something about Guy's downbeat tone that suggested he wasn't too thrilled to be tasting it a second time.

Yeshi laughed. 'Think of it as soup,' he suggested.

And that, it transpired, was the solution to drinking this concoction of churned yak butter and salted black tea that so frequently turns the stomachs of foreigners. As a cup of tea, it was truly unspeakable. But taken as a kind of thin cheese soup, one could swallow it without vomiting, at least. Mixed with tsampa, it made a soothing, cereally gunge.

Outside, a row of pilgrims wrapped in coarse woollen robes squatted on the pavement and warmed their hands round white enamel bowls of butter tea that they ladled from a black tin urn.

'Butter tea and tsampa are all they eat,' Yeshi explained. 'They bring with them a brick of tea and a container of tsampa, and then they buy the butter as they need it.'

It seemed a meagre and monotonous form of sustenance. I was glad that Guy and I were taking the luxury tour and would have a bit of yak meat and rice thrown in to supplement our diet.

We reached the trailhead after another two hours' driving along a vertiginous cliff road. In many places the surface had fallen away, tumbling off down the steep terrain, hinting sickeningly to the traveller that he or she might soon follow and join the splintered stones in their unforgiving grave far below. In other spots, boulders littered the way having crashed down in landslides from above. Laden pilgrim trucks hurtled up the middle of the steep road trying not to lose momentum as they ascended with their heavy loads. I closed my eyes and hoped for sleep.

'You want to ride a mule?' Yeshi asked when we arrived at the beginning of the track.

'Sure,' I replied. I was quite buoyed by the idea. Here was a form of Chinese transport I hadn't yet tried.

My steed was prepared with a multicoloured mat and an old red-and-white carpet slung across its back. As with most creatures in China, it wasn't a large animal (when Ernest Hemingway visited China with Martha Gellhorn in the early 1940s, he apparently decided his horse was so tiny as to be useless, so he picked it up and carried it). But my mule had a velvety, white nose and soft, slowly blinking eyes, and it carried me up the hill without so much as a whinny.

Maybe Hemingway's behaviour was still remembered in China and male Western visitors had henceforth been blackballed because Guy wasn't offered transport, but was made to climb the mountain on his own two feet. Fortunately, our luggage and equipment found a ride so we didn't have to carry it, and Numey, Adro and Ah-ping went ahead with the little, ambling caravan to prepare the camp for our later arrival.

We walked for five or six hours that first day. After lunch – hard-boiled eggs, flat bread, and cold spiced yak meat – I opted to give the mule an afternoon off and walked the rest of the way. The mule ride had been entertaining to start with, but the air was cold and we had been journeying in the shade of the forest. And, anyway, this was supposed to be a pilgrimage of sorts, and surely you gain no points with the unearthly powers that be if you make some poor beast do all the work?

Soon after lunch, we reached the pass, after which the path descended. Here, at the track's highest point, the trees were laden with prayer flags draped from every branch and trunk so that they formed a thick, fluttering, multicoloured canopy. From overhead, the sun shone through the curtain so that those gently undulating flags flew bright with colour, the reds, greens, yellows and whites of their fine fabric lit up against the deep blue sky. We stopped to tie our own strings from one tree to another, leaving our tiny, indiscernible mark on this spot rich with religious significance.

This was a year of the sheep in the eastern zodiac, considered to be an especially important year to complete the *kora* at Khawakarpo; tens of thousands of pilgrims were expected to make the journey before the year was out. That day the paths were busy. Every few minutes we passed a group hiking up the slopes, heading in the direction from which we had come. They walked with the aid of thin branches of bamboo that they had picked up along the way. One behind another they climbed the hill, their lines of upright staffs weaving down the slope like a spindly, teetering fence.

An old man beamed at us, his dark skin creasing into a thousand tiny rivulets. His front four teeth were missing so that his incisors formed stark, white goal-posts against a dark, rectangular cavity. Tiny wooden balls were strung round his neck in a rosary. On his head, he wore a bulky fur hat like a protective helmet.

Another man sported a singlet of long, white raggedy sheepskin, like the photographic negative of Rastafarian dreadlocks. A third, younger pilgrim was dressed in a V-neck yellow sweater over a diamond-print shirt with long, nose-diving collar points. His fur hat had a drooping fringe that sat like long, bushy eyebrows above his yellow wraparound shades.

The women and girls wore multicoloured aprons. Many carried babies strapped to their backs.

'*Tashi delek.*' The pilgrims called out the Tibetan greeting as they passed.

'*Tashi delek, tashi delek,*' we replied again and again.

Now, in the middle of the day, the sky was deep blue with just the occasional wisp of cloud. The air was clear, the light sharp and vibrant. Beneath the electric sky, the white cap of the mountains shimmered and the lush green of the foreground valleys seemed to burst with a vital verdancy. This, surely, was Shangri-La.

We camped that night near a village, in an emerald-green meadow at the foot of the snow-sprinkled mountains. When we arrived, our tent was already up, the fire was built, and water for coffee was burbling in a charred tin kettle. We thought sympathetically of the real pilgrims enduring yet another supper of yak butter tea and tsampa as we tucked into minced chilli yak, stir-fried broad beans, aubergines, courgettes, broccoli and potatoes.

As the evening grew dark, we drew up our chairs round the fire and washed our meal down with barley alcohol. Adro and Numey danced and sang exuberant Tibetan songs in praise of the local firewater while we gazed up at the phenomenal display of stars overhead.

I soon regretted the alcohol, of course. I'd only drunk a tiny cupful, then washed it down with copious amounts of water, but we were high here and no sooner had the fire hit my veins than the effects of the altitude, eager to claw their pernicious way under my skin, seemed to seize upon this one chink of weakness and follow the spirit into my bloodstream.

I felt almost instantly nauseous; a tight headache cramped my skull. As soon as we had retired for the night I found myself lying wide awake and queasy in the tent I was sharing with Guy. My sleeping bag was one of those down, mountaineer's kinds: it had a hood for the head and tapered in tight around my feet. Affected by altitude and alcohol, I felt confined, claustrophobic, too closely swathed for comfort.

The water had drained through my system. It seemed that the fluid had been so keen to cascade towards my ballooning bladder, where it now pooled and pressed uncomfortably, that it had entirely overlooked its hydrating role as it went. The night was cold: the temperature had dropped to around minus five. The last thing I wanted to do was to venture outside.

In the end, I could delay no longer. I broke out from

237

my sleeping bag, peeled back the tent doors, and rushed outside. The cold air, suddenly, was a relief. My bladder blissfully empty, I did my best to creep back into bed and lay there for several minutes more.

'Are you awake?' Guy's voice emanated across the darkness.

'How are you feeling?' I asked.

'Terrible.'

There was a short pause as we both lapsed into a self-pitying silence.

'Do you have any Nurofen?' Guy asked.

I dug out my emergency supply, we swallowed the pills and, minutes later, we both fell into deep, un-disturbed sleep.

We were up at daybreak again, woken by the un-familiar sound of yaks and mules lumbering past our tent with their neck-bells softly chiming. As the sun rose behind us, the snowy mountain in front glowed pink against the dusky-blue dawn sky. Small clouds of white smudged the surface where the wind whipped up distant snow storms. Between our sweet-smelling meadow and the rose-coloured peaks soared lower mountains that had not yet caught the sun's rays, which cast sharp, black silhouettes against the snow. In the meadow where we'd camped, Spanish moss hung from the trees and shone pale green in the early-morning light.

Adro had, incredibly, baked fresh bread for break-fast which we ate with eggs, potatoes and local honey that was stiff with cold. As we finished, a skinny woman with a pink woollen headscarf crossed through the field, bent over like a bony boomerang as she carried a heavy load of branches on her back. She stopped and sat on a rock to rest, taking in the scene and wondering, no doubt, who were these strange-looking people eating such extravagant food.

As we left the campsite a short while later, we took a little detour to a nearby river where Yeshi showed us how the villagers used the flowing water to turn a mill that rotated a weighty, circular rock that ground their barley into tsampa. He also showed us a rather unremarkable, green plastic container that was sitting in one part of the stream with cables running out from it.

'It's an electricity generator,' he explained. 'Each family has one. They put it in the water and the flow creates enough power for them to light their houses. Some of them have televisions, too.'

We walked through the village, past a gargantuan dozing sow, several sprightly dogs and countless clucking chickens. A group of small girls carried a shiny aluminium bucket slopping over with water, its handle suspended from a pole that they carried one child to each end. One wore a navy-blue knitted jumper featuring the smiling face of a fleecy sheep. They grinned, bright, toothy, and excited to see us.

Yeshi and his cohorts had seemed keen that I climb the steeper part of the mountain by mule as I had done yesterday. Without actually saying it in so many words, they seemed to think the ascent might be a bit much for me. But I wanted to walk; the mule had been fun but today I felt like taking some exercise.

Continually, the entourage stopped to help me, to offer me the ends of their sticks to pull me up a rocky bank. They refused to allow me to carry a thing. Unfortunately all this attention brought out the worst in me. Somehow, for no good reason at all, I felt the need to prove that girls too can climb hills. Letting pride get the better of me, I strode up the mountain leaving Yeshi and the guides far behind; Guy panted but kept up, occasionally complaining between rasping inhalations.

We stopped at the pass to let the others catch up and I took the rucksack that Guy and I were sharing. The guides looked profoundly shocked.

'You're letting *her* carry it?' they gasped.

'Yes,' said Guy, a little crossly.

On the way home, we stopped at the village where Thupten's girlfriend lived. She was building a guesthouse and we sat in a room that looked onto the central courtyard and ate yet more yak meat and flat bread, and again drank yak butter tea. By now, this curiously rancid drink was becoming almost palatable.

The guesthouse, like all the Tibetan buildings we had seen, featured ornately carved windows and screens, and vibrantly coloured pillars. In the corner, an old man – the girl's father, perhaps – stood over a tall cylindrical urn and churned yak butter with a long pole, as though he were plunging a vastly enlarged dipstick to repeatedly check his oil.

We finished our meal and continued our journey to Deqin via a brightly painted monastery where we lit butter lamps that we hoped would guide the spirits, shedding light on their paths to the next world. The burning butter smelt sour, but the light cast by the hundreds of tiny flickering flames that lined the temple was enchanting.

We drove the next day from Deqin to Zhongdian via a tiny school. A monk from a nearby monastery had set up the place and was dedicating his life to the education of children from poor rural families. Many of the pupils here were either orphans or from households where the parents had divorced. In these parts, where livelihood can be precarious, the absence of even one land-tilling parent can create severe deprivation. Although in China primary education is compulsory, parents have to pay towards the cost. In rural areas, far from the reach of the administrative mandarins, the offspring of poor families simply can't afford to go to school.

When this monk realized that so many of the children in the hill villages surrounding the monastery were receiving no education, he decided to do something about it. He originally operated from a tiny wooden shack with a plastic drape pinned across the door; however, a few years ago, a representative of the World Wide Fund for Nature happened to drive by and stop. She liked what she saw and managed to raise funds for a two-storey brick building with dormitories on the upper level and classrooms beneath.

At the time of our visit, there were forty-eight children in the school and the monk's running costs came to the equivalent of seven or eight thousand pounds a year. That worked out at about a hundred and fifty pounds per child per year, including their food, board, clothing and school materials. Even in these low-cost parts, that still wasn't a lot of money and the living here was frugal. The children all wore matching blue or red tracksuits that had seen better days. The older ones, aged twelve or thirteen, took it in turns to cook the meals. They stayed here for eleven months of the year and learnt to read and write Tibetan. There was nothing luxurious about this spartan building on a dusty roadside, but the children seemed happy enough and everything, though old, was glisteningly clean. We were offered tea which we drank, and duly made our monetary donations.

*　　　*　　　*

Back in Zhongdian, we checked into the Gyalthang Dzong Hotel which was part-owned by Yeshi's brother, Tashi. It was a beautiful place furnished with old Tibetan dark-wood chairs and bureaus, elegant silk drapes and rugs from Tashi's factory in Lhasa. Unfortunately, a hot bath after the rigours of the last two days was out of the question because the hotel didn't turn the hot water on until the evening. Neither did they put on the heating unless a guest insisted. It was a stylish place but they seemed to be economizing on fuel rather more assiduously than one might hope at an altitude of 3,200 metres at the onset of winter. At night, it was colder here than in the Khawakarpo mountains; it was only November, but already temperatures were dropping to minus ten before morning. The Tibetans, though, seemed to be inured to such hardships.

'The heating in my apartment has broken,' Yeshi told us in a resigned tone. 'I sleep in layers of fleeces and a woollen hat.'

In any case, we didn't have the opportunity to rest for long as Yeshi had arranged a night of feasting and dancing in his business partner Dakpa's village, Trinyi, a few kilometres out of town. Dakpa's and Yeshi's company had funded a community centre there. They wanted to revive the old customs of dancing and singing among the villagers, and to provide a place for them to meet. There was even a basketball court that, they hoped, would lure the teenagers so that boredom didn't drive them to the degenerative refuge of alcohol in the karaoke bars in town.

We sat at a wooden table in a spruce, pale-wood room with freshly carved ornamentation. In an adjacent lean-to, a small hive of villagers swarmed about cooking traditional hotpot and vegetables.

We ate well and drank barley wine. As we finished our meal, a pink-turbaned head popped round the doorway. I caught the woman's eye and smiled; she rapidly withdrew. Over the next few minutes, more outlandishly clad heads bounced in and out round the doorposts, like ornately swathed ping-pong balls batted to and fro by invisible bats. And then, at last, they filed in.

The women wore fuchsia woollen scarves, twisted and coiled round the tops of their heads like crowns, and gowns of peacock-blue satin that were embroidered with bold pink and green flowers in panels down their fronts. Some of the men had donned tall hats like upended buckets that were covered in glittering gold brocade and finished with soft, fur brims. One wore a flamboyant brown busby so full and bushy it looked as though a small bear had taken up residence on his head. Again, they all had outstanding teeth. There had to be something powerful in that yak butter.

After the first couple of minutes of nervous giggling and shuffling in our presence, the villagers seemed to forget we were there and threw themselves into a foot-stamping, high-kicking, jubilantly bellowing extravaganza. The dance routine, if you could call it that, seemed to consist simply of the men all linking themselves arm to shoulder in a line on one side of the room, and the women facing them in similar formation on the other. They positioned themselves like two very long lines of opposing, upright rugby scrums, with pink wool and gold brocade standing in for mud-drenched jerseys. The men would sing a raucous line, kicking their legs high to the rhythm, then the women would reply.

A three-year-old girl, also dressed in pink, wobbled through the door.

'That's Dakpa's daughter.' Yeshi laughed as she tottered over to hug him. Then she swayed over to the end of the line and, amidst much hilarity, attempted to mimic the dancers.

It was a joyful spectacle. It wasn't brilliant or polished, but the performers seemed to be having the time of their lives. In fact, it soon started to look as though they might go on all night. The hours ticked on and we were ready for bed. Each time a song drew to a close, Yeshi would clear his throat and just about manage to get out an 'Um . . .' before they rampaged enthusiastically into another number.

Yeshi looked at us and grinned.

'It's rather difficult to stop them once they get started.'

16

Reconstructing Paradise

Guy returned to Beijing early the following morning. I checked my email in the hotel's office where the staff were working in a glacial four degrees centigrade. My fingers were soon numb with the cold, and the painfully slow computer seemed to be seizing up in sympathy. The Malaysian boy working in the office seemed positively congealed. He sat stock-still, his skin white with the horror of it all, like an oriental Lot's wife who had made the mistake of looking back to sunnier times.

In reception, the staff stood stiffly behind the counter, immobilized by layers of gloves and hats. Above their heads loomed great, cubic ventilation systems. I asked why they didn't turn the heating on.

'We only turn it on when we have big groups staying,' they replied in strained voices, as though moving their mouths might cause their frozen faces to crack.

I was waiting in reception for Kesang, one of the hotel's guides, who was going to show me round the town and the surrounding area. He appeared and we went out to the car. Its windscreen was thick with ice. Curiously, in a country that froze over with chilling regularity, the driver had no tools for scraping it off. He just stuck his head out of the open window, his body contorted sideways like an Egyptian dancer's, and drove along that way.

'Don't worry, it will clear as soon as we get into the sun,' Kesang assured me with a nonchalant smile. Kesang was in his early twenties, well dressed and good-looking. He was half Tibetan, half Nepali, and must have come from an affluent family. Like Yeshi, he had been educated in India, in his case at boarding school. His family, like so many others, went into exile after the Chinese invaded (or, in their terminology, liberated) Tibet in 1950. The Chinese occupation of Tibet is still an issue fraught with emotion: the Dalai Lama's Bureau of Information reckons that more than a million Tibetans have been executed, tortured, or have died in labour camps since the 1950s; women have been raped and children taken away from their families for 're-education' in China. More than a hundred thousand Tibetans still live in exile, including their spiritual leader, the Dalai Lama. Meanwhile, Chinese resettlement projects mean that Han Chinese now outnumber the Tibetans in their own land: even if an election were to be held, the vote may well favour Chinese rule. The Chinese and Tibetans don't live easily side by side.

'The Chinese are terrified of the Tibetans,' Kesang told me. 'The Tibetans carry knives. They're tough people.'

Kesang had a relaxed confidence and easy charm. His greatest passion, he told me, was film. Every evening, he took out two DVDs from the local rental shop and sat till the early hours of the morning immersed in their faraway, fantastical worlds.

We drove out to the Ringha monastery, about

fifteen kilometres out of town. The road was in the process of being rebuilt and we took frequent diversions down dirt tracks and at one point even had to ford a small stream. The countryside was idyllic. Rivers and tributaries ran sparklingly clear. Along the edge of the road, small black-haired pigs with long ears that flopped forward over their eyes foraged for tasty morsels. They had long, thin, raggedy tails that wagged like a dog's as they walked, and endearing little faces.

Tall wooden stands were scattered sporadically over the land. Weaved into their slats, the drying barley crop created narrow walls of sandy thatch. The grass now, in the autumn, was sparse and golden but in the summer it would be thick with wild flowers of all colours – purple irises and blue poppies, yellow and magenta primulas, roses and azaleas. Even the ice-cold Malaysian in the hotel office had conceded that Zhongdian was pretty in summer. Herds of yaks and horses grazed on long stretches of flat meadow, then the land rose steeply into the mountain ranges that drew up around us.

'The yaks all belong to different families – most families just have one male which they use to plough and work the fields. But they graze together because this is common land,' Kesang explained. 'When evening comes, they each know where their home is so they just go there and butt their heads against the door, or kick it with their hoof and the family lets them in.'

It was a charming idea, the family yak coming home in the evening and knocking on the door, clamouring the yak equivalent of, 'Honey I'm home.'

At the Ringha Monastery, we bought incense and lit it. I asked Kesang if I should say a prayer as I planted

247

my spray of glowing pink sticks into the mound of ash.

'Yes,' he said with great sincerity. 'For the world peace.'

I gave it a try.

We moved on to visit the adjoining village. Kesang explained that the people who lived here continued to practise their traditional burial rites for the dead: they chopped the corpse into small pieces and threw it into the river.

'Is that legal?' I asked.

'Strictly no, but it is only one small village and the government pretends not to see.'

We walked up to a wooden house where Kesang greeted an old woman like a long-lost friend. She seemed delighted to see this good-looking boy who brought strangers to her home. We climbed the steps to the family's living quarters on the first floor. The houses here had no windows; the only light was cast by the embers of the open fire that burned constantly in one corner.

In the dim, smoky light, the old woman prepared butter tea over the flames. She wore traditional dress: a bright pink headscarf over a black hat lined with gold brocade, silver hoop earrings, a dark red tunic with gold and red decorative panels that fastened just beneath her shoulder, and a stained blue robe over the top. On her feet were tied worn white plimsolls. We sat on narrow wooden benches round the open fire and watched as the woman tipped boiling water from a coal-blackened jug into a tall wooden cylinder, agitated the mixture within with a long stick, and then poured the butter tea into chipped bowls and presented them to us. She also offered us her home-made yak cheese – curled, dried, yellow scrapings that looked to me like the toenail clippings of a very elderly man. I have never eaten old men's toenails, but the cheese had what I should imagine to be a similar consistency. Ever charming, Kesang pronounced it delicious and tucked in with gusto. I nibbled gingerly at one small sliver as slowly as I could.

From the rafters above the fire, gnarled chunks of yak meat hung on hooks to smoke. It was shrunken and purplish-black, and looked at least a hundred years old, the kind of flesh one might expect to find if one were to exhume a corpse buried a long time ago. Fortunately, we were not offered any. I was concerned, as it was, to have sampled the cheese.

As we drove home, Kesang told me more about Tibetan burial rituals.

'When I die, I will have a sky burial,' he declared and then went on to describe the process in lurid detail. 'First they remove the bones from the body. Then they put the flesh, about this big' – he held his arms in a circle in front of him – 'in a white material and the monk carries the flesh and the bones onto the mountain.'

'Does the family go too?' I asked with morbid fascination.

'The immediate family – the mother, father, brothers and sisters – don't go, but the uncles and cousins and so on climb the mountain with the monk. Then, on the mountain, the monk peels the flesh from the skin and soaks up the blood with tsampa. Then he chops the flesh into little pieces and lays it out on a rock for the vultures.'

The bones are smashed to splinters with a mallet, mixed with tsampa, and fed to the birds as well.

Kesang was telling me this in a very cheerful, matter-of-fact way. There was neither bloodthirstiness nor revulsion in his delivery. It was just the way things were, the way his people disposed of their dead, the way he, too, would eventually meet his end.

'First of all,' he continued, 'the head vulture circles round, and then he swoops down and takes the first piece of flesh. None of the other vultures will touch it until the head vulture has started. But as soon as he does, they all dive in.'

'And how long does it take for them to eat it all?'

'About thirty minutes.'

It sounded a gory way to go – but no worse, I'm sure, than being burned and stuffed in a pot in the ground. Still, I imagine it would be extraordinarily gruesome to watch one's relative being chopped up and fed to the vultures. I asked Kesang if he had attended a sky burial.

'Yes, when my uncle died,' he said, and smiled.

He seemed relaxed and happy about it – but then the Tibetans, in general, seemed unperturbed about death. For them, after all, this life is merely a stage and they are always looking forward to the next step in the cycle of reincarnation.

Back in Zhongdian, we took a walk around the old town. It was a building site. Houses were being renovated, roads ripped up and rebuilt. From all sides picks crashed and drills hammered, saws howled and cement mixers caterwauled. Great heaps of thundering boulders blocked the roads. The government had found its Shangri-La and was rebuilding it; those hoping to spread a little happiness into their bank accounts had bought up the creaking houses and with a rattling, clattering, earth-rending upheaval they were turning them into bars, restaurants, guesthouses and shops. By next year, the 'old' town would be entirely renewed.

We went into one teetering building. It was apparently three hundred years old. An elderly man and his wife lived here – they had been thrown out of this, their home, during the Cultural Revolution and the house had been used by the Red Guards as an office. The couple had lost everything except one wooden pot which they showed us with reverential pride.

On the warped wooden wall hung a poster featuring the disembodied faces of Mao Zedong, Deng Xiaoping and Jiang Zemin. I found it strange that this couple, who had suffered under the Chinese, should choose to display the Party leaders' images in their home. Then, next to the poster, I noticed a much smaller photograph. Rather faded now, it featured Chairman Mao meeting a youthful Dalai Lama. The picture was taken in the 1950s, before relationships between the Dalai Lama and the Chinese authorities soured as irrevocably as the Ringha woman's yak cheese.

The old man and his wife were ethnic Tibetans, and nurtured a deep and heartfelt respect for the Dalai Lama – yet still they seemed to hold the ideals of Communism close to their hearts. Somehow, in a very understated way, this yellowing photograph spoke more clearly of the complex loyalties and tangled affiliations of this area of eastern Tibet than any politician's speech ever could. For while the Tibetans may oppose the occupation of their land, the issues here are not black and white. The current government represents the latest stage in centuries of foreign rule in Tibet – by the Mongols, the Nepalis and briefly the British. Historically, Tibet and China have not always been enemies: when, in 1717, the Chinese arrived on the plateau and overthrew the occupying Mongolian forces, the Tibetans welcomed them and declared their land a protectorate of China – the basis on which the Communists reoccupied the plateau two hundred and fifty years later. Nowadays, most Chinese seem genuinely to believe that their occupation of Tibet has been beneficial to its people, bringing schools, hospitals and roads to the roof of the world. The Dalai Lama, on the other hand, accuses the Chinese of cultural genocide.

'I respect Mao,' the old man said. 'I like what he did for China. But out of those three' – he waved an age-spotted hand at the poster – 'the one I like best is Deng Xiaoping, because his reforms meant that I got my house back.'

17

Confucius Says *What*?

The view from the window of the bus that took me from Zhongdian to Lijiang the following morning would have been much improved had the girl in the seat in front not vomited quite so violently. Every few minutes, pale-faced and pinched, she would pull back the window and lean out. As the bus moved forward, the contents of her stomach sprayed forth and deposited orange-coloured flecks across my own window behind.

Despite the spots of sick, however, the scenery was pretty. The land at first was flat and brown in front and mountainous behind, the plains scattered with jet-black yaks. Then for an hour or so the road followed the path of a small stream whose rivulets ran clear over soft, smooth pebbles, the shallow water breaking and babbling as it slipped around the contours. It was now late November but the trees' leaves were still turning in this high land. Some were green, others flaming gold or blazing scarlet. Then the stream flowed into the mighty Yangtze and we clattered alongside in our vomit-speckled bus. Now the land started to rise around us into undulating, stepped rice terraces. Some were muddy and brown where the crop had been recently harvested; in others, tiny, pert tips of lush green were just beginning to peek above the line of the water and were bursting into the world with a new-born scream of vitality. We left the paddy fields and drove through a pine forest before finally arriving five and a half hours later in Lijiang.

The journey wasn't supposed to take five and a half hours, of course. We were held up by road works, once again. The authorities had decided that the route to Utopia was to be a smooth one and a new highway was being built that would cut the trip to just two hours. In the meantime, however, there were delays and diversions via dusty dirt roads.

Lijiang was a very touristy, very pretty little town whose 'ancient' quarter received its cosmetic surgery way back in the late 1990s, before such operations even became fashionable in China. The reconstruction was in this case provoked by the damage wreaked by an earthquake in 1996. Now, after renovation and the opening of an airport nearby, bars, restaurants and souvenir shops lined the maze of flagstone streets and narrow babbling canals that flowed through the town.

Dappled sunlight filtered through the trees and reflected from the surface of the clear water; over the canals, simple wooden bridges led from the stone-paved streets onto terraces furnished with rattan armchairs and tables with gingham cloths. From the overhang of the grey, curved-tile roofs descended strings of red lanterns. Above the market square the streets rose steeply; a haphazard hotchpotch of sloping slate roofs coated the hillside. The streets were immaculately, sensationally, spotlessly clean.

Naxi women wearing traditional blue cotton caps and aprons strolled through the streets among the tourists, carrying their goods in large wicker baskets on their backs as they have for centuries. The Naxi are the ethnic minority native to the land around Lijiang; they originally descended from the Tibetan Qiang tribes. As do most Chinese minorities, they speak their own language among themselves. More unusually, the Naxi also have their own pictographic writing system – the only hieroglyphic language still in use today – which features easily recognizable people, animals, flowers and birds. The pictograph for 'to ride' shows a stick figure astride a delightfully grumpy horse; 'kill' depicts a man brandishing a sword towards another who bends backwards in apparent terror. And, endearingly, 'discuss' is a drawing of two stick figures in skirts with long back lines, symbolizing tongues, sticking out from their heads and crossing each other.

Until recently Naxi society was matrilineal; even though rulers were male, it was indisputably the women who ran the show. Confucian values, which demote women firmly to subservience, don't seem to have had much effect among these strong-willed matrons.

'The shops were run, with very few exceptions, by women,' wrote Peter Goullart in his book *Forgotten Kingdom*. Goullart was a Russian who had escaped from the revolution in his homeland to Shanghai, then moved in 1939 to Lijiang where he worked as Depot Master for the Chinese government. 'They were shrewd and aggressive and knew how to clinch a bargain. When the woman had to go away, she asked her husband to take over. He was usually to be found at the back of the shop nursing a child and his emergence was a calamity to the business and a trouble to himself.'

Goullart also noted the Naxi people's propensity for suicide.

'There was not a family who did not number a suicide or two among its members. Suicide was looked upon as a convenient and desirable way of escape from a tangled love affair, a severe loss of "face", a grievous quarrel, a mortal insult, an unhappy married life, and from a host of other unfortunate situations.'

Goullart reckoned that four out of five suicides in Lijiang were pacts between runaway lovers. Their preferred method for killing themselves was to imbibe a concoction of the root of black aconite.

'It did cause great suffering, but it had the advantage of paralysing the larynx instantly so that no cries or groans could betray the whereabouts of the expiring suicides to any search parties,' Goullart explained.

Having checked into my hotel, I wandered out among the surviving Naxi and the tourists who now greatly outnumbered them. I soon lost myself quite delightfully in the tiny cobbled lanes linked by waterways and bridges that to a newcomer with a poor sense of direction seemed like a maze. I found a 'traditional' restaurant advertising the old Naxi favourite, deep-fried grasshoppers. Intrepid adventuress? Gastronomic brave? Mettlesome bug-munching explorer? Maybe not. I opted instead for a home-baked pizza in a cosy little restaurant with an English menu.

I had intended to dedicate the following day to rest and relaxation – a little strolling through the lanes of Lijiang, a lot of stopping in cafés for coffee and cake. I was still tired after the rigours of shopping in Shanghai and then the trekking trip. By the time I was ready to leave my hotel the following morning, however, I had discovered that its hot water was tepid, most of the lights didn't work, the heating was broken, and several of the buttons on the TV remote control had fallen off. Admittedly, I couldn't have understood any of the programmes even had I been able to channel-surf through them, but still, the state of the gadgetry didn't inspire confidence. I was in one of the most touristy towns in China; competition between establishments was fierce. I felt sure I could do better than this. And so I spent the first few hours of the day checking out rival hostelries, before finally settling on one just round the corner that had opened three months earlier and in which everything worked. It was an old-style courtyard house and immaculately pretty; it was also brand-new which, in China, is usually the safest option.

I changed hotels; I sent a box home containing the Tibetan nomad's coat among other things; I spent hours trying to book a flight out of Lijiang to Jinghong, which is in the far south of Yunnan and very poorly served by road. I heard the words '*mei you*' more times than I cared to count, then persisted for a few hours more, then changed my plans and booked a sleeper bus to Kunming, the province's capital city, instead. I wasn't intending to move on for a few days yet, but transport could easily sell out in these parts and it seemed a good idea to assure myself of an exit ahead of time. I rewarded myself after all that with a coffee and a huge, steaming bowl of apple crumble and then my relaxing day was over.

The next morning, I went to one of the cafés that advertised bicycle rental as I was planning to pedal out to the nearby village of Baisha. This tiny muddle of houses used to be the capital of the Naxi kingdom; today it still holds fast to traditional ways despite the hordes of tourists that come here to gad about and gaze.

My allotted bicycle was an old heap of rust with ropy brakes and recalcitrant gearing. As I was checking it out, another English girl, Tanya, appeared. She had been teaching English in Japan for the last few years and had saved up enough money to travel round Asia for several months. She also wanted a bike, and she was also planning to cycle to Baisha. We went together.

Baisha was only nine kilometres from Lijiang and, even given our rickety transport, the ride was an easy one. We pedalled gently along a straight country lane lined by fields where farmers watered their crops by dipping giant scoops into irrigation canals, then swinging them so that a spray fanned out over the land. These scoops were as tall as the farmers themselves; at the end of the straight log handle, the aluminium bowl was the size of a bathroom basin. It seemed an arduous way to water the plants.

Cranky farm vehicles, noisy, smelly and slow, clunked along the road beside bicycle carts carrying logs, hay and children, sometimes all at once. Women carried remarkable loads in straw-woven baskets on their backs: sticks, vegetables and, in one case, a weighty cargo of curved, slate roof tiles.

Baisha was a picturesque place, backed by the craggy, snow-spotted peaks of Jade Dragon Snow Mountain, one of the easternmost hills of the Himalayas. The houses were built with mud bricks that glowed golden in the sun. Piles of deep-yellow corn were laid out along stone walls to dry on their cobs. Water ran alongside the main street of the village in a fast-flowing canal, bridged every now and then by stone walkways. A woman squatted over the cold, clear ripples and peeled vegetables; another scrubbed clothes. Three ducks tried to swim upstream, frantically flapping their wide, webbed feet as they struggled against the current.

A few souvenir stalls had been set up in the main square, but this wasn't really a place that had embraced innovation. Old women sat around with baskets of apples for sale. They squatted on low wooden stools or roadside steps, dressed almost identically in big, blousy blue-cotton caps, blue aprons and blue or black trousers. On top, over coarse blue or brown tunics and jackets, they wore a kind of cape with straps that criss-crossed across their front by which they carried baskets and children on their backs. An old man, his delicate crinkly skin spotted with age, sat on a step and smoked a thin bamboo pipe the length of his arm. On his head he wore a tall, brown fur hat.

As we walked through the village, we heard the sound of music emanating from behind a low, mud-brick wall. Peering over and down into a barn whose floor lay well below the level of the road, we saw perhaps ten or twenty men and women dancing to a tape recording. They formed a semicircle and, holding hands, shuffled round crossing one foot over the other in their seemingly spontaneous barn dance. A younger man dressed all in black gave instructions to begin with; then he joined the end of the line and capered alongside the rest.

Tanya and I found a tiny restaurant that perched on the roadside, on the other side of the canal. Simon and Garfunkel crooned from the stereo. There was no menu in Chinese or otherwise. We wandered into the kitchen to pick out our food.

'You like fish?' asked a youngish woman, perhaps in her mid-thirties, wearing a standard Naxi blue apron. She had a kind, smiling face. She pointed at a washing-up bowl on the kitchen floor. Inside lay two fish that glistened like disco balls. We said we'd have them.

'Vegetables?' she asked, holding up two colanders that overflowed with vibrant, greener-than-green Chinese spinach. 'They came from that field there.' She gestured towards the neat, luxuriant rectangles on the other side of the road. They stretched into the distance, across the plain towards the misty grey-blue hills beyond.

The fish arrived stewed in a delicious gravy with garlic, ginger, chillies and coriander. We sat on a tiny, narrow balcony overlooking the road, while Chinese tourists passing by stopped to point at us and take photographs of their friends posing in front of the two big-nosed foreigners.

That evening I went with Tanya to a concert of traditional Naxi music. I usually avoid such events having failed to appreciate so many worthy cultural experiences in the past – a water puppet show in Hanoi had turned out to be incomprehensible and went on roughly for ever; Chinese opera had made me want to reach for my earplugs. But I had nothing else to do that evening and I had a new friend who already had a ticket, so I joined her.

I bought my ticket and met Tanya in the hall.

'There's a film crew here,' she told me excitedly. 'They're English. They just told me to get out of the way!'

I looked around; the hall was scattered with cameras and giant booms whose furry microphones would relay traditional Naxi music to the world in full sonic techni-tone.

'Ah,' I said – and then I spotted him. 'And that man they're clipping a microphone to looks awfully like Michael Palin.'

'My goodness, so it is!' exclaimed Tanya.

In order to visit the loo before the performance began, we had to shuffle right past his second-row seat. Wearing little glasses that gave him an almost professorial air, he was writing efficiently in a small, hardback notebook. What was he writing? I wondered. For certain, it would be something clever, witty and slick. I looked around the concert hall. All I could see was a bunch of boring-looking people sitting in rows. I sighed. Michael Palin, no doubt, was concocting a brilliant satirical portrait of some character on the twenty-second row.

And then, to my total horror, Tanya stopped right in front of him. The gangway we were edging through was narrow. Tanya was in the lead. There was no escape.

'Mr Palin!' she called out cheerily. I shrank. Mr Palin carried on writing.

'Mr Palin!' she cried again. She wasn't giving up.

Poor Mr Palin looked momentarily confused as he surfaced from his scribblings.

'Ah, um, yes?' he said.

'I just wanted to tell you how much I enjoyed your show!' gushed Tanya.

'Well, thank you very much,' said Mr Palin, smiling now and being charming.

'And Polly here' – she gestured to me with both hands – 'is a travel writer!'

I was horrified. Really, I didn't want to be brought into this. I prayed for the ground to swallow me.

'Oh, really?' said Michael Palin, feigning interest. 'What kind of travel books do you write?'

I wished I could just disappear. I willed the large gong on the stage behind me to topple over and squash me flat.

It didn't.

'Er, well, um, you know, kind of humorous travel stuff really,' I muttered with spectacular ineloquence.

Michael Palin's eyes gave a little twinkle behind the erudite spectacles. 'Ah,' he said, 'competition!'

I stuttered through a few vigorous denials, a couple of banal observations, and made good my escape. But I couldn't go far. It now transpired that, perhaps because I had bought my ticket so late, I had been allocated a seat in the almost-empty first row – by some perversity, directly in front of him. It seemed excessively rude just to plonk myself in his view when most of the row was empty, so I scuttled along a bit and observed him from a distance. His jacket didn't seem to have reached nearly the same shameful shade of grungy black that mine had. His shoes were respectable leather; I was wearing a pair of trainers that had gone grey beneath a couple of months' worth of Chinese street grime. In all, Michael Palin looked immensely tidy. He looked quite professionally in control of the situation, in fact.

The concert began with a long, rambling monologue from a man in a long blue robe. The Chinese audience guffawed with laughter. He translated his speech into English – or at least a precis of it, for the English version was very much shorter than the Chinese. The English-speaking members of the audience clapped politely and tried to work out what the joke was.

I snuck a sideways glance at Michael Palin. His face bore an air of benign amusement. He must have understood something I had missed. Damn.

There was a mournful wail from a creaking geriatric

sitting before a bank of gongs and the orchestra started up. This music was supposed to date from the Tang dynasty and, judging by appearances, so did some of the orchestra's members. With their white hair, long pointed beards, and pink-and-gold silk robes, they appeared to have travelled by time warp from a bygone age. They looked like withered little elves wrapped in coloured tin foil. On their faces, they wore spectacularly dour expressions. They didn't seem to think much of sitting in this hall, providing a cultural spectacle for ignorant tourists. One of them frequently screwed his face up as though he had just chewed a particularly astringent segment of pomelo. Whether he was experiencing musical ecstasy or whether his wincing was an expression of agony that his musical career should have descended to this, I couldn't tell.

The first clanging, twanging offering thankfully drew to a close and we were treated to another witty monologue from the man in the blue robe which, again, I could understand nothing of. Then: '*Waaaaaahhhhhaaahh.*' A woman stood up to perform a solo voice number – a shrieking, agonizing din in which she slid down the musical register in a kind of continuously falling scale. It was similar to the sound one might expect her to make if she were to plummet down a very deep well. She would have been pushed, perhaps.

Blue Robe stood up and enthusiastically delivered more well-chosen words. A lot more. I noticed that one or two of the hoary-headed veterans had by now fallen asleep. Their heads hunkered slightly into the stiff, upright collars of their tunics, their eyes closed. I wondered if they might start to dribble. Then, '*Donnnngggg!*' Creaky Bones bonged his gongs, and the old men juddered into wakefulness, picked up their wooden flutes, their *erhu* and their zithers and scraped crustily through another number.

But maybe I just missed the point. I have no idea what Michael Palin made of it.

18

A Brutally Bruising Bus

The lowest point of the journey to Kunming was when the driver let slip a bloodcurdling, terror-stricken scream. I was taking an overnight bus, though the term 'sleeper' really was a misnomer. Sleep was out of the question.

The bus was furnished with three rows of bunk beds running lengthways down the vehicle. Two narrow aisles struggled to squeeze between them. The bunks were two-tiered; I was on the upper bed nearest the door, just across from the driver. On the trains, the upper bunks were best. On a bus, I soon discovered, they weren't.

The pallet was ridiculously short and narrow. I couldn't lie flat with both arms pinned to my sides because only one arm would fit. I had been told that robbery was a problem on these sleeper buses so I started the journey trying to cram all my luggage into my bed with me. I was left crouched in an upright foetal position somewhere in the middle of the painfully thin mattress. It didn't seem a very good position for sleeping. Then the bus went over a pothole and my rucksack leapt from the bed and crashed to the floor below. At this point I gave up sharing my accommodation with my luggage, but even once I had the bed to myself I couldn't quite lie straight.

In addition to being designed for stunted anorexics, the upper bunk had no effective railing to keep its incumbent from falling out. There was a tiny metal bar that ran along the outside of the mattress from my head to my ribs, but it was very low – shallower by far than my body – and pathetically short. I could see no chance that it would stop me from flying out of bed and splintering on the floor at the first rut in the road.

And ruts there were many. We rattled along, the bus bouncing and bumping. The hard plank on which I lay jolted and juddered. As the bus's wheels flew acrobatically over the road's ramps and divots, my body jerked up into the air, then thumped back down. I felt like a heart attack victim receiving a particularly violent dose of CPR. I was spectacularly uncomfortable – and the bus was full, so there was no chance of relocating to a less perilous berth.

When the bus left at eight o'clock it was already dark but, unlike the trains where I could read until the lights were turned off, the bus had no lights so all I could do was lie there, praying for unlikely sleep.

My phone rang. It was Clive, sitting in a hotel room in God knows where. Maybe he felt like talking to somebody who was having an even less entertaining evening than he was.

'Where are you?' Clive asked with entirely inappropriate cheer.

'I'm on a sleeper bus from Lijiang to Kunming,' I hissed bitterly. I went on to describe the incommodious arrangements.

'Ah. When do you arrive in Kunming then?' asked Clive.

'Oh,' I said airily, 'just another eleven hours to go.'

There was a short silence from Clive.

'Oh dear,' he said.

Diagonally across from me, in the bottom bunk behind the steering wheel, the reserve driver slept soundly. He was making truly incredible noises. He snuffled, spluttered and snored at astonishing volume. His colleague at the wheel hawked more loudly than anyone I had ever heard, and then spat the sputum he had mustered through the window. He did this with remarkable frequency – every five minutes or so. As he brought up the phlegm, a terrifying rattling noise echoed within him. It sounded as though tiny gremlins were firing machine guns in his lungs. With anxious paranoia, I wondered whether he had TB, and whether I could catch it from this distance. And then, miraculously, I went to sleep.

I woke up at two o'clock in the morning as we pulled into a great, concrete bus park. It was an eerie place, ill-lit except for the beam of bus headlights that reflected off the slick, grey ground. Ghostly silhouettes walked stiffly between them; these figures too had just awoken from sleep and made little conversation, just lit cigarettes whose orange tips glowed luminescent in the darkness. In one corner of the depot, stallholders huddled through the night selling unsavoury-looking objects on sticks, fruit, nuts and water. They didn't speak much either. There was something strangely sinister about the place (dank, silent and dark, location unknown) that suggested a sleeper-bus purgatory, a place out of this world where those vehicles whose flesh had finally crumbled sat and expiated their manifold sins – the brutal tenderizing of passengers' flesh, taking too gleeful pleasure in their pain, perhaps. It was almost as if that terrified shriek from the driver's lips really had indicated our collective demise, and this was what lay beyond.

I forced myself from my bunk and out into the cold night air. I limped to the washrooms; it seemed foolish not to make use of the opportunity. Then I returned to the bus and lay back down on the impossibly narrow bunk. And waited.

We stayed there for about an hour; the driver, presumably, was living it up with his buddies in the canteen. They were probably shouting and laughing as they slurped their noodles. The bus park, however, was silent except for the ceaseless thrum of diesel engines and the shrill, cutting cries of a woman who strode around with a megaphone directing drivers to their bays. When each bus had successfully parked, she would climb up the steps into the gangway and bark out some kind of information to the groggy passengers. I couldn't understand what she said, but presumably it went something like: 'Good morning, passengers. It is two a.m. and you have arrived safely in hell. You will not leave here for a seemingly interminable time, because Driver Number One is hungry, and Driver Number Two appears to have died. You will therefore lie here in the darkness and contemplate your bruises in a silence punctuated only by my own gloriously amplified screeching. Please make sure you have stowed your bodies securely in the overhead bunks. Have a nice night.'

Finally, the first driver returned, shook the second driver who was still snoring, and they changed places. I didn't sleep much for the rest of the journey. The road surface was unspeakably bad – perhaps it was under construction and we had been diverted via yet another dirt track. Whatever the reason, we hurtled over holes and leapt from the crests of little jumps that seemed to have been laid out solely to test the resilience of our bones.

When we arrived in Kunming at seven-thirty the following morning, I felt as grey as those silent silhouettes who had shuffled through the bus depot. It wasn't just the lack of sleep. Eleven and a half hours of heavy battering had left my insides shaken and my flesh a pulp. I went to my hotel and climbed straight into bed.

A couple of hours later, feeling not much better, I decided I ought to go out and take a look at the city. I hadn't seen much of the place that night I'd spent between planes on the way to Zhongdian; I'd arrived late, left early and purposely stayed in a hotel within spitting distance of the airport. Now I had a few days here, while I tried yet again to sort out a flight to Jinghong. Hopefully, from here, the capital city of the province, flights should be easier to come by. In the meantime, I had plenty of time to check out the town.

Kunming seemed a pleasant place. The little green men at pedestrian crossings here didn't gallop like those in Nanjing, nor march like their less frantic counterparts elsewhere. These were so relaxed that they performed a kind of dope-induced backward moonwalk. Their wavering arms extended outwards, and their front legs rose and fell like slow-motion cyclists in reverse.

Wide, clean boulevards flanked by department stores contrasted with higgledy-piggledy backstreets whose creaking timber buildings were curved and warped with time. Occasionally, elegant stone carvings lay below the eaves. In the bird market the high-pitched chirruping of thousands of birds rose up in a deafening clamour; cage upon cage of brightly coloured plumes created a riot of colour. I wondered if somebody might have dyed the birds, like that poor dog in Suzhou which had had its ears and tail coloured pink.

I came upon a huge flower market under a permanent awning where aisle after aisle was packed with blossoms of every imaginable hue. There were pink, yellow, white and orange lilies, roses, gerberas, carnations and endless others that together filled the air with a heady perfume.

I browsed through some tea shops as Yunnan is famous for its tea. In one I bought a selection of tiny crackle-glazed cups. In another I sat at a low, carved table and sampled the leaves from two or three of the barrels. A shop attendant – a refined urbanite with unblemished skin the colour of a fine jasmine infusion – sat opposite me. She boiled the water and poured it over leaves in one brown, clay pot, then ceremonially tipped the liquid into another pot, then into tiny cups. But this was just the first brew, and not good enough to taste, so she tipped it away and poured more. Finally, after much tipping and pouring, she served the tea into two tiny, white thimbles, one for her and one for me, and together we drank. In the background flowed the gentle strumming of *erhu* chords.

Feeling somewhat soothed, I strolled down to the Muslim quarter for lunch. There are twenty million Muslims in China. Some descend from traders who settled in the southern trading ports and along the Silk Road; others, the Uyghurs of Turkic descent, moved into the north-west Xinjiang region during the Tang dynasty. Racks of lamb carcasses hung outside shops; men in white skullcaps barbecued kebabs, stirred great vats of noodles and kneaded the dough for flat breads. Tiny shops sold Arabic calligraphy and paintings of

Mecca. The sweet smell of one huge fruit shop seeped into the street outside; inside heaps of pomelos lay alongside oranges and pineapples. I stopped at a tiny hole-in-the-wall and sat at a makeshift table behind a grill while the restaurant owner served me succulent, piping-hot kebabs spiced with chilli and herbs.

At the end of the street lay the Yunnan Provincial Museum. I'd been into quite a few Chinese museums by now and was beginning to form the opinion that they were all very much the same. With the occasional exception, such as the brilliant Shanghai Museum, they were cold, cheerless buildings with dim, un-welcoming foyers and dusty staircases. They seemed usually to be entirely unpopulated apart from a solitary fossilized creature who sat near the door behind a glass cabinet containing faded, dog-eared brochures. Each establishment seemed to have one room dedicated to porcelain, one to bronze, and a display of calligraphy or old coins or ethnic minority clothing. This particular place also had rather a meagre exhibition of Buddhist art. There were very few items on display – four or five old carved frescoes, a few headless clay torsos and a couple of decapitated heads that looked remarkably similar to the limbless, headless bits of statue I'd seen elsewhere. It would be a good idea, I should have thought, if all the museums in China staged some kind of co-operative body parts fair. Who knows, they might find that the head in Kunming matched the torso in Chengdu, and that Hefei had the arms and legs. They could spend a good couple of days engaged in macabre bartering – 'My right leg for your left arm' – and perhaps piece some of these statues together.

I went for a swim that evening; it seemed a shame not to take advantage of the one night I was staying in a hotel with a pool. Anyway, it seemed appropriate to swim at least once in China. The Chinese are fond of the sport, though their prominence at international sporting events has in recent years been marred by drugs scandals. Mao Zedong was a keen swimmer: he had a heated, Olympic-length pool built at Zhongnanhai, the compound next to the Forbidden City where he lived in a seventeenth-century Qing palace. Over the years, most of the luxurious residences across the country that had been set aside for Mao were similarly equipped. Mao spent much of his time lounging by the pool, reading and working. Among his aides, the words 'swimming pool' were synonymous with the Chairman. 'You're wanted at the swimming pool,' was the summons Li Zhisui first received before being ushered into Mao's presence to be appointed as his personal physician.

Once, when he was feeling particularly annoyed with Russia, Mao even held a meeting with Khrushchev in his swimming pool. The incident followed a disagreement between the two Communist powers regarding the building of a Chinese navy. The Chinese had asked the Russians for assistance; the Soviet ambassador Yudin had responded that his country would contribute but would assume overall command. Mao was furious; Khrushchev flew to Beijing to backtrack. Harrison Salisbury describes the incident in his book *The New Emperors*:

> Mao decreed that the parties would meet at his swimming pool. In fact, not 'at' but 'in' the pool. Khrushchev had never swum in his life. He was fitted out with a pair of baggy green trunks and a bulky life preserver. Mao, his boxer swimming trunks comfortably enfolding his well-developed

belly, swam about like an elderly porpoise, propelling himself with a powerful sidestroke. Khrushchev was led into the water and floundered helplessly in the wake of the Chinese leader. Interpreters scurried around the rim of the pool, trying to convey Mao's husky Hunanese to Khrushchev without tumbling in themselves. Khrushchev spouted his Ukrainian-accented responses through gulps of water . . . Finally Mao relented and permitted the sodden Khrushchev to follow him to a wooden shed beside the pool.

I slept for twelve hours that night but none the less woke up exhausted. I'd been in China for just over six weeks now and a deep-rooted fatigue was boring through me. I had spent a day longer than I'd needed to in Lijiang to recuperate, but one bad night on a bus had sent me plummeting back to square one. It wasn't lack of sleep; except for those nights in trains and buses, I was sleeping like the dead. It was the continual alertness, the constant requirement to address new situations. It seemed feeble, really, that I should be quite this taxed by a few weeks on the road. Perhaps, I considered, the problem was that I had a very unfit brain, one that collapsed panting at the merest glimpse of having to think and adapt. Maybe my nervous system lacked the flexibility and endurance required for China, just as my limbs had failed at kung fu. Perhaps, before my next trip, I mused, I should attempt to increase my mental agility through assiduous practice of crosswords and chess.

In the meantime I tried to shake myself into some form of life and went out to the Bamboo Temple, twelve kilometres from Kunming. The temple dates back to the Tang dynasty but, during one of China's many periods of upheaval, was burned down and subsequently restored. The story of the temple's genesis relates that two brothers of royal lineage were out hunting one day when they saw a rhinoceros. They gave chase to this extraordinary beast, but lost sight of it and found instead a monk; when they drew close, the monk planted his walking stick in the ground and vanished. When they returned the next day, the walking stick had sprouted into a bamboo grove. The brothers understood the message: this was a holy spot and they must build a temple here.

The most interesting figures here, though, were not the temple's founders but the five hundred life-size Buddhist arhats, or enlightened ones, who were created by Sichuan master sculptor Li Guangxiu and his students at the end of the nineteenth century. These figures were in their day so mould-breaking as to be scandalous. Unusually for Buddhist sculptures, they were modelled on human life with all its hopes and pleasures, hardships and imperfections. Each of the five hundred sculptures was unique and shouted its own character. One bleary-eyed monk rode a mule, his unshaven jowls sagging below his half-open mouth. Some were fat; they sat sprawled, their robes asunder and their flesh billowed in capacious folds. Others were so skinny that their ribs poked through. One was pious, another was sad, another rolled his eyes in terror. They were sick and healthy, amused and sad. One figure lasciviously ate a luscious piece of fruit, another fought with a fearless warrior's bravado, his left leg drawn up, his right out straight as he leapt from the wall delivering a mighty kung fu chop.

In the main temple the principal sculptures formed an extraordinary collage on the walls, either side of a seated gold Buddha. Surfing great three-dimensional waves, these characters leapt, screamed, kicked and lunged from the brickwork. They were incredibly vibrant, astonishingly realistic in their depiction of the human condition – and yet surrealistic as well, decades before the 'real' surrealists started delving into their subconscious on the other side of the globe. The monks rode mythical beasts; they surfed on the backs of crabs, sharks, turtles and an array of brightly coloured, bulging-eyed fish. One flew astride a pink bird with flowing tail feathers.

It was all too way out for Li Guangxiu's contemporaries. They didn't approve at all and, shortly after these astonishing pieces were completed, the sculptor disappeared off the face of the earth.

I moved on to see the remainder of the sculptures that were housed in two rooms flanking the gateway to the temple. Here, a couple of hundred of these ancient figures leapt with vigour on dusty shelves behind dirty glass. Angry and pious, tidy and dishevelled, exuberant and weeping, they silently enacted their colourful, characterful stories of life on earth.

An old woman sat woodenly on a chair by the door. Her hands were folded in her lap. She seemed to be sleeping. Perhaps deceased. It could have been rigor mortis.

19

A Dog's Dinner

And then I seemed to be in Thailand. The weather was hot, palm trees flanked the streets, wooden houses stood on stilts and women wore conical straw hats as they cycled slowly down the red-dirt lanes. Yet, remarkably, this was still Yunnan, the same Chinese province that enveloped Zhongdian on the Tibetan border, Lijiang and Kunming. This was the southern Xinshuangbanna region. Bordering Burma and Laos, it is inhabited by the Dai people who are of the same ethnic group as the Thai, and it has a very different vibe to other parts of China. The bus journey here was supposed to take anything from twenty to twenty-five hours. Given the state I'd been in after less than twelve hours on the bus to Kunming, I had flown.

The taxi driver who took me from Jinghong airport into town was immensely friendly – perhaps because he was charging me several times the usual fare – and spoke to me in slow, clear Mandarin. We almost managed a conversation about the weather. ('Is it cold in Kunming?' . . . 'Here it is hot') and we established that I was from England, which elicited an enthusiastic thumbs up and the response, '*Yingguo hau.*' England good.

Jinghong seemed pretty good too. It was, as the taxi driver had said, gloriously hot and I was delighted to find that my hotel, which I had selected solely because it was cheap, had a fabulous outdoor swimming pool and poolside bar. Both were deserted. I changed into my shorts and wandered to a nearby Thai restaurant where I ate chicken and vegetables in coconut milk with jasmine rice and a spicy green papaya salad. At the table next door, ten Chinese men were enjoying a long, alcohol-fuelled lunch.

'*Ganbei!*' they chorused as each downed a small glass of a very noxious-looking clear liquid, then winced as though it were a bitter medicine.

'*Ganbei!*' They did it again.

Two of the men had turned a livid, purplish colour; their eyes were bloodshot and red. One of the two soon stood up, staggered away from the table and bid his slurred farewell. The Dai waitress smiled pityingly.

After lunch, I took a tour of the town. I wanted to find a guide who would take me trekking in the jungle for a few days. I'd heard that Jinghong's tourist trade was booming; I'd rather expected to be bombarded by guides touting treks the minute I set foot in town. I'd thought I would be able casually to pick the person I liked best. Unfortunately, this didn't seem to be the case. On the contrary, it was beginning to look as though I might have to put in some legwork and hunt a guide out for myself.

I very soon became lost in Jinghong. It was a small town, whose characterless boxy buildings blared of Chinese expansion behind the palm trees. Strangely, though, I couldn't find any of the roads along which I wandered on my map. I walked and walked. This place seemed a lot larger than I had assumed – and clearly I was in the wrong part of it. Then I came to a roundabout with a park on one side and a large post office branch on the other. These landmarks corresponded exactly to the big roundabout on my map; surely there couldn't be two with parks and post offices in exactly the same spots? No, I decided, it was the same roundabout. It was just that somebody had come along and changed the names of all the streets.

After I had made this momentous discovery, navigating my way around Jinghong became very much easier. I finally tracked down the one 'traveller's street' which was home to two or three cafés and a couple of seedy-looking guesthouses. It was a dusty, dilapidated place.

'Dorm beds on 3rd floor, 12 yuan,' a faded, painted board advertised. The building was a precisely rectangular, concrete block. It was very grey. The second floor had been gutted. Inside lay heaps of crumbling brick; plaster hung from the decimated walls. The third floor appeared to be lined with ashen, spartan cells.

'Bamboo huts, Dai style,' proclaimed another signboard. Next to it an arrow pointed down a dingy alleyway that screamed of mangy cats, fat rats and plump, lazy cockroaches.

I climbed the stairs into the Mekong Café on the first floor of a wooden building. It was a simple place with a concrete floor, wooden tables and bamboo lampshades, but it was amenable. A Dai woman with soft, brown muscovado skin and dark round eyes like plump dates brought me a freshly squeezed pineapple juice which I drank to the background music of eighties anthems. At least it made a change from *erhu* and Boney M. I was the only person in here. I wondered where all those booming tourists were hanging out; it wasn't here.

I asked the girl in the café if she knew of any trekking guides. Yes, she said, she would telephone her at once. She came back from the telephone: I was to meet the guide here in the café at eight o'clock tomorrow night. All being well, we could leave for the jungle the first thing the following morning.

Back in my hotel room, the telephone rang at twelve minutes past nine. I picked up; the line went dead. We were back to this again. I looked sadly at my bed. The joy of climbing between the covers, snuggling up and falling to sleep would be shattered by the grimy reality of what so many Chinese men must have paid for there. In the bathroom, the usual lotions sat alongside the shampoo and the shower cap. And then, above the kettle and the small pot of green tea bags, I spotted two small, square boxes.

'Healthy and antiseptis [sic] pants common size,' pronounced the black lettering on the box. 'Condom-inclosed.' On the front of the box a man modelled the garment, thrusting forward his hale and hearty genitalia for the camera.

'UNCOMPLIMENTARY – 30 yuan,' proclaimed the box.

Feeling that there must be at least a couple of men I knew whose wardrobes were incomplete without such an item, I gathered up the boxes and stuffed them into my rucksack. I fully intended to pay for them. In the juvenile state to which my mood had descended after so many weeks of solitude, I was rather looking forward to the exchange when I checked out.

'Have you taken anything from the minibar?' the girl on reception would ask.

'No,' I would say and then add very earnestly, 'but I

have taken two pairs of uncomplimentary, healthy and antiseptic underpants.'

But to my great disappointment, when the time came to leave I forgot and unwittingly I stole them.

Given that I wasn't meeting my guide-to-be until eight p.m. the following evening, I had a whole day to while away. At one of the travellers' cafés, I hired a bicycle and headed out to the jungle villages just outside Jinghong.

The road out of town soon turned to a dirt track and the square, breeze-blocked houses gave way to Dai villages whose houses teetered on red-brick stilts. Their pitched, slate roofs stretched long and low. I cycled along the track until I came to a rickety bamboo bridge that hung in a wobbly way over the Mekong. Three or four Dai people squatted on low stools under an awning at the entrance to the bridge. I paid them the requisite one yuan to cross. This was a toll bridge, Xinshuangbanna style.

I walked my bike over the bridge: it was narrow and its uneven bamboo slats suggested that I might take an unplanned dip in the Mekong if I tried to ride. On the other side the track continued for a while through a flat valley. Every tiny chink of land was planted with a rich array of fruit and vegetables: cucumbers, tomatoes, and many green stalks that I couldn't identify. They all lined up in perfect rows in their rectangular patches. In the distance the hills rose in a hazy blue light. The morning had been overcast but now the clouds were lifting and the sun was beating through the mist. Scrawny chickens clucked in consternation and hurried out of the path of my bike, running comically on their long, skinny legs.

Then the track began to climb through the hills. The

vegetation here was lush, bold and immoderate. Banana trees sprouted bright green leaves two or three metres long; their fruit curved upwards in tight waves of unripe, yellowish-green beneath.

A magnificent poinsettia tree sprang from the bank at the side of the path. It was truly enormous, a brash and riotous rush of scarlet that soared as high as a house and stretched several metres wide. It leapt irrepressibly from the rusty soil, its bright red bracts bursting uncontained in all directions. A little further on, a water lily floated motionless in an utterly tranquil irrigation pond. Lusciously plump, its bulging, shocking-pink petals reached up for the sky.

I cycled for about three hours through this land so different from the various versions of China I had seen before. Every now and then I cut through a village where children scrabbled and chickens scrounged in the dirt. Once I passed a woman leading a herd of water buffalo. A small, lone calf stopped dead and stared at me with wide, frightened orbs of eyes, then set off in a knock-kneed gallop on its spindly legs. Good Lord, I thought, can even a buffalo calf see that I look strange?

Even here, though, they were building a road. Near the point where the track turned back to Jinghong, the path widened. Every couple of minutes, a truck laden with red dirt would clunk down the hillside throwing up choking clouds of dust in its wake. This new road would link the hills with the shiny new concrete bridge that crossed the river from the town. It didn't seem to lead anywhere at all, though. It just rose up into the jungle, then stopped.

Maybe this was what Chinese men did to pass the time. Perhaps, when they squatted on the pavements with their jars of tea, their conversations ran: 'So, Old

282

Li, what are you doing next week?' Old Chang hawks, spits loudly and slurps his tea.

'Nothing much.'

'Fancy building a road?'

'A road? Heck, I *love* building roads. Where were you thinking?'

'Aw, nowhere much, just up into the jungle among the banana trees.'

There were three Dai temples on the road back to town. The Dai follow a different branch of Buddhism from the rest of China. To the north, most Chinese are Mahayana Buddhists; the Dai (along with the Burmese, the Thai, the Laotians and the Cambodians) follow the Theravada path. The main difference between the two is that the Theravada Buddhists believe that the path to enlightenment is a solitary one and Buddhas can only show the way; they emphasize monastic life. In the countries that practise this faith, temples often provide schooling for boys and nearly all will spend some period of their childhood in the monastery. The Mahayana school believes that all humankind is linked, that all existence is one, and emphasizes collective salvation over personal enlightenment. Bodhisattvas play a large role in the Mahayana system: they are enlightened beings who have given up nirvana to lead others. Tibetan Buddhism, with its emphasis on Lamaism, is a mystical strand of Mahayana Buddhism.

I stopped at the first temple. Its ornate red and gold painted buildings with their high, steeply sloping roofs made for a very different sight from the Mahayana temples I had visited elsewhere. The gleaming, glittering gold Buddhas with soaring cranial protuberances that rose in a point towards the heavens seemed different creatures altogether from the rounded Buddhas of the north. Having looked around and run the gauntlet of the souvenir shops, I sat in the shade of a tree in the temple grounds and drank a Coke. A monk in a bright orange robe and blue flip-flops sauntered by.

The following two temples were older and shabbier. A teenage monk chatted on a mobile phone outside the first; in the entrance to the second a group of boy monks played cards with childish animation. I went inside and looked at the faded frescoes that ran round the walls telling the tale of some tortured soul's rocky path to enlightenment in the days before telephones and top trumps.

We left for the jungle early the next morning. My guide, whose name was Lijuan, met me in the lobby of my hotel. She was in her mid-twenties and had learnt English working in the Mekong Café. She had had to leave school at fifteen because her father had fallen ill and her family had needed her to help support them; later, when better times smiled on her family again, she had spent a year in Beijing studying English. She brought with her one of her relatives. His name was Hao Liu or, in English, Number Six, as he was the sixth son in his family. It's quite normal for Chinese parents to number off their children in this way.

'But what about in school?' I asked Number Six. 'It's OK if you're Number Six – presumably there are fewer of you. But what about Numbers One and Two? If the teacher says, "Number Two!" there must be about fifteen boys who leap to attention.'

Number Six giggled and revealed that the boys all have regular, given names too, but these are considered excessively formal for familiar use.

The government's one-child policy wasn't always

very effective here in the boondocks, or indeed in other remote parts of China. The laws are in any case relaxed for ethnic minorities and for farming couples whose first child is a daughter because they may need a son to help work their land. Where couples go ahead and have children outside these provisions, they are heavily fined. When they can't pay the fine, the authorities routinely knock down their house or force them to leave their village. While the houses are simply constructed and families can usually rebuild them, it is more difficult for them to replace family and social structures. But whatever the punishment, I thought six sons was pushing one's luck.

Number Six was a quiet, shy boy. Perhaps he had been beaten into submission by Numbers One to Five. He looked younger than his twenty years, and was wispily effeminate with a high-pitched sing-song voice. He'd been in Jinghong for just two months; before that he lived with his family in the countryside. He was boyishly excited about the prospect of coming trekking. He had seen that the foreigners who passed through Jinghong liked to do it, and was eager to experience the treat for himself.

Lijuan, Number Six and I took a bus to our first port of call, Man Fei Long. Our fellow passengers were country folk travelling between town and village. One lugged a sack containing live chickens. From within the hessian emanated a plaintive squawking. A woman dragged a weighty sack of pig feed. On the front was a picture of an enthusiastically gobbling, bright pink pig. Its tail defied all laws of gravity, pointing upwards and spiralling with perfect symmetry so that it resembled a stick of fusilli.

Another woman carried a bicycle for a very small child. Every couple of minutes she would glance down at it – electric-blue, sparkling-new, still without a scratch beneath its protective, plastic wrapping – and her face would flush with emotional anticipation as, presumably, she imagined the euphoria of the little son or daughter who was soon to receive it.

We drove through endless paddy fields and banana trees, then through a rubber plantation where neat rows of straight trunks grew tall. Their bark was slit diagonally and a small cup tied at the bottom of the cut so that the rubbery sap could be collected drip by gummy drip.

At Man Fei Long we visited a pagoda that dated back to AD 1204. A slim golden Buddha stood with his palm facing out; a few metres away stood a statue of a Dai goddess with long flowing locks – according to legend, her hair reached down from the heavens to the earth and fed the people. Next to her, a peacock symbolizing a beautiful woman shook its tail feathers beside a sturdy elephant which, in Dai imagery, represents a strong and vigorous man.

We ate lunch in this tiny roadside town. Orange-robed monks large and small hurtled past the door on mopeds and bicycles; most Dai boys are educated in the temple from the age of six until their late teens. We sat on tiny plastic stools at a round, low table. Given that there were no hand-washing facilities, I pulled out my germ-blitzing gel. I offered a dollop to Lijuan and Number Six. Lijuan politely took a little and rubbed it into her hands. Number Six looked blatantly horrified.

'What is it?' he hissed to Lijuan in a terrified whisper.

'It's for cleaning your hands,' she replied.

Number Six shook his head with some agitation. He appeared really quite frightened by the concept.

We ate Dai barbecue – fried chicken and a kind of minced pork that was similar to sausage meat – then went to a market to buy food for our dinner. The village in which we would spend the night was very poor and we wouldn't be able to buy food from the villagers.

Lijuan selected a stallholder who stood wielding a manky chopper in front of a grimy wooden table. Personally, I didn't think his stall looked like a great choice. A single blubbery slab of pork lay before him. It consisted almost entirely of fat, which wobbled like a thick layer of pale, rubbery custard above a tiny, pink pin-stripe of meat. In the case of this pig, the expression 'lard-arse' took on a whole new meaning.

'Do you like pork?' Lijuan asked blithely, and smiled.

What? While I had been thinking, 'Good Lord, that pig should have had liposuction,' she had been eyeing it up as a tasty proposition for tea.

'Er, yes,' I replied in a spineless display of confrontation avoidance, and Lijuan started to negotiate. Almost immediately, I noticed a very funny thing. The conversation that Lijuan held with the stallholder almost perfectly mimicked the dialogue I had learned in Chinese class back in London. At the time I had thought it an exaggerated, drawn-out, rather silly conversation; now I saw that it was nothing short of vital for survival in rural China. It went something like this.

Lijuan: 'How much is this pork?'

Stallholder: 'Eight kwai for one *jin*.'

Lijuan: *(Gasps loudly.)* 'Eight kwai? That is very expensive.' *(Wrings hands for good measure.)*

Stallholder: 'Eight kwai is very cheap. Last week's pig cost ten kwai for one *jin*. (The stallholder looks Lijuan unwaveringly in the eye in the vain hope* *that this will fool her into thinking he is telling the truth.*)

Lijuan: 'I cannot possibly pay so much! I have elderly parents, fifteen hungry children, and a whole houseful of starving chickens to feed. If I part with eight kwai, I will have no money for grain and we will all perish. I will give you six kwai.'

Stallholder: '*Six kwai?* For the flesh of my finest pig? If that's all you've got, I can give you the trotters – they'd make a tasty stew.' (*The stallholder picks up his chopper, whether to lop off the trotters or to lay into us for insulting his pig, I'm not entirely sure.*)

Lijuan: 'Oh, all right. How about seven?'

Stallholder: (*Inhales through his teeth to imply hard decision making.*) 'Oh well, just this once, you're getting a bargain mind . . .'

The bus from Man Fei Long to Dongfang, where the road ran out and our walk began, was meant to leave at two o'clock. When Lijuan enquired as to its whereabouts, however, the man at the restaurant said it wouldn't depart until four. This second leg of the bus journey would take two or three hours. That meant we wouldn't even start to walk until six or seven o'clock, by which time it would be dark, and it would take us a further two hours to walk through the jungle to the village we were to stay in that night. I wondered whether Lijuan knew the way well enough to negotiate the route by night. And then I had a better idea: we could take a taxi.

Lijuan managed to negotiate the fare down to eighty yuan. The bus would have cost thirty for the three of us anyway. Entirely delighted, I paid the difference and we set off, bouncing and bumping along the truly terrible road. At one point Number Six was catapulted from the seat and hit his head on the ceiling which elicited a squeaky yelp of pain. Still, only a few brain cells shorter, we arrived at Dongfang at three-forty-five – before the bus would even have left – and we set off down the path into the jungle in glorious sunshine.

'Watch out for the bears.' Lijuan grinned a little manically. They were still roaming wild round here, apparently. 'The villagers told me, if you see a bear, stand very still, edge slowly backwards – and then *run*!' Lijuan shrieked with nervous laughter.

To take our minds off the possibility of having our skulls crushed by the powerful paw of an Asiatic black bear, I asked Lijuan about her family. Her grandmother, she said, had spent three years in jail during the Cultural Revolution: her Chairman Mao badge had fallen off and landed on the ground where a chicken had defecated on it. Somebody denounced her to the authorities and for her carelessness she was incarcerated. She talked of her mother's stories of the Great Leap Forward.

'She told me she was so hungry she had to eat the leaves from the trees.'

'Do the people still like Mao, then, given all the suffering he brought them?' I asked.

'The local people think he is a god.'

'And you?'

'I think he was half right, half wrong. I don't think he was a god.' Lijuan paused. 'I am very lucky,' she went on. 'I was born in 1979.' That was three years after Mao's death and a year after Deng came to power, abolishing the communes and allowing the peasants to profit from their labours.

'Do people still talk about what happened, or do they prefer to forget?' I asked. During my first weeks in China, I hadn't liked to delve into these questions.

It had seemed discourteous to pry too closely into these people's painful past. I had felt that to ask them to reopen the wounds inflicted by the latter decades of the Mao regime would seem excessively voyeuristic. I had thought that they wouldn't want to share such horrors with a foreigner. But now I was beginning to think that they really didn't mind. The people I had talked to were phlegmatic: it was terrible; it is past.

'Sometimes they talk about it.' Lijuan shrugged. 'One time I brought a group of people from Shanghai out here. They had all been sent here to do hard labour during the Cultural Revolution. They wanted to come back and see this place again.'

'What kind of work were they made to do?'

'Difficult work. Clearing forests and hard work they were not used to. They were city people. It was very bad for them. When I brought them back here, they cried.'

We arrived in Yakou, a village of the Akha tribe, at a little after six in the evening. This was a new village. It was built in 1999 when the three hundred inhabitants moved here from their old homes because the land was better for growing rice, and the track that led here was navigable by tractor so they had better access to the road. We walked down the tiny mud lanes, between the stilted houses with slate pitches that ran so deep the buildings seemed to be just roofs on legs.

'This is where we stay.' Lijuan pointed to a house that was slightly larger than the others. It had a state-of-the-art concrete extension. 'This is the village leader's house.'

'Are they expecting us?' I asked.

Lijuan laughed. 'No. There aren't any telephones in

the jungle. But I have been here before. I know these people.'

We climbed the steps and poked our heads round the doorway of the large, main hut. The room – dark except for the flames from the fire and the glow of one exceptionally dim bulb – was packed with old men squatting on low stools and eating. One of them leapt to his feet, came out, and talked to Lijuan. It turned out that we had come on a busy day. They were doing their village audit: the elders had gathered with three government officials to go over the accounts.

In addition, there were two men who had come about a cow – or, more precisely, three cows. They had walked that day from the next village and, in between the headman's sums, they had negotiated with him the purchase of the cows for seven hundred yuan each. The next day they would walk back with the doubtless reluctant cows to Dongfang where they would sell them at the meat market for between 730 and 750 yuan.

That didn't seem to me to constitute a very great profit. The men shook their heads. No, they said, the money wasn't good. It was much better to buy cows from Burma and bring them back over the border. The Burmese border was only five kilometres away from the village we were in now, and the cows on the other side were much, much cheaper. The problem was that if they were seen by the Burmese soldiers who patrolled the area, they would be shot for smuggling. They therefore only dared go about once a year.

With improved infrastructure in this border area, smuggling has become rife in recent years – though the importation of narcotics from the Golden Triangle bothers the Chinese government rather more than the occasional cow. Still, despite disputes about heroin and cattle, relationships between Burma and China are good. Burma was the first non-Communist country to recognize the People's Republic after the Communist victory in 1949. In return, the Chinese government has become one of Burma's chief trading partners, and their main supplier of arms. Other than a brief breakdown of relations during the 1960s, the two countries' cordiality has strengthened over the decades: China supported the military regime when it seized power in 1988 and renamed the country Myanmar, and was one of the few foreign powers that did not condemn the junta for its failure to recognize the general election victory of the democratic leader Aung San Suu Kyi in 1990.

We moved on from the perilous topic of Burmese soldiers to linguistic matters. The Dai word for a cow, the cow men said, was 'Moo'. This was because Dai cows say moo.

'English cows say moo as well,' I told Lijuan, who translated for the cow men. It was comforting to think that, were I to have an English cow handy, our cows would have been able to speak to each other even if we couldn't.

We sat on the flat roof over the new concrete extension and sipped our green tea while the accountants in the hut finished their meal. Below, along the mud track that ran between the houses, dogs and puppies of all sizes frolicked among black pigs who rooted around with their incredibly long snouts. It was as though they had been involved in a tussle with some fearsome creature, like the Elephant's Child in the *Just So Stories*, and had had their snouts painfully stretched. Chickens scrabbled in the dirt; colourful cockerels strutted and crowed. The villagers made their way home from their day in the fields; every now and then a woman would pass with the traditional black Akha headdress piled high on her crown.

The undulations of the deep green jungle hills rolled out before us. In the low, evening light, the earth was flushed with a warm amber lustre. Great, billowing banana leaves reflected the setting sun with a yellowish tinge. In the background, the hills rose and fell, gradually turning from green to ever softer hues of blue as they grew distant in the haze. Wisps of white smoke curled up from the village chimneys and blended with the evening mists. As the sun dipped lower, a glint of lucent pink gleamed along the upper edges of the clouds. The hills grew darker until just the furthest peak was lit with a shaft of dying light. The trees along its ridge climbed and dipped with the contours of the land, standing as stark silhouettes against the slowly fading, pastel-pink sky.

It was truly dark now. The cow men stood and smoked, and chatted between themselves. They were talking about me. Again, Lijuan translated.

'They are wondering what you do.' She paused for a moment. 'He is asking the other one if he thinks you know how to plant rice.'

The two men were looking at me now, and laughing uneasily. I grinned at them. Clearly they couldn't work me out at all.

'She writes books,' Lijuan told them.

'Ah!' They nodded, entirely satisfied. That seemed to them a suitably esoteric occupation for a strange-looking woman.

They debated some issue hotly between themselves for a short while, then asked, 'In your country, do you have the same sun and moon, and stars?'

It was a difficult question. Sun and moon, yes. But

293

the stars? For sure these men knew an awful lot more about them than I did.

'They're the same, but they've moved round a bit,' I said. The two men gazed up at the sky sprayed with sparkling white glitter and considered the matter, explaining their thoughts to each other with movements of their hands.

We were offered stewed dog for supper. They had killed one or two in honour of the village audit and served us the remains alongside our own unappetizing pork, vegetables and rice. I ate two small pieces: it was tough and heavily spiced. It was hard to distinguish from the meat of any other aged, skinny beast.

'Sometimes in this village they even eat rats. The people here are very poor,' Lijuan told me.

The headman's son dined with us. A bony cat slunk round the low table looking for scraps.

'Do they eat cats here, too?' I asked Lijuan. She translated.

'*Cats?*' The son looked appalled. 'No way!'

I later found out this was not because a cat was classed as any less tasty than a dog or a rat, but because cats catch mice and are therefore considered useful.

The audit continued after supper. Somebody had provided a calculator that played a jarring, tinny jingle each time the equals sign was pressed. It cut piercingly into the peaceful jungle night. The men were going to be up for some hours yet, so they gave us the headman's sons' bedrooms – tiny box-like cells in the concrete extension. As we would normally have slept in the main room with the rest of the family, we were deeply grateful.

*   *   *

The stewed dog made a reappearance at breakfast the next morning. I declined to eat any – I find seven a.m. a bad time of day for culinary experimentation – and stuck to the rice and vegetables.

We set off after breakfast towards a village of the Hani tribe (who are closely affiliated to the Akha) called Wei Dong. Lijuan was keen to try out a new route through the jungle that she had not walked along before. I expressed a fervent hope that we wouldn't get lost. We were, after all, only five kilometres from the Burmese border and I was profoundly unenthusiastic about the idea of ending my days at the wrong end of a renegade soldier's rifle. Fortunately, another of the village leader's sons – he seemed to have several – offered to show us the way, and so the four of us set off in single file along a tiny track.

The headman's son walked in the lead. He was a lean, sinewy boy, perhaps in his late teens or early twenties, with a proud, upright posture. He was dressed in camouflage trousers, army plimsolls, a white T-shirt and a khaki-coloured cotton hat embroidered with daisies. Across his body he wore a bag made from a plastic washing-powder sack. He also had a rifle slung from his shoulder.

'What's the gun for?' I asked Lijuan. I was wondering if he was intending to save us from slaughter at the hands of trigger-happy militiamen.

'It's for the bears!' Lijuan paused for a moment and looked at me with wide eyes, then pealed with laughter and added, 'Actually, I think he wants to shoot some birds for his supper.'

At a cracking pace, we marched through the jungle. For an hour and a half, the three of us almost skipped along, such was our eagerness to keep up with the headman's son. Finally, we joined the path that Lijuan knew from her previous excursions. The boy and his gun went on their way to shoot supper and we continued our own journey.

Great bushes of deep yellow flowers danced jubilantly around us and rocketed over our heads. Lijuan reckoned they were some kind of wild chrysanthemum but they bore little resemblance to the biddable blossoms I associated with that plant. These flowers were the size of my hand. The bushes were anarchically spawning, propagating to a quite indecent degree. They were rowdy, unruly and spectacularly out of control. Spotted among them were towering, tumbling poinsettias in shameless scarlet. I thought they were fabulous.

I was still thinking about our accommodation last night. The headman was clearly a powerful person. His house was the only one in the village with a concrete extension for bedrooms. All the other families would have slept together in their main huts.

'How did he get to be the headman?' I asked Lijuan.

'He was elected. All the villages elect their leaders.'

At local level, she said, Chinese society is very democratic. The villages elect their heads and these officials wield considerable power over the people's everyday lives. They even exert a strong influence over the regional government.

After a short while, we stopped at a village belonging to the Bulang tribe, the second biggest ethnic minority in this area after the Dai. They weren't very populous in this village that afternoon, though. It was a poor, downtrodden-looking place. There were no new slate roofs here, just battered, tattered thatch. The only sign of life was a very old man who squatted on the threshold of his hut weaving baskets. Beneath his jaunty brown fedora, his clothes – a threadbare brown jacket, blue T-shirt, baggy grey trousers and the ubiquitous green army plimsolls – hung from his gaunt, skeletal frame. His cheeks were sunken and skin sagged from his neck, yet he had a glint of amusement in his dark eyes and a perpetual half-smile on his lips. He was smoking a long, bamboo pipe. I wondered whether something in it was making his indubitably hard life seem somehow rosier.

Lijuan shouted a greeting to the old man and asked if we could have some tea. He beamed a welcoming smile and we clambered up onto his bamboo canopy which, like the other houses in this region, stood on stilts above ground level. The flooring was ramshackle and shaky; as I edged up the rickety old ladder I hoped I wouldn't put a foot wrong and fall right through.

The old man abandoned his basket-making and disappeared into the hut. Everyone else in the village, he explained, was out working in the fields. He reappeared a while later with three chipped bowls containing black tea. Dirt was floating visibly in the red, clear liquid. Number Six widened his eyes and refused to take so much as a sip.

'I feel embarrassed,' Lijuan told me. 'I asked him to make us tea but now it is dirty and I don't want to drink it.' She valiantly kept face and started to sip.

As for me, I'm afraid to say that I decided a few minutes' loss of face was preferable to a couple of days of wrenching stomach cramps and the accompanying loss of bowel control. And so, hoping this man knew nothing of the history of tea exportation, trade imbalances, opium wars and the like, I pretended that English people don't drink such a peculiar beverage and left the strange concoction untouched.

We trekked for only another hour or two before we

reached our destination for the night. By now, both Lijuan and Number Six had fallen rather quiet.

'My toes hurt,' whimpered Lijuan limply. 'They keep hitting the front of my shoes when we walk downhill.'

Number Six was no more cheerful. A very different figure from the exuberant boy with the melodious voice of yesterday morning, he was now sad and silent, and entirely at a loss to figure out why foreigners pay good money just to go for a walk in the woods. His legs were sore, he bleated. He quietly confided to Lijuan that he hated trekking.

Finally we arrived in the village. Our host family showed us to the balcony where we sat and drank tea, and nibbled fruit and nuts. I hoped this would revive my guides' flagging spirits.

This family's hut was divided into two rooms as is the Hani custom: men and women live and sleep in separate areas, each with their own fire. It seemed a fluid arrangement in this case, however, and most of the living seemed to be done in the women's quarters where the food and tea was to be found. Most of the family was away from home this afternoon, though. The villagers were building a new house up on the hillside and it was the custom for everybody to lend a hand.

This house-building seemed to be a well-organized affair. Construction always took precisely nine days, after a month or so of planning and preparation, and on the ninth evening a big housewarming party was held. All the houses in these villages were designed in exactly the same way, and each roof was topped by what looked like a horseshoe.

'They are horns,' Lijuan told me. 'During the Warring States period, a general captured Yunnan and the Hani people were very happy to see him. They have honoured his memory ever since by decorating their houses with the horns from his helmet.'

After our rest and refreshment, we walked a little further to bathe in a waterfall. It was good to have the opportunity to wash after a couple of days in the jungle. I even managed to convince Lijuan and Number Six of my certifiable insanity by washing my hair in the freezing cold water. Lijuan stopped at her feet and face. But the whole experience was too much for Number Six. I wore a swimming costume in an attempt not to alarm him too horribly – I was afraid that the sight of a semi-naked woman might give him nightmares for weeks – but it was not enough. Terrified of the prospect of seeing women even partially unclad, he refused to come near and sat on a rock round the corner. When we returned to collect him, he had fallen asleep.

There was a small puppy in the house where we stayed. According to the family, it was just four weeks old. With its velvety tan fur, its little tail that waggled when it walked and silken ears that flopped forward onto its face, it was a winsome creature. The family was obviously fond of it. As the evening grew cooler, the woman of the house picked it up and put it by the fire to keep it warm. When the youngest boy in the family, aged about six, came to sit by the fire he took the puppy on his lap and petted it. The mother and father dogs padded round the fire and joined the family gathering.

'Will you eat that dog when it's older?' I asked. Really, I was joking. I was being very naïve.

The oldest son had just come in from a hard day's house-building. He looked astonished. 'Of course!' he replied. He seemed staggered that anyone could ask such a silly question.

'There were five puppies, but the other four died,' said the woman. The family collectively looked sad. I wasn't sure whether they were sorry because they liked the puppies or because a good supply of food had expired. It was probably both. These people were, after all, fond of their dogs, and their habit of eating them when they grew old was a simple practicality in this poor land where in recent decades millions had starved to death.

'Some Hani people eat snakes.' The grandmother picked up the conversation. She was a hunched little woman with the posture of a garden gnome. She was approximately the same size, too.

The eldest son shuddered and muttered. He didn't seem to be a great fan.

'The Hani people are very superstitious,' Lijuan explained as she translated. 'They believe that snakes can understand human language and that it is bad luck to eat them.'

'About ten years ago, three men in our village found a really big snake,' the grandmother went on with a grave expression. 'They killed it and ate it. Immediately, they were all rendered mute and were completely paralysed. They never spoke again.'

'Are they still alive?' I asked.

'No. One died about two years afterwards, the next soon after – but the last one didn't die till last year.'

We were sitting on stools round the fire. All the family members nodded in solemn agreement. If this happened only ten years ago, all the adults present must have been able to remember the men and the incident clearly. It was hardly an apocryphal tale.

'Do you believe her?' Lijuan asked me. She was clearly used to Westerners and our cynicism.

I shrugged. 'They seem pretty sure.'

Out of interest, when I arrived home, I emailed Graham, a doctor friend of mine who specializes in unpleasant diseases and tropical horribleness, and asked if the story sounded feasible. He replied that it was.

'In the south of China there are several species of snake with varying degrees of nastiness,' he wrote. 'These include vipers, kraits and cobras, whose victims suffer paralysis, particularly of the muscles controlling the eyelids, eye movements, palate and tongue – which might explain why they couldn't speak. It's similar to "curare" which you might have heard about – a sort of poison that South American Indians add to their spears to paralyse prey.

'The interesting question would be whether they bothered to cook the snake. My guess would be that they didn't and, I don't know for sure, but it seems reasonable that if you eat one of these things without knowing what you're doing, you save it the bother of having to bite you (a somewhat pyrrhic victory for the snake, I grant you).'

Little wonder the villagers were superstitious.

We only walked for three hours the next morning, along a well-defined track to a dusty, decrepit town from where we would take a bus back to Jinghong. It was a horrible, shabby, one-street place. All the restaurants seemed closed and the bus wouldn't leave for another two and a half hours. I was keen to leave immediately: in Jinghong there was pizza, beer and massage, but in this humdrum hole there were no private vehicles that could even be bribed to take us.

In a roadside shack, we managed to buy some noodles – thin, white, wiry specimens that suggested intestinal worms drowning in an anaemic soup. Then

301

we sat and waited. The bus appeared. I took a seat; Lijuan and Number Six settled themselves in the row behind me. We were determined to stake out our territory early – this bus would doubtless be full, as Chinese country buses always were, and we didn't want to sit in the aisle.

An old man with a bamboo broom climbed on and swept away the crunchy carpet of sunflower seed husks that the previous incumbents had thrown down. We sat and waited some more.

It was forty-eight kilometres to the main road; when, finally, the bus croaked into action, it took us three hours to cover them. We trundled painfully down a bumpy dirt track stopping at every round-shouldered slump of a village on the way.

It was truly remote out here. Every now and then, we would pass women in conical hats planting rice in the fields, or a group of men working on the roadside in straw hats with wide, floppy brims. I was tired after three days of walking and two nights sleeping on the floors of villagers' huts, but dozing off was out of the question. Several of the passengers crammed onto the seats and into the aisle had puppies with them that they must have bought in whichever villages their journeys had taken them to. One woman carried a basket containing four or five tiny, wriggling creatures with skins sleek as otters who lay entangled one with another. Another dog, slightly larger, sat on its new owner's lap and whimpered each time the bus clattered through a ditch.

'And this isn't the worst of it,' I thought morosely, looking into its doleful brown eyes. 'They've only bought you so they can turn you into stew.'

Finally, after three long hours, I saw in the distance a tiny strip of black asphalt winding like a thin lace of liquorice round a hillside in the distance. The main road! I never thought I would be so happy to see tarmac and other cars. At last, the ride was a little smoother. We travelled for a further hour, then reached a town with a station where we changed buses for Jinghong.

During the last leg of our journey, the sun began to set. In the evening light, the water of the irrigation ponds lay perfectly still, rendering on its surface an immaculate reflection of the banana trees and chrysan-themum bushes. As the sun dipped lower, for just a minute, the pinkish-orange of the sky perfectly reflected the rust-red of the earth.

20

An Awfully Long Train Ride

Back in Kunming, Christmas had been declared in my
absence. It was 2 December and, suddenly, there were
fake fir trees everywhere. From the airport I went
straight to the hotel where I had been staying a few
days ago. The woman at the travel desk had organized
my overnight train ticket to Guilin and I had arranged
to go there to pick it up. The lobby which, a few
days earlier, had been all marble and good taste, now
flaunted a choir of six-foot polystyrene angels.

The train from Kunming to Guilin would take
eighteen hours, the woman at the travel desk had told
me. As I was about to pay, it suddenly occurred to me
to double-check.

'What time does this train arrive in Guilin?' I asked
in a tone that was far too trusting.

The woman paused as she leafed through her time-
table. She was a straight, streamlined figure, almost
two-dimensional in fact. She looked as though she'd
been ironed. Her face was as featureless as freshly
rolled pastry; her body entirely lacked contours.

She found the right page. 'Two o'clock in the morning,' she said, flatly. 'On Thursday.'

Thursday? It was only Tuesday today. That wasn't eighteen hours; if the train left at ten to nine this evening as planned, that would be nearly *thirty* hours on the train.

'You told me before it was eighteen hours,' I squawked in strangled horror. Foolishly, though, I still thought the situation might be salvageable. I harboured an optimistic suspicion that there must be two trains; an express one and a second that stopped at every station. If that was the case, I could just wait a little longer in Kunming and then take the fast train tomorrow, perhaps.

The hour that followed was one of the most frustrating of all my time in China. Rather than accept that she had made a mistake, the woman opted for a face-saving but tortuous route. She decided that, instead of telling me the stark truth – that there was no alternative train – it would be much more amusing to spend an hour of her life attempting to convince me that from eight p.m. on Tuesday to two a.m. on Thursday was, as she had said, eighteen hours.

'Yes! Eighteen hours!' she trilled with confidence and apparent ease. She almost, but not quite, smiled.

I paused. Could she really not count, or was she trying to fool me?

'Nooooo,' I said very slowly and carefully. 'From eight o'clock on Tuesday night to two o'clock on Thursday morning is thirty hours.'

'No! Eighteen hours!' This time the very flat face remained impassive and unwrinkled.

I tried to repeat my point in Chinese. It didn't really matter. I didn't want to teach her maths, I merely wanted to know if there was a faster train. But she just wouldn't let go.

She made many telephone calls. I was forced to

speak to countless people on the other end who professed to speak English. Repeatedly, I asked my one simple question: was there another train? But what was the matter with this nice train, they twittered. It only took eighteen hours, after all.

The flat woman took me over to the cashier at the hotel reception; he spoke better English than she did. She explained the problem; he nodded earnestly.

'The train takes eighteen hours,' he informed me with the utmost sincerity.

'Look,' said the woman, feigning infinite patience. She took a piece of paper and a pencil. Then, with the cashier as witness, she drew out the hours from the train's departure time. Under the heading 'December 2' she wrote, '9, 10, 11, 12.' Then she scored a line and wrote a new heading 'December 3' and underneath, '1, 2, 3, 4, 5, 6, 7, 8, 9, 10, 11, 12.' Then another line and the heading 'December 4', and '1, 2.' Then very slowly, as if she were talking to a very stupid child, she counted the numerals.

'You see,' she said. 'Eighteen hours.' Her pancake face cracked to reveal a self-satisfied smile.

'*But you've missed out the whole of the afternoon!*' I jabbed my finger at the column marked 'December 3'. In contrast to her apparent calm, I was wide-eyed with astonishment and fast becoming breathless with frustration.

The woman looked confused. How was I failing to understand such a simple concept? She made some more phone calls. She handed me the receiver.

'There is another train,' said the disembodied voice on the other end. 'It takes eighteen hours.'

Hooray!

'It leaves at two a.m. in the night, and arrives at two a.m. the next night.'

'But that's not eighteen hours!' I almost screamed down the phone. 'That's twenty-four hours. *There are twenty-four hours in a day!*'

There was a short silence. 'Oh.' The voice shrugged. 'I don't know.'

The flat woman sighed heavily, took back the phone, punched some numbers and began to jabber once more. Really, her fortitude was astonishing. She was refusing to cave in. She would have been brilliant under torture. She should have applied for the SAS.

I, on the other hand, probably shouldn't. I'm not made of such stern stuff. I slumped forward, my elbows on the desk, my head in my hands. Unwittingly, I found myself making pathetic whimpering sounds. In fact, I noticed, I was making a noise alarmingly similar to that of the puppies on yesterday's bus. But the worst thing was that I was beginning to wonder: were there really twenty-four hours in a day? Why was it that every person I had spoken to agreed with the woman at the desk? I knew I was tired. Could it be me who was wrong? It was horribly unsettling.

Perhaps, on the other hand, I considered, I was an involuntary participant in some kind of bizarre social experiment in obedience. Maybe a sinister arm of the Chinese government was lurking with its cameras and bugging equipment behind a false wall, intent on discovering how long it would take to brainwash a weary, travel-worn Westerner into believing that there were, in fact, only twelve hours in a day. They could use the results to treat those poor, deluded individuals who still insisted that something nasty happened one night in Tiananmen Square, perhaps. Could it be that the six-foot polystyrene angels that had taken up residence in the lobby were merely a front, a grotesque façade for Christmas that harboured not seasonal goodwill but an occidental Stanley Milgram who was, at this very moment, muttering instructions into a radio mouthpiece to turn the dial up further and increase the pain?

And then, suddenly, unexpectedly, the ordeal was over. The woman changed her mind.

'Oh,' she said, putting down the phone. 'You are right. The train to Guilin takes thirty hours.'

But by this stage my grasp of logic had deserted me entirely. With hindsight, all I was being asked to do was to lie around in a nice, comfy bed reading and eating for a day or so. It wasn't so much to bear. But by now I had it in my head that to spend thirty hours on a train would be equivalent in terms of hardship to hopping on one leg to the North Pole, or swimming solo round the globe while harpooning my own fish for lunch.

With much the same level of reasoning that persuaded Van Gogh he'd look cute with just one ear, or convinced Mao that green was a good colour for teeth, I suddenly decided that I would not, after all, go to Guilin. I'd go instead, I thought, to Guiyang, the capital of Guizhou province. Geographically, that was a little more than halfway to Guilin. I had read in my guidebook that there was a morning train from there to Guilin that took three or four hours. That meant I would arrive there late Wednesday morning instead of the early hours of Thursday. Deep down, I knew this couldn't be right. The distance was too great; the guidebook had to be wrong. But the rational part of my brain was no longer working: where once thoughts had ticked over, cool and collected, grey matter now seethed in a bubbling cesspit of overboiled gunk.

*   *   *

I travelled soft sleeper to Guiyang. It was the first time I had upgraded myself to such dizzy heights. Everyone I had talked to about Chinese trains had concurred that it wasn't worth the extra money. Soft sleeper, they said, was no better than hard. It was full of fat Chinese businessmen and, they reckoned, it might not be a good idea for a single woman to travel alone with such creatures in a small cabin with a locked door. But tonight the man-eating glare in my eye was such that no-one with a modicum of self-preservation instinct would have dared come near.

In any case, I soon came to disagree wholeheartedly with those worldy-wise sages who favoured hard sleeper. The soft bed was no softer – in fact, it was almost identical – but there were two vital features that made shelling out the extra cash worthwhile. First, the cabin was quiet. There were no dribbling noodle-slurpers, no children playing with toys that played tunes, no groups of hawking, squawking, card-slamming men.

Secondly, in soft sleeper I was allowed to control my own personal light switch. This meant that I could lie in my bed and read when the mood took me and, better still, I didn't have to wake up at five a.m. when the powers that be decided it was time to rise and make one's face shine through vigorous scrubbing. On the down side, there was an annoying PA system in the cabin which rattled out a blend of reedy Chinese flute music and the twangings of a tremulous *erhu* interspersed with frequent information announcements. Happily, I couldn't understand them.

I shared my cabin with three Chinese men. They dressed for the night, attiring themselves in the ubiquitous long johns and T-shirts. They then made a great display of slouching around the cabin, their capacious, dimpled bellies sagging like old cushions whose stuffing has slipped, their legs splayed wide. The man in the upper berth opposite mine wore slightly stained, pale green Y-fronts. He read his book lying on his side with his back to me. His underwear, I noticed, had a slit down the back which reached right round, so he never had to take down his pants whichever way he wished to relieve himself. Repeatedly, he scratched his bare buttocks through the slit. I closed my eyes, turned off my light, and settled down for an early night.

We arrived at Guiyang at eight the next morning. I made straight for the ticket office, hoping to catch an express connection straight to Guilin.

The queue was, more accurately, a brawl. A surging mass of highly agitated humanity pressed down on the ticket window. Once near the front, the idea was to cram one's hand under the glass – alongside ten or so other hands – and proffer one's money while screeching a destination. But I didn't know how much money to clasp or what to yell. God help me, I needed to ask a question. When was the next train to Guilin? How long would it take?

I planted myself robustly in the line, Mandarin phrase book in one hand, money in the other. For good measure, I then swung around a little with my rucksack and rather ungenerously bashed a few prospective queue-jumpers on the head. There was uproar. Ten or twenty enraged Chinese started to scream at me. I stood stoically in their way, protecting my spot in the queue, refusing to allow them to barge past. By the time I reached the counter, there was a small riot in the ticket hall.

'*Ni hao.*' I smiled benignly at the woman behind the counter, trying to pretend that the rumpus behind had nothing to do with me. 'Could you tell me, when is the next train to Guilin?'

They were kind and wise people in the station; given the pandemonium breaking out in my wake, they opened a new window especially for me. Therefore I bought my ticket for Guilin in relative calm. The train was due to depart in half an hour and would arrive at – I could have guessed it – two a.m. the following morning.

I fought through the waiting hall and boarded my train. I battled with the carriage attendant to change my ticket – I had asked for soft sleeper and had been given hard. I survived near heart failure induced by the man in the next carriage who insisted that I had boarded the wrong train. And then, finally, I reached my cabin.

By some extraordinary stroke of luck, I had a four-berth compartment to myself. I shut and locked the door, huddled on the bed with my knees up to my chin, and wrapped the duvet around me. That one last fight had almost finished me. I was feeling horribly overwrought, desperately harassed. The PA system was jangling with some *erhu* number. And then it faded out and through some truly surreal twist of humour, a string of strangely familiar notes tinkled out. It was *The Jungle Book*'s 'Bare Necessities'. I laughed for about five seconds, then all the pent-up frustrations of the last day surged to the surface and, in a sudden and unexpected release of tension, I burst into tears.

It turned out to be an exceedingly pleasant day. All I had to do was lounge around my private cabin snoozing, reading and writing. Many hours of enforced idleness were exactly what I needed right then. I

312

wandered down the corridor to the end of the carriage, holding the empty railway thermos. The carriage attendant leapt up from her place and filled it with hot water. She seemed to have singled me out as needy of kindness. I hoped she hadn't seen me cry.

Back in my compartment, I broke into the pretty pot of jasmine tea that I had bought as a gift for someone else. I drank many cups of the pale yellow infusion, watching with pleasure as the tiny, tightly curled balls of jasmine swelled and branched outwards, filling the bottom of my cup with its own underwater world.

I had bought two large pizzas in Kunming to eat on the journey. They were now cold and rather battered, of course, but none the less fabulously tasty and comfortingly doughy. Between snoozes, I'd rip off another chunk of pizza, and chase it down with a couple of tangerines. For several hours, I just sat and stared out of the window, gazing at China passing by – mile after mile of cabbage patches and brown hills, and rundown shacks the mere thought of living in which made me shudder.

Every now and then, a dilapidated and frightening-looking factory would scar the landscape. Beside the concrete blocks with smashed windows that surely should have been abandoned decades ago, chimneys belched thick smoke whose waste painted the surrounding countryside a scorched, lifeless white.

As we crossed the border from Guizhou into Guangxi province, the hills started to rise into more interesting shapes and high domes, then as we headed south the land flattened once more. It was a hazy day, with the sun trying hard to break through the clouds. As we drew away from each town and trundled further into the countryside, the sky became a clear, watery blue and the horizon grew more distant.

It was a relaxing scene, and I thought I might augment my newfound sense of well-being by ambling gently to the restaurant car and buying a beer. I looked at my watch; it was ten to six.

'Ah.' The involuntary thought crept up on me. 'Better give it another ten minutes.' And then I thought, 'What?' Here I was, juddering through the middle of nowhere on a Chinese train. I had been travelling, on this train and the last, for nearly twenty-three hours. And yet that very peculiar, strangely British piece of cultural baggage had followed me all the way here, that odd element of our etiquette that says if you drink before six p.m., you'll slide irretrievably into the gutter. I took a firm stand against such nonsense, strode directly to the restaurant car and bought my beer at five minutes to.

21

Reaching a Peak – or Two

'POLOY EVANS.' The driver's placard stood firm among a gaggle of touts as I battled my way out of the station.

From the train, I'd phoned my hotel in Yangshuo – sixty-five kilometres south of Guilin – and asked them to send a driver. It was an extravagance, but in my current state of mind I didn't fancy hanging round the station till the buses fired up at six.

The car picked me up exactly as planned. Within a couple of minutes, we were roaring out of Guilin and through the limestone peaks that have over the centuries brought poets, artists and, latterly, tourists to the area. The driver was a brisk character who seemed keen not to be kept from his bed a minute longer than was absolutely necessary. He slammed his foot down hard and we careered along the straight, empty road. We were at the hotel in Yangshuo by two-forty-five. I checked in, took a bath, and was tucked blissfully into bed by a quarter past three.

The fact that my room looked out over a stagnant pond filled with scum and rubbish against a backdrop of the bus station was not representative of Yangshuo.

The small town, nestled among towering karst spires, is really an incredibly pretty place. The gradual erosion of these soluble limestone hills has created remarkable formations that loom in the mist. Some seem to rise vertically upwards, others descend in series of ever-diminishing cones. Beneath them, on the river, cormorant fishermen with simple wooden boats send their birds after the catch as they have for centuries.

Nowadays, the farmers and the fishermen are outnumbered by those plying the tourist trade. Yangshuo was one of the first places in China that catered to the foreign backpacker market; even today, there are very few such centres in the country. On the pedestrianized main street, cafés selling banana pancakes, offering internet access, and showing English-language videos on cranky television sets elbow for space among souvenir stalls, clothes shops, and cut-price CDs. On my first day there, I did little more than saunter between them with a sense of relief verging on euphoria. I drank coffee, sent emails, and wandered round the tiny market that fronts the river.

I met up with Annie the following morning. Annie is the guide that Guy and Nancy employ to show their Imperial Tours guests round the area. She had offered to take me to her village, ten kilometres out of Yangshuo, where her family owned kumquat orchards and a tea plantation.

'Would you like to go on my moped, or by bicycle, or walk?' Annie asked. I opted to walk. It was only ten kilometres, after all, and after several days' travelling it would be pleasant to stroll for a couple of hours among the karst pinnacles.

We headed out of town via a market where Annie bought a bag of tangerines to sustain us on our journey.

It was a hazy day and the hills were enveloped in mist but as we hiked up the dirt road that led to the village we were granted idyllic views of the distant peaks silhouetted softly in the milky light. We passed countless paddy fields, brown at this time of year as the rice here had been harvested just a month or two earlier, in October. In Guangxi farmers manage to eke two rice harvests per year from their crop, in June and October, whereas in the colder north they can only raise one crop annually. (Further south still, on Hainan Island, the people enjoy a bumper three harvests each year.)

We climbed higher. Now the hills were dotted with speckles of tiny bright orange kumquats, the sweet, diminutive oranges native to China.

'Kumquats are the main form of agriculture in this area, with pomelos,' Annie told me. 'When I was younger, I used to carry my family's kumquats from the village to the market in Yangshuo.'

'That's a long way,' I remarked. 'How many kumquats did you carry in one go?'

'Fifty or fifty-five kilos.' Annie laughed at my astounded expression. That was equivalent to her carrying *me* (less an arm or a leg) for ten kilometres – and she was at least a head smaller than I was. 'I carried them in two baskets on either end of a bamboo pole that sat on my shoulder.'

She paused for a moment and then added, more seriously now, 'I am lucky. I escaped.'

Since those days, Annie has stopped walking and has found other means to move up in the world. She talked of her investments in kumquat fields and in her brother's tea-growing business. She wore good clothes and had just finished building her own house. Two months previously, she had bought a brand-new moped. Motorized transport had taken its toll on her fitness. At the two-kilometre marker, she started to complain – her feet hurt, her back ached. My heart sank. We had another eight kilometres to go.

Annie told me about her son. He was four, but spent each week from Monday to Friday living with her brother who ran a kindergarten a few kilometres outside Yangshuo. She was divorced and seemed to have a low opinion of men.

'Is it easy to divorce in China?' I asked.

'Yes, very easy.' Annie shrugged. 'If both people agree, you just go to the notary and sign the piece of paper. It only takes an hour or two.'

Now Annie had a new boyfriend. He was twenty; she was thirty-five. His family, she said, was very unhappy that their only son was dating a thirty-five-year-old divorcée with a child.

We finally arrived in the village after two and a half hours; since the eight-kilometre post, Annie had stopped grumbling about either miles or men and had taken to laughing hysterically instead. We walked down a tiny path among pomelo trees towards her house. It was a large building.

'I have three brothers!' Annie exclaimed in explanation. But even given that her parents were sharing the house with her brothers' families, the house was spacious by rural Chinese standards. We walked through the forecourt where chickens pecked and into the downstairs room that adjoined the kitchen.

Annie introduced me to her mother, a small, smiley woman. The room was bare concrete with no decoration other than two rough calligraphy posters that were taped to the walls. The only furniture was a small dining table and a sideboard; against the walls, heaps of farming equipment sat waiting for use. No interior design shop would make much money out here, I mused, if even the affluent families had no desire to ornament their homes with anything more than a pile of old machinery.

Annie's mother had prepared lunch for us. A fabulous array of dishes covered the entire surface of the table: pork liver, fried chicken, vegetables with tofu, and minced pork balls fried with tofu and water chestnuts. We ate well, Annie's mother pressing ever more food upon me. Beaming, she fished around in the bowl with her chopsticks and selected for me the choicest of the plump, sweet water chestnuts; when I pronounced them delicious her smile grew broad and the soft, wrinkled skin round her eyes crinkled into a hundred tiny tributaries. We drank tea, delicate and refreshing, that had been grown on the family estate and then, when we really could eat no more, we went out into the fields to survey the family's land.

We had to hike across a long hillside of orchards before we reached Annie's parents' domain; every family in the village farmed kumquats, she explained, as we picked our way between the trees laden with the tiny ripe orange globes. The branches were covered in white plastic sheeting to keep off the rain which would rot the fruit. Walking among them, it seemed as though we were exploring a never-ending, fruit-filled tent. Finally we arrived in her parents' orchards and found her father hard at work watering the trees and feeding the chickens that lived in a coop on the upper reaches of the hillside.

Leaving Annie's mother behind, we thanked her for lunch and proceeded to clamber higher over the mountainside. Soon the spotted landscape of kumquats gave way to orderly stripes of green tea hedges that snaked round and round the conical, rising hills. The bushes were flat on top. Pruning encouraged the spring growth that would be harvested and dried to make tea for drinking, Annie told me. As we reached the top and walked along the wide path between the bushes, the peaks and troughs of the tea-covered hills stretched far into the distance.

Annie didn't want to walk back to Yangshuo – in fact, she declared that she was never going to walk along that dirt track ever again, as long as she lived – so she phoned her brother from the tea factory and asked him to send some transport in the form of two boys with mopeds. It was already five-thirty in the afternoon; it would soon be dusk and I was wary about weaving our way in the dark with no helmets down that rutted, rocky road, among the farm vehicles without lights and the lumbering water buffalo. I suggested that we might therefore leave sooner rather than later and not spend too much time sampling tea in the upstairs room of the factory.

'You are afraid of riding in the dark?' Annie asked.

I kept my answer simple. 'Yes.'

We managed most of the journey in daylight. Farm workers made their way home, crammed into the back of clattering trucks and tractors. Others wandered home on foot along the dusky red road. Boys led their water buffalo down to the paddy fields for their evening bathe in the irrigation ponds. With their heads craned forward on the water's surface, the buffaloes' smoothly curved horns rested against the skin of their necks. They wallowed there, silent and perfectly still, their huge grey humps rising up from the cool, brown water.

As if Annie's legs hadn't taken enough punishment, the next day we arranged to go cycling. She assured me she would be fine as cycling uses different muscles from walking. We met in the lobby of my hotel; noticeably, Annie had arrived today without her moped.

'It's broken down,' she said.

'But it's only two months old!'

'Yes, Chinese things, you know . . . Chinese factories.' Annie laughed.

This was one of the problems with the Chinese gallop into the modern age. They built everything in such a hurry that frequently they didn't do the job as well as they might, yet nobody expressed any surprise or outrage when things collapsed. That morning, in the hotel, some part of the electricity circuit had gone down. Neither my room's heating nor the dining-room toaster had worked, but nobody had batted an eyelid. They just seemed to accept that things here were shoddy and continually falling into disrepair.

We hired bicycles from a stand opposite the hotel and set off out of town. Soon we took a right turn down a tiny mud path that ran between two paddy fields. Even in that day's dull weather, the scenery was breathtaking. The karst spires soared overhead as we cycled along a tiny bridge that crossed a lake; in the distance, a lone fisherman on a small wooden boat cast his net.

Annie's hands started to hurt from the vibration of the handlebars.

'Look,' she kept saying to me, holding up her reddened palms. 'Blood!' I didn't seem to be doing much for the health and comfort of my guides on this trip: Lijuan had had painful toes, Number Six sore legs; yesterday Annie's neck, lower back and legs had hurt; today it was her hands.

Luckily, we soon passed a man selling sugar cane to give us an energy boost. He pedalled slowly down the narrow, packed-earth track on his creaking old bicycle.

On either side of the back wheel, metal panniers held the tall, skinny stalks upright, like vastly enlarged sticks of sweet seaside rock. Annie called for him to stop and bought a cane. The vendor took out a small knife with a gleaming square blade, hacked the purple branch into shorter lengths, and peeled them. We stood by the side of the path, with the karst hills receding in the background, bit off chunks of flesh and sucked out the delicious sugary sap.

We stopped for lunch at an ancient village. We wandered through a doorway where a woman washed plates at a hand-pumped well in a courtyard. In an adjacent roughshod room an older woman, her mother perhaps, was busy flipping food on a sizzling wok.

'May we have a chicken?' Annie asked.

The old woman emerged from the kitchen wiping her hands on her apron and pushing back wayward wisps of grey hair from her face. She pointed at a coop in the corner of the yard where four or five fowl were enclosed behind a wire grate.

'Which one would you like?' she asked. We had to buy a whole one; you cannot, after all, slaughter half a chicken.

Annie selected our lunch and, while the old woman's husband slew, plucked, washed and cooked it, we took a tour of the village. The houses were about two hundred years old, and none showed any sign of renovation. The ornate wooden panelling was crumbling and dull from years without polish. The rooms inside were plain and draughty like hollowed out breeze blocks. We went into one house where a young woman sat among rows of square trays. She was making bean curd. She soaked the soy beans for many hours before mashing them and pressing the pulp into its familiar, rectangular form. Annie bought some but still, as we left, an old woman tried to charge me for having entered her house. A stout, unyielding woman with an unsmiling face, she was not unlike a breeze block herself.

'We just went to buy some bean curd,' Annie remonstrated.

The woman argued for a while, then turned stonily and disappeared through a dilapidated doorway.

Unfortunately this turned out to be something of a theme of the day in these tiny villages that have so recently been beset by tourism. I was charged fifty yuan for the chicken which seemed a lot considering that it was a scrawny creature. When I commented that the price seemed steep, the old woman retorted that it was a very special chicken.

'It is free-range. It was not reared in a factory,' she declared with an entrepreneurial zeal that made me roar with laughter.

We cycled back to town via Annie's brother's kindergarten so that she could pick up her son for the weekend. I walked into the room where twenty-two three- and four-year-olds sat transfixed in front of the television. One of them saw me and turned to stare. Slowly, silently, the whole room twisted round and gaped, fixated, seemingly astonished.

'Ni hao.' I smiled and waved at them. They gave not a flicker, not a blink of an eyelid in response but continued steadily to scrutinize the unlikely creature that had entered their domain.

We cycled back along the tarmac road into town. Annie's son kept up a barrage of questions from his child seat over his mother's back wheel.

'Do frogs feel cold in winter?'

'How do hens lay eggs?'

'Who makes the hair come out of your head?'

As far as I know, he didn't ask why it was that my skin was so white and my eyes so round – but maybe Annie just chose not to translate.

I went the next day for a calligraphy class. The teacher was a kindly, gentle man, with the beginnings of grey hair sprouting round his temples. He seemed blessed with an infinite patience garnered, no doubt, from many years of trying to instil graceful expression into the brushes of clumsy students.

He laid on the table a pile of crisp, delicate sheaves. Unhurried, he went over to another table and thoughtfully selected brushes. With great care, he poured black ink from a large plastic container into a tiny round porcelain dish. His every movement seemed suffused with elegance. Perhaps the fluid style of calligraphy was something that rose up through the energy channels of one's entire body, I mused. In that case, I was surely doomed.

The teacher took the first sheet of paper, clasped his chosen brush in an upright position, dipped its tip with mindful precision into the ink and, with a concentrated flourish, inscribed:

Ren. It means person – the two strokes are a simplified pictograph of a pair of legs. It looked pretty simple, to tell the truth. Just two strokes of the brush. The way he had written it, it also looked rather beautiful, two plain strokes of bold black ink tailing off to perfectly stylized points on the fine, white paper.

The teacher took a second brush and dipped it in the ink. He carefully passed it to me and told me to copy. With total concentration I took the brush and attempted to mimic what he had done. But my efforts came out blotchy and irregular. The tails of my strokes didn't flatten before petering out as the teacher's did.

I tried again, and again, that same simple character. Once, I did one that wasn't too terrible. But then the next few were awkward and bumbling once more.

We moved on to *kou*, mouth:

Now that was just a square. Anyone could draw a square – couldn't they? But the problem was, when written in style, each stroke was supposed to be infused with character. It was no good just to make a straight line. The base line had to be slightly curved in just the right way; the end of each stroke should have been signalled by a slight depression, then a flick of the brush.

'Don't worry,' smiled the teacher when I failed miserably for the tenth time in a row. 'Most Chinese people have very bad calligraphy too. I have been teaching in middle school for many years, and in each school, maybe two or three students have a tiny bit of talent.'

Times have changed since a polished calligraphy was vital for success in the Chinese world; nowadays the students all write on computer keyboards – they use a software program by which certain combinations of keys create the characters.

The receptionist came in. The teacher, ever charming and friendly, asked her if she wanted to try.

The girl blushed. 'No, no,' she stammered. 'My calligraphy is very bad.'

Frankly, I didn't believe her. She could write Chinese, couldn't she? She had to be infinitely better than I was, at least.

The girl took the brush. To my astonishment, her attempts were almost as clumsy as mine. Ink blobbed; graceful, wispy flourishes came off the brush as heavy black lines. Once she even inscribed her strokes for a simple character – *shan*, mountain – in the wrong order. This was a cardinal sin if my teacher's wrath in London was anything to go by.

And so the three of us together persisted for an hour or so. It was a serene, peaceful, all-consuming activity, sitting there, drinking tea and trying to create a single, elegant line with ink and brush. In that small room, there was no need to think of the world outside. There was no need to exclaim over the scenery, or to make conversation, or to attempt to buy food or tickets. It was delightful that afternoon to lose myself absolutely in the free-flowing lines of ink and to forget, just for a while, about the demands and expectations of my journey.

22

Over and Out

The bus from Yangshuo to Guangzhou was quite
simply the best I had travelled on in my life. It was
a brand-new, freshly upholstered coach. The seats
reclined almost to couchant, and there was enough
leg room for the lankiest of travellers. There was air
conditioning, smoking was out of the question – and
I had only four fellow passengers. An hour or so
into the journey, an attendant came round and served
small packets of biscuits and cartons of soya milk.

It was extraordinary to think of the contrast between
this, the last bus I took in China, and that first juddering
minibus full of smoke that I had taken from Wutai Shan
to Taiyuan all those weeks ago. That had certainly been
the least comfortable bus journey I had ever suffered
through while this one hurtled off the other end of the
spectrum. My journey to Guilin had been long, but
the last leg had been the most luxurious train trip I'd
ever taken: I had never before had a private sleeper
cabin entirely to myself, with an attendant on hand to
make sure I had plenty of hot water for my tea. Yet on
that same train, the hard-seat carriages would have
been crammed full of the ordinary, country-dwelling,

hand-to-mouth-living Chinese. The Chinese transport system really did seem to be symptomatic of that vast country's contrasts and contradictions. With every technological advance, with each sparkling BMW that spun out of the company's new Shenyang factory, the gap between rich and poor stretched and China groaned beneath its growing pains as the seat springs twanged on an ageing country bus.

Outside the window, though, nothing had changed. Cabbage patch after endless dreary cabbage patch rolled on by, followed by brown paddy fields whose rice had been harvested so that now only straw-coloured sticks poked up through the earth. Water buffalo grazed as they had for centuries. We glided in our hermetically sealed slice of modernity past rivers and mountains, and then more cabbage patches. We scooted, unstopping, through drab towns with sprawling moped dealerships and worn-out, concrete buildings. We drove by a few fields of sugar cane whose long purplish stalks and sprays of unruly leaves stretched up towards the clouds. And then there were more cabbage patches.

We arrived in Guangzhou. My hotel room looked fabulous but felt freezing. I fiddled with the heating operations in my room for a while. Icy air blasted from the vents. As I passed through reception an hour or so later, I thought I'd mention it to the man on the desk.

'The heating in my room doesn't seem to work,' I said. 'Is it possible to send someone to mend it?'

The man looked astonished. 'No,' he said. 'There is no heating in the whole hotel. We do not turn on the heating until the temperature reaches five degrees.'

I spent most of the following day walking. I must have covered at least twenty miles on foot that day, after which I was so exhausted I would have slept soundly even if the temperature had been *minus* five.

Superficially, Guangzhou was an ugly city, but there were pockets of faded charm. Off the main roads with their monstrous grey tower blocks and concrete flyovers lay narrow cobbled alleyways whose low-rise houses peeled paint. This seemed to be where Guangzhou really came to life: this haphazard maze of streets buzzed with bicycles and little shops tucked into scarcely accessible corners – a hairdresser's, a snack stall, or a kindergarten.

I headed south to Shamian Dao, a curious anachronism off the northern bank of the Pearl River. This was where the foreigners of yore lived and traded. The British East India Company, which held a monopoly on British trade with China, conducted business here from the early eighteenth century, well before the Treaty of Nanjing after which the subsequent treaty ports were opened.

The foreigners, most of whom were British, were allowed to trade only with certain named merchants. They were forbidden from keeping Chinese servants or learning the Chinese language: it was this latter prohibition that gave rise to the extraordinary pidgin that blended English, Chinese and Portuguese. In addition, they weren't permitted to venture into the main city but were restricted to living and working in this area on the river front. In 1861, matters improved for the foreigners but took a nose dive for the Chinese when the island was ceded to the British and French as a concession. Now the foreigners lived under the rules of extraterritoriality; that is to say, by their own laws on Chinese soil as they did in Shanghai and the other treaty ports.

Shamian Dao is today as then a world apart from

the Chinese city. Its leafy tranquillity and grand colonial buildings seem to exist in some kind of erroneous time warp on this tiny stretch of land only three streets deep, connected to the real world by a series of stone bridges. The great Victorian edifices still stand as testament to the brash confidence of their founders, but now house offices and apartments.

But the most striking thing about Shamian Dao was its lack of soul. The city over the bridges may have been grey and choked with pollution, but life at least was lived there. Shamian Dao seemed to me now, as a century ago, to be a rarefied delusion, a dream created by foreigners for foreigners who wished to convince themselves that they weren't in China at all, but cocooned in the familiar entrapments of home.

By now, I was ready for some home comforts myself. Hong Kong was less than two hours away by train. It's no longer a British colony but is a former home to me and home still to many of my friends. I'd had enough of striding round Chinese cities, of struggling to find good places to eat and clean spots to sleep. It was impossible for me to enjoy Guangzhou knowing, as I did, that just two hours' journey away my friends Sheena and Duncan's spare room would be made up with clean sheets, and that finding food and wine there would be as simple as pulling open the fridge door. I felt almost physically tugged, as though drawn southwards by some gravitational force, compelled, perhaps, by my inner wimp to seek a more comfortable life. China had been wonderful; it had been fascinating. At times it had been fun. But it had been hard work. I was exhausted; it was time for me to move on.

I took a taxi to the train station. As the driver pulled up, two men approached. The first was stout and had a

330

brutal, determined expression. He had just one leg and hobbled along with the help of a pair of rickety, wooden crutches. The other, in contrast, was slight and shifty, constantly swirling like a reedy willow sapling in the wind.

As the driver and I went to the boot of the car to retrieve my luggage, they approached.

'*Qian,*' money, demanded the one-legged man. He jabbed a grubby, calloused hand palm-up towards my chest.

I ignored him and continued to collect my baggage from the boot.

'*Qian,*' he said again, and this time pushed me lightly on the arm.

His willowy companion closed in on me, trying to carry my luggage.

'*Qian!*' The one-legged man shoved me a little harder.

Both men were now standing uncomfortably close to me, just by my right shoulder. They seemed to be trying to stop me from gathering my belongings. They were emphatically blocking my path. My driver stood there ineffectually and laughed, for this was the new China which no longer frowned on private enterprise, on a person's desire to make himself a quick buck.

I reached into the boot of the car, picked up my rucksack, and swung it onto my back, narrowly missing clipping the one-legged man who was standing precariously close. As he hissed and the willowy creature hooted with laughter, I made my way to my departure gate.

I passed through passport control. I boarded the train; with a slight judder, it departed. An hour and a half later, the train arrived in Shenzhen, the high-rise border town built by the Chinese as a Special Economic

331

Zone in the 1980s. Then, as the train chugged through the station, along the platform, the signboards changed. 'Lo Wu' they announced – Hong Kong's border post. We gathered speed as we drew out of the station, leaving behind the malls and office blocks of China and pulling out, instead, into the green countryside of Hong Kong – for nobody on this side of the border has ever thought to build on the land this far north.

Less than two hundred years ago, this lush, tropical greenery covered the whole of Hong Kong. But this jungle-clad hillock off the south China coast was at first seen by the powers-that-be not as a paradise, nor as a strategically brilliant trading post, but as a rotten apple in the glorious Empire's cart.

'A barren island with hardly a house upon it,' spluttered the foreign secretary of the time, Lord Palmerston, when he learned that his underlings had settled for Hong Kong at the Treaty of Nanjing. The monarchy saw it as an entertaining little joke, a fungous stump in the imperial orchard.

'Albert is so much amused at my having got the island of Hong Kong,' the newly crowned Queen Victoria crowed to her uncle, King Leopold of Belgium.

Hong Kong didn't stay barren for long. The colonialists constructed government offices and godowns, clock towers and cathedral spires. As the buildings rose, storey by storey, year on year, the population grew too. With every surging wave of China's turbulent history – the Taiping Rebellion of the mid-1800s, the civil war and Japanese invasion, the famine that followed the Great Leap Forward, the draconian purges of the Cultural Revolution – mainlanders fled over the border.

Pirates and other criminals, who found the British

justice system attractively lenient compared to the punishments meted out on the mainland – strangulation, decapitation, 'death from a thousand cuts' and being lowered slowly into a vat of lime – flocked here too. When the Communists seized power and drove out the Triads, Hong Kong became their base. In 1900, Hong Kong's population had stood at three hundred thousand; by 1962 three million people lived here, and that's risen to more than seven million today.

Now, I was following them. And suddenly, as those men and women persecuted by war, famine and politics had before me, I felt almost light-headed with relief. I loved China, I was enchanted by it. But it had been gruelling. I had been lonely. And now, I was back on home ground among friends. I was seized with a curious desire to leap from my seat and run up and down the aisle whooping for joy as familiar sights came into view. The schoolchildren in their outmoded sailor-suit uniforms; the public housing estates with their hideous salmon-pink wall tiles; the hillsides sprayed with foreboding grey concrete in an attempt to tame the jungle and prevent landslides: all looked to me at that moment like the plump peaches of paradise.

As we glided southwards, the towns became denser, higher, uglier, yet all quietly told their own stories of China's past. We glided through Shatin, one of the 'new towns' of the 1970s that were built to rehouse the hundreds of thousands of squatters who had poured over the border and lived in poverty and squalor. We passed the racecourse, that curious blend of traditional British sport with the Chinese love for gambling. The racecourse is the only place one can bet legally in Hong Kong – and the two courses here generate more money per race than anywhere else in the world.

We reached Kowloon. Now we were surrounded by concrete and neon-light boards advertising everything from watches to dim sum to girls. The hub of Kowloon screams sheer, unadulterated commercialism – and is stifled by the crowds that come with it. For this is emphatically a Chinese city, despite a hundred and fifty years of British rule. With their unceasing appetite for hard work, their incredible energy, their remarkable resilience and their refusal ever to accept defeat, the Chinese who immigrated to escape a troubled Motherland have generated wealth and opportunity here – and the world over – like no other race on earth. And now, as the tight bonds of government loosen over the border, their mainland cousins too are seizing the entrepreneurial spirit and galloping towards prosperity.

'When we fight, we first use bullets; when the bullets are gone, we use bayonets; when the bayonets are dull, we use the rifle barrel; when this is broken, we use our fists; when our fists our broken, we bite,' chanted one Chinese warlord's troops in the 1920s. In the decades that followed, in the face of great adversity, those soldiers' countrymen have followed their spirit.

The train was slowing down now. We drew into Hung Hom station on the edge of the Kowloon peninsula, the very tip of the Chinese mainland. After all those weeks on buses and trains, this was my final stop. I had travelled by bicycle, by plane and on the back of a mule. I had driven along brand-new highways and along pot-holed rural tracks. I had ridden in countless crawling, clanking buses, and on the fastest train in the world. And now, with a mixture of regretful nostalgia and a profound sense of relief, I had reached the end of the line – for now, at least.

Sources

Dragon Lady / Sterling Seagrave, Vintage.

Forgotten Kingdom / Peter Goullart, John Murray.

Generalissimo / Jonathan Fenby, The Free Press.

Journey to a War / W. H. Aulden and Christopher Isherwood, Faber & Faber.

Lost Horizon / James Hilton, Pocket Books.

Shanghai / Harriet Sergeant, John Murray.

The Dragon Syndicates / Martin Booth, Bantam.

The New Emperors / Harrison Salisbury, HarperCollins.

The Private Life of Chairman Mao / Zhisui Li, Arrow.

The River at the Centre of the World / Simon Winchester, Penguin.

The Rape of Nanking / Iris Chang, Penguin.

The Soong Dynasty / Sterling Seagrave, Corgi.

When China Ruled the Seas / Louise Levathes, Oxford University Press.

IT'S NOT ABOUT THE TAPAS
Around Spain on Two Wheels
By Polly Evans

Disenchanted with her job as a senior editor in Hong Kong, Polly Evans exchanged the shiny red cabs of Hong Kong for a more demanding form of transport – a bicycle – and set off on a voyage of discovery around Spain. From the thigh-burning ascents of the Pyrenees to the relentless olive groves of Andalusia, Polly found more adventures than she had bargained for. She survived a nail-biting encounter with a sprightly pig, escaped over-zealous suitors, had her morality questioned by the locals, encountered some dubious aficionados on the road and indulged her love of regional cooking.

0 553 81556 3

'A hilarious account of her epic adventure around bike-mad Spain'
Daily Express (Book of the Week)

KIWIS MIGHT FLY
Around New Zealand on Two Wheels
By Polly Evans

When Polly Evans read a survey claiming that the last bastion of masculinity, the real Kiwi bloke, was about to breathe his last, she was seized by a sense of foreboding. Abandoning the London winter she took off on a motorbike for the windswept beaches and golden plains of New Zealand, hoping to root out some examples of this endangered species for posterity. But her challenges didn't stop at the men. Just weeks after passing her bike test, Polly rode from Auckland's glitzy Viaduct Basin to the vineyards of Hawkes Bay and on to the Southern Alps. She found wild kiwis in the dead of night, kayaked among dolphins at dawn, and spent an evening on a remote hillside with a sheep-shearing gang.

0 553 81557 1

BANTAM BOOKS